D0981284

Mountain Biking
Southern
California

Mark A. Ross and Brad L. Fine

FALCON®

HELENA, MONTANA

A FALCON GUIDE ®

Falcon® Publishing is continually expanding its list of recreational guidebooks. All books include detailed descriptions, accurate maps, and all information necessary for enjoyable trips. You can order extra copies of this book and get information and prices for other Falcon® books by writing Falcon, P.O. Box 1718, Helena, MT 59624 or calling toll free 1-800-582-2665. Also, please ask for a free copy of our current catalog. Visit our website at www.FalconOutdoors.com or contact us by e-mail at falcon@falcon.com.

©1999 by Falcon® Publishing Inc., Helena, Montana
Printed in the United States of America.

1 2 3 4 5 6 7 8 9 10 MG 04 03 02 01 00 99

All black-and-white photos by the authors unless otherwise noted.

Cataloging-in-Publication Data
Ross, Mark A., 1968–
    Mountain biking Southern California / by Mark A. Ross and
Brad L. Fine.
        p.   cm. — (A FalconGuide)
    Includes index.
    ISBN 1-56044-807-5 (pbk.)
    1. All terrain cycling—California, Southern—Guidebooks.
    2. Bicycle trails—California, Southern—Guidebooks. 3. California,
    Southern—Guidebooks. I. Fine, Brad L., 1969– . II. Title.
    III. Series: Falcon guide.
    GV1045.5.C2R67   1999
    917.94'90453—dc21   99-12361
                                                                  CIP

CAUTION

Outdoor recreational activities are by their very nature potentially hazardous. All participants in such activities must assume responsibility for their own actions and safety. The information contained in this guidebook cannot replace sound judgment and good decision-making skills, which help reduce risk exposure, nor does the scope of this book allow for disclosure of all the potential hazards and risks involved in such activities.

Learn as much as possible about the outdoor recreational activities in which you participate, prepare for the unexpected, and be cautious. The reward will be a safer and more enjoyable experience.

♻ Text pages printed on recycled paper.

Contents

Map Legend

Interstate		Hill/Rock	
U.S. Highway		Campground	
State or Other Principal Road		Picnic Area	
		Ranger Station	
Forest Road			
Interstate Highway		Buildings	
Paved Road		Peak/Elevation	4,507 ft.
Gravel Road		Bridge/Pass	
Unimproved Road		Gate	
Trail (singletrack)		Parking Area	
Trail (doubletrack)		Lake/Reservoir	
Trailhead			
Trail Marker		Map Orientation	N
Waterway		Scale	0 0.5 1 MILES

Southern California Locator Map

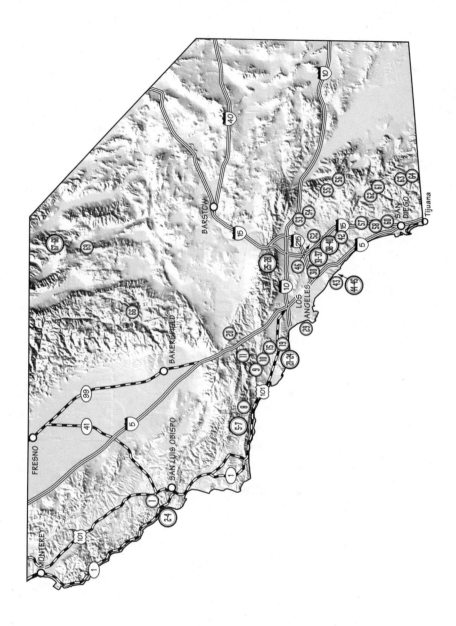

Introduction

Welcome to *Mountain Biking Southern California*. Mountain biking is truly an awesome sport, and there's no better place to enjoy it than Southern California, whose name conjures up images of sunshine, blue skies, pristine sandy coastlines, and vast networks of pine-covered mountains.

This book encompasses mountain bike trails of all levels. It takes you from San Diego near the Mexican border in the south, to Morro Bay in the north, to Mammoth Mountain in the High Sierras. Whether you're a rookie or an experienced rider, the most frustrating part of finding new trails is getting lost as a result of a bad trail description or an old, unreliable map. Well, we have gotten lost so that you do not have to. How many times have you ventured out with a new trail guide only to find trail diversions that were not described in the book? Well, we have taken care of that for you. Every confusing trail diversion is accounted for so that you can enjoy the trail rather than spend time worring about getting lost. This does, however, require that you bring the trail description with you; don't rely on your memory.

There are a wide variety of trails included in *Mountain Biking Southern California*. These range from short, mellow dirt roads for the entire family, to steep, grueling climbs for the masochist, to fast technical singletrack for the adrenaline junky. Whether you are a beginner or an advanced rider, there are trails in here for you. Please bear in mind that the difficulty rating we have provided is subjective. While we, the authors, are advanced riders, we have tried to portray the trails as an intermediate rider would view them. Your view of the trail may differ substantially depending on your riding ability and aversion to fear.

While mountain biking is a challenging and fun sport, it can be dangerous. We suffered many scrapes and bruises during our trail adventures, and, we have known and seen other riders with broken bones as a result of a bad fall. Always wear a helmet. If mountain biking is new to you, stay within your limitations. Do not venture onto 20 miles of technical singletrack if you are not prepared. Mountain biking requires a great deal of confidence in your riding ability. One bad spill could ruin your riding confidence and forever impair your ability to reach for the hardest trails. Slowly build your way up. There is no hurry. If you are an experienced rider, do not take your rookie friends on the toughest trails. They will not enjoy the experience and you will loose a potential riding partner. Just be patient and in a short time you will have a strong riding partner who enjoys the tougher trails.

Trails in Southern California are extremely volatile due to the weather. This book was written during an El Niño season, which caused massive damage to many trails. Several trails that had been mapped prior to the storms had to be removed due to trail destruction. Other trails are slowly getting back to solid riding form. While most of these trails can be ridden year-round, you should always wait at least two days before riding after a big rain storm. Riding wet trails causes irreparable damage and erosion to the trails. Please be aware that these trails were accurately portrayed in this book as it went to press but may suffer severe storm damage in subsequent seasons. It is always a good idea to contact a local land manager such as a park or forest ranger to obtain the latest trail conditions.

Trail access is also a big concern in Southern California. Disputes between mountain bikers and equestrians have lead to the closure of certain trails. Mountain bikers must respect other trail users, including hikers. Regardless of the fact that most of these rides are on public property and that we all have a right to use them, mountain bikers are relatively new to the trails and, like all newbies, they are the least respected. With your respect for other trail users and the continued support of bike groups organizing trail maintenance crews, we will soon gain the respect we deserve and trail access will no longer be a problem.

Before you hit the trail, you should make sure you have the right equipment. The most important part of mountain bike riding is a solid bike, as well as a helmet. There are a wide variety of mountain bikes on the market these days. Prices range from $100 to several thousand dollars. While most bikes in the lower range should stay on the bike path at the park, you can still get a lot of bike for a reasonable amount of money. Mountain biking is an abusive sport. Your body and your equipment will take a lot of bouncing and banging. For a beginner, the $500 price range is a good place to start. If you spend anything less, you will get a bike that will fall apart with a little abuse. The larger manufacturers have more to offer in the low-to-middle price range. Their buying power allows them to use better components for the money. The more money you spend, the longer the bike will last. Not only will it hold up better, but as your skill level increases you will continue to enjoy your bike. If your first bike is on the low end, you will soon want a newer, more expensive bike and your initial investment will be wasted.

A bike's single most expensive part is the frame. Entry level bikes are often made out of steel while most bikes in the mid-to-high range are made with aluminum frames. Some of the higher-end frames are built of more unique materials such as aircraft grade titanium, metal matrix, and carbon fiber. These materials offer lighter weights without a loss in strength. A good frame can last many years and other parts can be replaced as they break or wear out. The rest of the bike is composed of parts like shifters, derailleurs, brakes, cranks, pedals, hubs, rims and tires. While the frame is the most expensive part, the quality of these other components can significantly impact price. The lower grade components will be heavier and more likely to break. Additionally, the lower grade shifting systems have fewer gears, do not shift as well, and require more frequent adjustment. The higher level components are lighter and stronger and make riding a much more pleasurable experience. Most bike manufacturers will price different levels of bikes by using the same quality frame with component groups of varying quality. This is an excellent way to get a good frame at a lower price and then upgrade components at a later time.

Once a budget has been determined, the biggest question is suspension. While full-suspension is becoming increasingly popular and is excellent for rocky descents, it is not necessary. It is not even recommended unless you have a budget around $1,000. Often you will find a full-suspension bike under $1,000 but in order to compensate for the expensive frame, the bike comes with cheap components. The cheaper components will not work as well and will not last as long. However, for under $1,000 you can get a front-suspension bike with race-ready components.

Enough of that! A lot of effort was been put into finding a wide variety of quality trails to enjoy. Over 12 months of research, travel, riding and writing have been put into this book. We hope you enjoy *Mountain Biking Southern California* as much as we do. Remember, keep the rubber side down!

RULES OF THE TRAIL

If every mountain biker always yielded the right-of-way, stayed on the trail, avoided wet or muddy trails, never cut switchbacks, never skidded, always rode in control, showed respect for other trail users, and carried out every last scrap of what was carried in (candy wrappers and bike-part debris included)—in short, did the right thing—then we wouldn't need a list of rules govern to our behavior. Most of us don't need these rules, but we do need knowledge. What exactly is the right thing to do?

Here are some guidelines—we like to think of them as reminders—reprinted by permission from the International Mountain Bicycling Association (IMBA). The basic theme here is to reduce or eliminate any damage to the land and water, the plant and wildlife inhabitants, and other backcountry visitors and trail users. Ride with respect.

IMBA RULES OF THE TRAIL

1. Ride on open trails only. Respect trail and road closures (ask if not sure), avoid possible trespass on private land, obtain permits or other authorization as may be required. Federal and state wilderness areas are closed to cycling. The way you ride will influence trail management decisions and policies.

2. Leave no trace. Be sensitive to the dirt beneath you. Even on open (legal) trails, you should not ride under conditions where you will leave evidence of your passing, such as on certain soils after a rain. Recognize different types of soils and trail construction; practice low-impact cycling. This also means staying on existing trails and not creating new ones. Don't cut switchbacks. Be sure to pack out at least as much as you pack in.

3. Control your bicycle! Inattention for even a second can cause problems. Obey all bicycle speed regulations and recommendations.

4. Always yield trail. Make known your approach well in advance. A friendly greeting or bell is considerate and works well; don't startle others. Show your respect when passing by slowing to a walking pace or even stopping. Anticipate other trail users around corners or in blind spots.

5. Never spook animals. All animals are startled by an unannounced approach, a sudden movement, or a loud noise. This can be dangerous for you, others, and the animals. Give animals extra room and time to adjust to you. When passing horses use special care and follow directions from the horseback riders (ask if uncertain). Running cattle and disturbing wildlife are serious offenses. Leave gates as you found them, or as marked.

6. Plan ahead. Know your equipment, your ability, and the area in which you are riding—and prepare accordingly. Be self-sufficient at all times, keep your equipment in good repair, and carry necessary supplies for changes in weather or other conditions. A well-executed trip is a satisfaction to you and not a burden or offense to others. Always wear a helmet and appropriate safety gear.

Keep trails open by setting a good example of environmentally sound and socially responsible off-road cycling.

If you have any questions or comments, you can contact IMBA at:

IMBA
P.O. Box 7578
Boulder, CO 80306-7578 USA
Tel: 303-545-9011
Fax: 303-545-9026

HOW TO USE THIS GUIDE

Each ride description in this book follows the same format:

Number and name of the ride: Rides are cross-referenced by number throughout this book. In many cases, parts of rides or entire routes can be linked to other rides for longer trips or variations on a standard course. For the names of rides, we relied on official names of trails, roads, and natural features as shown on national forest and U.S. Geological Survey maps. In some cases, well-known local names are used.

Location: The general whereabouts of the ride in relation to well-known areas.

Distance: The overall length of a trail is described in miles.

Time: An estimate of how long it takes to complete the ride—for example: one or two hours. The time listed is the actual riding time and does not reflect rest stops. Strong skilled riders may be able to do a given ride in less than the estimated time, while other riders may take considerably longer. Also bear in mind that severe weather, changes in trail conditions, or mechanical problems may prolong a ride.

Tread: The type of road or trail—paved road, gravel road, dirt road or jeep road, singletrack or doubletrack. Many of the rides are on fireroads, which are dirt roads used by fire trucks and other vehicles.

Aerobic level: An estimate of the level of physical effort required to complete the ride—easy, moderate, or strenuous. (See explanation of the rating system on page 5.)

Technical difficulty: The level of bike-handling skills needed to complete the ride upright and in one piece. Technical difficulty is rated on a scale of 1 to 5, with 1 being the easiest and 5 being the hardest. (See explanation of the rating system on page 6.)

Hazards: A list of dangers that may be encountered on a ride. This includes traffic, weather, wildlife, trail obstacles and conditions, risky stream crossings, difficult route-finding, and other perils. Remember that trail conditions may change at any time. Be alert for storms, new fences, downfall, missing trail signs, and mechanical failure. Fatigue, heat, cold, and/or dehydration may impair judgement. Always wear a helmet. Ride in control at all times.

Highlights: Special features or qualities that make a ride worth doing—scenery, fun singletrack, chances to see wildlife.

Land status: Managing agencies and private holdings. Most of these rides are national forest, national parks or California state park land but some cross portions of private or municipal land. Always leave gates as you found them and respect the land, regardless of who owns it. (See Appendix for a list of contacts for land-managing agencies.)

Fees: All National Forests in California now require a Forest Adventure Pass. This can be purchased at or near the trailhead from a ranger or local merchant for $5 per day or $30 for an annual pass. There is a $100 fine for not having an Adventure Pass. Most California state parks have a $5–$6 day-use fee which is paid at the parking lot. An annual pass can be purchased for $75.

Services: Where to find bathrooms, food and other services near the trailhead.

Water: Whether or not there is water along the trail.

Maps: A list of available maps. Mostly USGS topographical maps in 7.5-minute quad series and Thomas Brothers maps to locate the trail.

Access: How to find the trailhead or the start of the ride from a well-known area.

Notes on the trail: A narrative description of the ride, how to find your way, and what to look for.

The ride: A mile-by-mile list of key points along the trail. All distances were measured to the tenth of a mile with a cyclo-computer (a bike-mounted odometer). Terrain, riding technique, and even tire pressure can affect odometer readings, so treat all mileages as estimates.

Remember, trails are changing all the time. The information presented here is as accurate and up-to-date as possible, but there are no guarantees out in the mountains. You alone are responsible for your safety and for the choices you make on the trail.

RATING THE RIDES

Falcon's mountain biking guides rate each ride for two types of difficulty: the *physical effort* required to pedal the distance, and the *bike-handling skills* needed to stay upright and make it home in one piece. We call these "Aerobic level" and "Technical difficulty."

The following sections explain what the various ratings mean in plain, specific language. An elevation profile accompanies each ride description to help you determine how easy or hard the ride is. You should also weigh other factors such as elevation above sea level, total trip distance, weather and wind, and current trail conditions.

AEROBIC LEVEL RATINGS

Bicycling is often touted as a relaxing, low-impact, relatively easy way to burn excess calories and maintain a healthy heart and lungs. Mountain biking, however, tends to pack a little more work (and excitement) into the routine. Fat tires and soft or rough trails increase the rolling resistance, so it takes more effort to push those wheels around. Unpaved or off-road hills tend to be steeper than the grades measured and surfaced by the highway department.

Expect to breathe hard and sweat some, probably a lot. Pedaling around town is a good start, but it won't fully prepare you for the workout offered by most of the rides in this book. If you are unsure of your level of fitness, see a doctor for a physical exam before tackling any of the rides in this book. If you are riding to get back in shape or just for the fun of it, take it easy. Walk or rest if need be. Start with short rides and add on miles gradually.

Here's how we rate the exertion level for terrain covered in this book:

Easy: Flat or gently rolling terrain. No steep or prolonged climbs.

Moderate: Some hills. Climbs may be short or fairly steep or long and gradual.

Strenuous: Frequent or prolonged climbs steep enough to require riding in the lowest gear; requires high level of aerobic fitness, power, and endurance (typically acquired through many hours of riding and proper training). Less fit riders may need to walk.

Many rides are mostly easy and moderate but may have short strenuous sections. Other rides are mostly strenuous and should be attempted only after a medical checkup and implant of a second heart, preferably a big one. Also be aware that flailing through a highly technical section can be exhausting even on the flats. Good riding skills and a relaxed stance on the bike save energy.

Finally, any ride can be strenuous if you ride it hard and fast. Conversely, the pain of a lung-burning climb grows easier to tolerate as your fitness level improves. Learn to pace yourself and remember to schedule easy rides and rest days in your calendar.

TECHNICAL DIFFICULTY RATINGS

While you are pushing up that steep, strenuous slope wondering how much farther you can go before you collapse, remember that the condition of your heart, lungs, and legs aren't the only factors that affect the way you ride to the top of the mountain. There's the tree across the trail, or the sideslope of ball-bearing–sized pebbles, or the place where the trail disappears except for faint bits of rubber clinging to a boulder the size of your garage.

Mountain bikes will roll over or through an amazing array of challenges, but sometimes we, as riders, have to help. And even more astonishing, some riders get off their bikes and walk—get this—before they flip over the handlebars.

The technical difficulty ratings in this book help to take the worst surprises out of backcountry rides. In the privacy of your own home you can make an honest appraisal of your bike-handling skills and then find rides in these pages that are within your ability.

We've rated technical difficulty on a scale from 1 to 5, from easiest to most difficult. We've tried to make ratings as objective as possible by considering the types of obstacles and their frequency of occurrence. The same standards were applied consistently through all rides in this book.

We've also added plus (+) and minus (-) symbols to cover gray areas between given levels of difficulty; a 4+ obstacle is harder than a 4, but easier than a 5-. A stretch of trail rated 5+ would be unridable by all but the most skilled (or luckiest) riders.

Here are the five levels defined:

Level 1: Smooth tread; road or doubletrack; no obstacles, ruts or steeps. Requires basic riding skills.

Level 2: Mostly smooth tread; wide, well-groomed singletrack or road/doubletrack with minor ruts or loose gravel or sand.

Level 3: Irregular tread with some rough sections; single or doubletrack with obvious route choices; some steep sections; occasional obstacles may include small rocks, roots, water bars, ruts, loose gravel or sand, and sharp turns or broad, open switchbacks.

Level 4: Rough tread with few smooth sections; singletrack or rough doubletrack with limited route choices; steep sections, some with obstacles; obstacles are numerous and varied, including rocks, roots, branches, ruts, sidehills, narrow tread, loose gravel or sand, and switchbacks.

Level 5: Continuously broken, rocky, root-infested, or trenched tread; singletrack or extremely rough doubletrack with few route choices; frequent, sudden, and severe changes in gradient; some slopes so steep that wheels lift off ground; obstacles are nearly continuous and may include boulders, logs, water, large holes, deep ruts, ledges, piles of loose gravel, steep sidehills, encroaching trees, and tight switchbacks.

Again, most of the rides in this book cover varied terrain, with an ever-changing degree of technical difficulty. Some trails run smooth with only occasional obstacles, and other trails are obstacle-ridden. The path of least resistance, or line, is where you find it. In general, most obstacles are more challenging if you encounter them while climbing than while descending. On the other hand, in heavy surf (e.g., boulder fields, tangles of downfall, cliffs), fear plays a larger role when facing downhill.

Realize, too, that different riders have different strengths and weaknesses. Some folks can scramble over logs and boulders without a grunt, but they crash head over heels on every switchback turn. Some fly off the steepest drops and others freeze. Some riders climb like the wind and others just blow—and walk.

The key to overcoming "technical difficulties" is practice—keep trying. Follow a rider who makes it look easy, and don't hesitate to ask for constructive criticism. Try shifting your weight (good riders move a lot, front and back, side to side, and up and down), and experiment with balance and momentum. Find a smooth patch of lawn and practice riding as slowly as possible, even balancing at a standstill. This will give you more confidence—and more time to recover or bail out—the next time the trails rears up and bites.

ELEVATION PROFILES

An elevation profile accompanies each ride description. Here the ups and downs of the route are graphed on a grid with elevation (in feet above sea level) on the left and miles pedaled across the bottom. Route surface conditions and technical levels are shown on the graphs.

Note that these graphs are compressed (squeezed) to fit on the page. The actual slopes you will ride are not as steep as the lines drawn on the graphs (it just feels that way). Also, some extremely short dips and climbs are too small to show up on the graphs.

TOPOGRAPHIC MAPS

The maps in this book, when used in conjunction with the route directions present in each chapter, will in most instances be sufficient to get you to the trail and keep you on it. However, these maps cannot begin to provide the detailed information found in the United States Geological Survey (USGS) 7.5-minute series topographic maps. Recognizing how indispensable these are to bikers and hikers alike, many bike shops and sporting goods stores now carry topos of the local area. If you're brand new to mountain biking you might be wondering, "What's a topographic map?" In short, these differ from standard "flat" maps because they indicate not only linear distance, but elevation as well. One glance at a topo shows you the difference, for "contour lines" are spread across the map like dozens of intricate spider webs. Each contour line represents a particular elevation, and each topo has written at its base a particular "contour interval" designation. Yes, it sounds confusing if you're new to the lingo, but it truly is a simple and wonderfully helpful system. Let's assume that the 7.5-minute series topo before us says, "Contour Interval 40 feet," that the short trail we'll be pedaling is two inches in length on the map, and that it crosses five contour lines between its beginning and end. What do we know? Well, because the linear scale of this series is two thousand feet to the inch (roughly 2.25 inches represent a mile), we know our trail is approximately four-fifths of a mile long (2 inches x 2,000 feet). We also know we'll climb or descend 200 vertical feet (5 contour lines x 40 feet each) over that distance. The elevation designations written on occasional contour lines will tell us if we're heading up or down.

The authors of this series warn their readers of upcoming terrain, but only a detailed topo gives you the information that enables you to pinpoint your position exactly on a map, steers you toward optional trails and roads nearby, and lets you know at a glance if you'll be pedaling hard to take them. It's a lot of information for a very low cost. In fact, the only drawback with topos is their size—several feet square.

Major universities and some public libraries also carry topos; you might try photocopying the ones you need to avoid the cost of buying them. But if you want your own and can't find them locally, write to:

USGS Map Sales
Box 25286
Denver, CO 80225

WHAT TO BRING

The following is suggested as an absolute minimum:

- [ ] tire levers
- [ ] spare tube and patch kit
- [ ] air pump
- [ ] Allen wrenches (3, 4, 5, and 6 mm)
- [ ] small flat-blade screwdriver
- [ ] chain rivet tool
- [ ] spoke wrench
- [ ] baling wire (about 10 inches, for temporary repairs)
- [ ] spare chain link
- [ ] spare nuts and bolts
- [ ] There are numerous tools on the market which combine many of these tools into one small and handy unit.
- [ ] It is also wise to keep a snake-bite kit. These can be found at most sporting goods or camping stores.

How to Beat the Burn

by Dr. Harvey R. Ross, DPM

OK, so there you are. Collapsed under the only shade tree within several miles. Sweating, shaking, cramped up and vomiting. The humility of it all! Your friends have left you and there is no catching up. Even if you have done this hill before, you are the "wimp" now.

Why? Dehydration, overtraining, heat exhaustion or even heat stroke. Dehydration which results in loss of as little as 2 percent of body mass can adversely affect a variety of physical functions and lead to performance decrements. Of particular importance is the association of dehydration with inadequate heat regulation, which could in turn result in heat exhaustion or heat stroke. Thus, dehydration during exercise should be avoided.

Although sweating is affected by various functions, including temperature, humidity, clothing, and altitude, it is not uncommon to lose 2 to 3 percent body mass, most of it water, during a typical mountain bike ride. During long rides, or repeated training at altitude, losses of up to 8 percent mass can occur when fluid replacement is inadequate. Your body warns you of this with the sensation of thirst. However, be aware that the sensation of thirst lags behind the need for water replacement. The recommendation for water replacement is approximately two cups every 30 minutes during long-term riding and repeated high-intensity racing and altitude riding. Water replacement is also needed during shorter rides of interval training periods in which smaller amounts of body water are lost.

Not only does the body expel fluid during training, but it also expels essential minerals, called electrolytes, found in bodily fluids. Extreme loss of electrolytes can upset the body's fluid balance, affect heat regulation, and distrupt the body's other functions. Electrolytes are usually available in sports drinks that also contain carbohydrates. Sports drinks are used to prevent dehydration, reduce any loss of electrolytes through sweating, and replace carbohydrates.

Certain hydration guidelines should be followed in order to avoid finding yourself embarrassed and left behind in a shivering and cramped-up mess. Eight to sixteen ounces should be taken 15 minutes before riding. Thereafter, four to eight ounces should be consumed every fifteen minutes. This can be done easily with the use of a backpack hydration system with an adequate bladder. Furthermore, after riding, an adequate intake of fluid must be continued. Sixteen ounces for every pound of body weight lost should be ingested.

Lactic acid build-up in the muscle tissue is also an important factor causing cramping. To avoid this there are several products on the market which buffer lactic acid. These sports drinks are available at bike, running and health food stores and are recommended over the use of plain water. They are highly advertised in bike magazines as well. Commercial sports drinks found in supermarkets and convenience stores also aid in fluid recovery but are not as effective as the more advanced drinks found in specialty stores.

One of the most important things in choosing a sports drink is to find one that tastes good to you. When it comes down to it, you will not drink what you don't like.

Energy bars and gels are also an excellent source of carbohydrates, electrolytes, and amino-acids which aid in muscle recovery. Most bars have similar composition and effect. You can choose higher protein, higher carbohydrates, or an equal amount of both. Bars are mainly differentiated by taste and the possibility of side effects such as diarrhea. So pick the one that is enjoyable and does not require regular stops behind the bushes.

Using the proper backpack with bladder and room for storage is recommended. This way you can have your fluid replacement and energy bars with you at all times. Water bottles are hard to use while riding, especially on technical singletrack. Furthermore, bottles often become contaminated from the dirt and mud on the trail. Hunter virus and other major illness-causing contaminants have been found on the tips of water bottles.

Overtraining is not just for the pro-racers or the Kamakazi downhillers. A weekend rider and even the more frequent rider is always prone to this syndrome. Symptoms are fatigue, bad temper, lack of stamina, and disinterest in work and fun. We call it "burn-out," but sometimes it's nothing more than overdoing it to keep up with your buddies. To avoid overtraining it is important not to go on long rides all of the time. Interval training is important. A long ride once or twice weekly and short rides in between are recommended. Vary your activities. Cross-training is a good shock to the muscles and builds strength and stamina. Work out at the gym. This will give you anaerobic training. Trail run for endurance and stamina. Whatever you chose, do it within your limitations. Warm-up to prepare yourself and to prevent injuries. It is important to warm up. This is agreed upon by professionals and weekend warriors as well. The short warm-up period prior to riding or cross-training can be considered a "mini" training session in which muscles and tendons are stretched, joints are lubricated, and the cardiovascular system is stimulated. Exercising regularly is extremely important. Preconditioning on a regular basis helps to avoid injuries and prevents failure of the cardiovascular system. Thus reducing the "wimp-factor." Unless the regimen of loosening up is done on a regular basis, the problem of injury and failure will be repeated. The weekend rider is most prone to injury and failure.

Lastly, it is important to cool down to avoid cramping and lactic acid build-up. Remember to replace fluids. Cooling-down exercise should be less active than the actual ride or cross-training.

So now you know how to beat the burn. Go out and train, ride, hydrate, and "kick ass."

Dr. Harvey R. Ross specializes in podiatric sports medicine and surgery. He is the sports podiatrist for the Huntington Beach Police Department's adventure racing and running teams. He is a native Californian who is active in mountain biking, adventure racing, skiing, rock climbing, and surfing. Therefore, he is well-acquainted with multidiscipline sporting methods and injuries. He is an author and has made several television appearances. Extreme endurance sports are his specialty.

San Luis Obispo County

Cerro Alto

Location:	In the Los Padres National Forest along California Highway 41 between San Luis Obispo and Morro Bay.
Distance:	4-mile loop.
Time:	40 minutes.
Tread:	Mostly singletrack.
Aerobic level:	Moderate to strenuous.
Technical difficulty:	3+.
Fees:	Forest Adventure Pass required.
Services:	Pit toilets in the campground near the trailhead. All other services approximately 8 miles in either direction.
Water:	Water available at the trailhead.
Highlights:	Fun singletrack descent. Views of Morro Bay from the upper ridge.
Hazards:	Hunters, poison oak.
Land status:	Los Padres National Forest.
Maps:	USGS Atascadero; Thomas Brothers San Luis Obispo, page 325.

Access: From California Highway 1 in Morro Bay take California Highway 41 east about 7 miles to the Cerro Alto Campground. Turn right into the campground and drive about three-quarters of a mile to the day-use area. As you drive in you first see the bridge trail to the right and then, farther toward the back of the campground, just before veering left to the parking area, you come to the AT&T Trail.

From U.S. Highway 1 in San Luis Obispo take CA 41 west about 8 miles to the Cerro Alto Campground. Turn left into the campground and drive about three-quarters of a mile to the day use area.

Cerro Alto

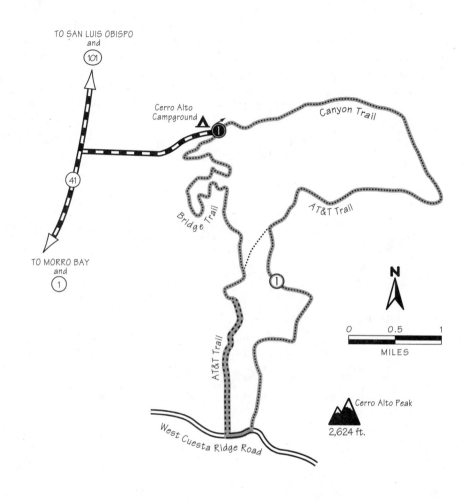

TO SAN LUIS OBISPO
and
(101)

Cerro Alto
Campground

Canyon Trail

(41)

AT&T Trail

Bridge Trail

TO MORRO BAY
and
(1)

N

0   0.5   1

MILES

AT&T Trail

Cerro Alto Peak
2,624 ft.

West Cuesta Ridge Road

Notes on the trail: The Cerro Alto is a fun, short ride requiring strong climbing skills. This combined with a fast, technical downhill and room for exploration makes this a great all-around trail. Begin riding along the AT&T Trail as it gently rollercoasters along the bottom of the canyon for about half a mile and begin a steep climb up toward the top. After 1 mile the AT&T

Trail forks: A narrow footpath heads to the right, while the left path switches around the left and reaches the top of the footpath, just above. The left fork is much easier. The trail then levels off for a short stretch, until you reach the Cerro Alto Trail at 1.8 miles and go left. Here the trail begins another steep climb to the ridge. At 2.3 miles you reach a junction and veer right, beginning a descent to the ridge. (A left at this junction would take you to Cerro Alto Peak within another 2 miles.) After passing through the gate turn right onto the ridge and then make another right on the AT&T Trail at 2.6 miles. At 2.8 miles veer right and pass through another gate as you begin a fast, steep descent down loose fireroad. At 3.2 miles go left onto the Bridge Trail to begin the final singletrack descent. At 4 miles you reach the bottom of the trail, back in the campground. Cross the bridge and head back to your car.

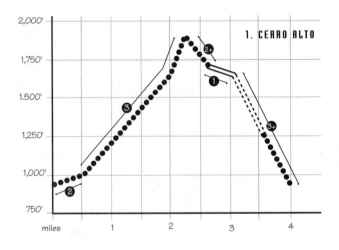

THE RIDE

- **0.0** Trailhead for the AT&T Trail.
- **1.0** Veer left as you reach the footpath to the right. The left fork switches back and takes you to the top of the footpath.
- **1.8** Turn left on Cerro Alto Trail.
- **2.3** Veer right and begin descent.
- **2.5** Pass through gate and turn right on ridge.
- **2.6** Turn right on AT&T Route.
- **2.8** Veer right and pass through gate to the right of the old tool house.
- **3.2** Veer left onto the Bridge Trail.
- **4.0** Back at the bottom of the campground. Cross bridge and head back to car.

Overlooking the ridge at Cerro Alto.

Cerro Cabrillo Trails

Location:	Eastern portion of Morro Bay State Park.
Distance:	4.1-mile loop.
Time:	35 minutes.
Tread:	Singletrack.
Aerobic level:	Easy to moderate.
Technical difficulty:	3.
Fees:	None.
Services:	All services back in the town of Morro Bay.
Water:	Water available at the Morro Bay Campground.
Highlights:	Cerro Cabrillo is a fun non-technical network of singletrack. The trails quickly run through rolling grass-covered hills. It is a great place to get a feel for race-type conditions except it lacks tough hills.
Hazards:	Hunters, lots of mosquitoes, ticks, and poison oak.
Land status:	Morro Bay State Park.
Maps:	USGS Morro Bay South; Thomas Brothers, San Luis Obispo County, page 631.

Cerro Cabrillo Trails

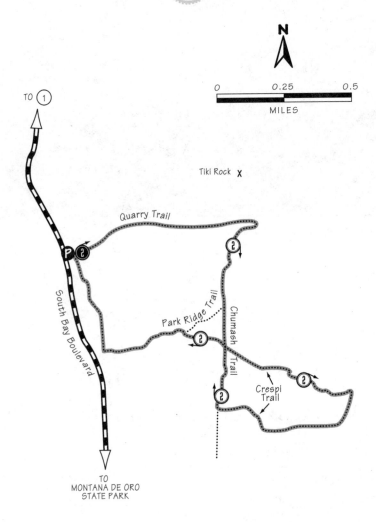

N

0   0.25   0.5

MILES

TO ①

Tiki Rock X

Quarry Trail

P ②

② →

South Bay Boulevard

Park Ridge Trail

Chumash Trail

②

Crespi
Trail

②

②

TO
MONTANA DE ORO
STATE PARK

Brad and the missus at Cerro Cabrillo.

Access: Approximately 1 mile south of Morro Bay and 12 miles north of San Luis Obispo, exit California Highway 1 at Southbay Boulevard. Travel west for approximately 1 mile. About one-half mile past the turnoff for Morro Bay State Park you see a small parking area to the left of the road, adjacent to the wetlands. Pull into the parking area and you see the trailhead to the left of the information board.

Notes on the trail: As you pass through the trailhead you begin a gradual climb up the Quarry Trail. Although this is the steepest, most technical part of the trail, it is still not terribly demanding. At approximately one-quarter mile you see a trail off to the left and continue to climb straight until the trail levels off at 0.5 mile. At 0.8 mile continue straight past the trail that climbs steeply up the hill to the left to Tiki Rock. At 0.9 mile turn right onto the Park Ridge Trail and continue straight past a trail merging in from the left. At 1.3 miles turn left at the junction and continue another 0.1 mile to another junction where you turn left onto the Chumash Trail. At 1.5 miles you reach a four-way junction and turn left on the Crespi Trail (the marker has been changed to read Pepsi Trail). At 1.8 and 1.9 miles, veer to the right past trails coming in from the left. At 2.8 miles continue straight past a trail that comes in from the right. At 2.9 miles turn right onto the Chumash Trail. After a short steep climb you find yourself back at the four-way junction that marked the Crespi Trail at 3.2 miles. Take the fork to the immediate left, merge with Park Ridge Trail, and continue down. At 3.6 miles you pass a trail sharply to the right. Continue until you get to the gate near the main road. Turn right onto Live Oak Trail and veer left after passing two trails to the right. You find yourself back at the parking lot.

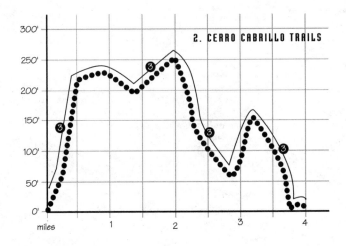

2. CERRO CABRILLO TRAILS

T H E   R I D E

0.0 Pass through trailhead and begin gradual ascent up Quarry Trail.

0.3 Continue straight past trail to the left.

0.5 Continue straight past Live Oak Trail to the right.

0.8 Continue straight past trail to the left, which climbs to Tiki Rock.

0.9 Turn right onto Park Ridge Trail.

1.0 Continue straight past trail merging in from the left.

1.3 Turn left, stay on Park Ridge Trail.

1.4 Turn left onto Chumash Trail.

1.5 Take the Crespi Trail to the left at the four-way junction.

1.8 Veer right at the junction.

1.9 Veer right at the junction.

2.8 Continue straight past the trail from right.

2.9 Turn right onto Chumash Trail.

3.2 After a short, steep climb turn left at the four-way junction.

3.4 While riding down, veer left past a trail to the right and merge with Park Ridge Trail.

3.6 Continue straight past the trail to the right.

3.7 At the gate near the main road turn right onto Live Oak Trail.

3.8 Veer left past the junction which heads back into the canyon.

3.9 Veer left past the junction which treads back into the canyon.

4.1 The end.

Montana de Oro State Park

Montana de Oro State Park is one of the most beautiful units of the California state park system. Sitting just south of Morro Bay, it faces the ocean with fantastic views of Morro Bay and Morro Rock. Its 7-mile-long shore combines sandy coves with rugged cliffs and headlands. The most popular beach area is Spooner's Cove, just below the historic Spooner Ranch House where the ranger station is located. With plenty of day-use parking, picnic tables, pit toilets and barbecues, Spooner's Cove is an excellent hub for a day of biking, swimming and just relaxing.

Montana de Oro State Park includes over 8,000 acres of undeveloped mountain and beach. California live oak and Bishop pine inhabit the chaparral-covered hills while willows, big-leaf maple, box elder and black cottonwood trees cover the stream-cut canyons. An assortment of wildlife inhabits the park, including rabbits, squirrels, skunks, raccoon, badger, deer, fox, bobcats, and, as we frequently encountered, snakes.

The park's 8,000 acres offer a variety of trails for hiking and mountain biking. The park is best known for the mellow but scenic Bluff Trail which meanders along the rugged cliffs overlooking the surf below. While the Bluff Trail is an excellent choice for the entire family, the park also offers more challenging rides. The Islay Creek Trail is an excellent choice for those looking for a solid technical ride. Don't be disappointed with the first 3 miles of flat fireroad on the Islay Creek Trail. The singletrack trail steeply climbs into the hills and meanders along the mountainous ridge before quickly dropping over ruts and bumps back to the ocean below.

Islay Creek Trail

Location:	Morro Bay, located approximately 20 miles west of San Luis Obispo.
Distance:	8-mile loop.
Time:	1.5 hours.
Tread:	The first few miles are fireroad, then the trail turns into singletrack.
Aerobic level:	Moderate to strenuous.
Technical difficulty:	3+.
Fees:	None.
Services:	Bathrooms and a ranger station where you can buy maps, books, etc.
Water:	Water available at park headquarters.
Highlights:	The biggest highlight of this trail is probably the 2 miles of insane arm-burning singletrack. Second to the singletrack are the views of Morro Bay and the Pacific Ocean.
Hazards:	Snakes, snakes, snakes. They were abundant.
Land status:	Montana De Oro State Park.
Maps:	USGS Morro Bay South; Thomas Brothers, San Luis Obispo County, page 651.

Access: From U.S. Highway 101 exit Los Osos/Baywood in San Luis Obispo. Travel approximately 12 miles west on Los Osos Valley Road. Los Osos Valley Road then becomes Pecho Valley Road. This takes you into the park. Once you see the Montana de Oro State Park sign drive another 2.5 miles to the park headquarters. You can either park by the beach if you plan on hanging out for a while, or you can park across from the headquarters. The trailhead is approximately two-tenths of a mile before the parking lot at the beach.

Notes on the trail: This trail has everything. From the trailhead ride along the fireroad for 3 miles. Just after passing a barn on the right at 2.9 miles, you come to the East Boundary Trail on the left at 3 miles. This is where you begin a steep singletrack climb until you reach the Ridge Trail. At 5.1 miles take a sharp left when you reach a sign that reads, "Ridge Trail." At 5.5 miles, after a fairly steep climb, you can turn either left or right. Turn left and continue on the Ridge Trail. After traversing the Ridge Trail for a while you begin a great downhill singletrack that lets you out on Pecho Valley Road, which is 0.1 mile above where you started.

Islay Creek Trail

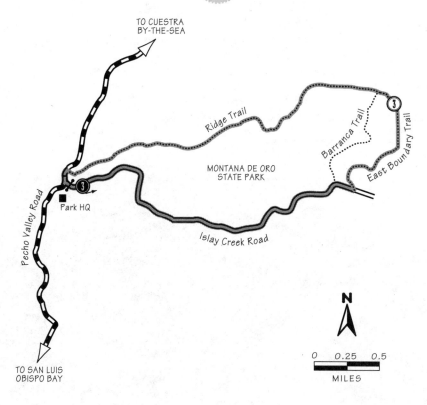

TO CUESTRA
BY-THE-SEA

Ridge Trail

Barranca Trail

East Boundary Trail

③

MONTANA DE ORO
STATE PARK

Pecho Valley Road

Park HQ

Islay Creek Road

③

TO SAN LUIS
OBISPO BAY

N

0   0.25   0.5

MILES

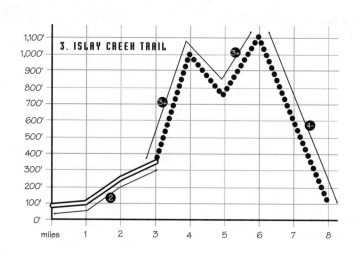

3. ISLAY CREEK TRAIL

1,100'
1,000'
900'
800'
700'
600'
500'
400'
300'
200'
100'
0'

miles   1   2   3   4   5   6   7   8

③+
③+
④-
②

THE RIDE

0.0 From the trailhead ride along the main fireroad.

2.7 Continue straight past a trail to the right.

3.0 Turn left on the East Boundary Trail.

4.9 Go straight past the Barranca Trail on the left.

5.1 Take a sharp left when you reach a sign that indicates Ridge Trail.

5.5 After a fairly steep climb you are able to turn either left or right. You want to turn left and continue on the Ridge Trail.

6.0 At the top of the ride begin your final descent.

8.0 The end.

Right before we ran over the rattlesnake on Islay Creek.

Bluff Trail

Location:	Morro Bay, approximately 20 miles west of San Luis Obispo.
Distance:	3.8 miles, out and back.
Time:	45 minutes.
Tread:	Fireroad with some offshoot sections that are singletrack.
Aerobic level:	Easy.
Technical difficulty:	2.
Fees:	None.
Services:	Bathrooms, camping and a ranger station where you can buy maps, books, etc. All other services back in Morro Bay or San Luis Obispo.
Water:	Water available at park headquarters.
Highlights:	The scenery is awesome. This is a great family ride. You can also pack a picnic and barbecue on the beach after your ride.
Hazards:	The trail is loaded with hikers so you cannot fly on this trail. You should heed the warnings on the bluff and not get too close to the edge.
Land status:	Montana De Oro State Park.
Maps:	USGS Morro Bay South, Thomas Brothers, San Luis Obispo County, page 651.

Not exactly their idea of a vacation, but the Bluff Trail was fun.

Bluff Trail

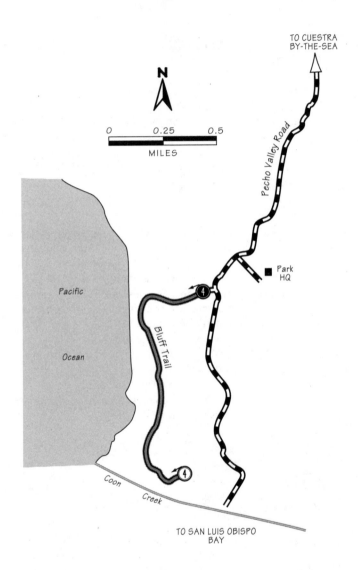

TO CUESTRA
BY-THE-SEA

N

0   0.25   0.5
MILES

Pecho Valley Road

Pacific

Ocean

Park
HQ

Bluff Trail

Coon   Creek

TO SAN LUIS OBISPO
BAY

Access: From U.S. Highway 101 exit Los Osos/Baywood in San Luis Obispo. Travel approximately 12 miles west on Los Osos Valley Road. Los Osos Valley Road then becomes Pecho Valley Road. This takes you into the park. Once you see the Montana de Oro State Park sign drive another 2.5 miles to the park headquarters. You can either park by the beach if you plan on hanging out for a while, or you can park across from the headquarters, which is where the trailhead is.

Notes on the trail: You find the trailhead approximately 100 yards up from the park headquarters. This trail is easy to follow. Bring your camera; the scenery is beautiful. While you ride along the cliffs you have the option to take little offshoot trails toward the bluffs, which slightly lengthen the ride. Ride all the way to Coon Creek where you turn around and take a leisurely ride back.

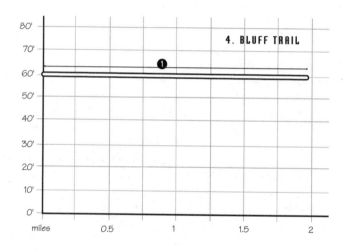

THE RIDE

0.0 Begin across from the park headquarters and ride along the bluffs.
0.7 You come to a bridge on your right that crosses a small crevice. Turn right and cross the bridge. Make an immediate right after you cross the bridge.
1.4 Veer right past the fork in the road with a sign that indicates Pecho Road.
1.9 Reach a fence marking Coon Creek. Turn around and head back.
3.8 The end.

Santa Barbara County

Nineteen Oaks

Location:	In the San Marcos Pass within the Los Padres National Forest.
Distance:	6.5-mile loop.
Time:	45 minutes.
Tread:	Fireroad climb with singletrack descent.
Aerobic level:	Moderate.
Technical difficulty:	4.
Fees:	Forest Adventure Pass required.
Services:	Pit toilets in the Upper Oso Campground. All other services back near U.S. Highway 101.
Water:	Water spigots in the Upper Oso Campground.
Highlights:	Spectacular views of the Santa Ynez Mountains.
Hazards:	Dirt bikes and other off-road vehicles. Hikers and equestrians.
Land status:	Los Padres National Forest.
Maps:	USGS Little Pine Mountain, San Marcos Pass; Thomas Brothers, Santa Barbara County, page 366.

Access: Take California Highway 154 north from U.S. Highway 101 for approximately 10 miles and turn right on Paradise Road. Continue on Paradise Road until you reach the Lower Oso Recreation Area just after the water crossing. Turn left at the first road which is marked to Upper Oso. Toward the back of the campground, on the right, is a green-gated trail and sign that reads, "Camuesa Buckhorn OHV Route." Farther back is a little singletrack past the campsites. Don't go there.

Notes on the trail: After passing through the gate at the trailhead begin to climb along the well-maintained, moderate dirt road. At 0.7 mile, as the road bends to the right, you see the Santa Cruz Trail straight ahead. Continue on the main road, ride past two trails merging from the left at approximately 1 mile. At 2.6 miles continue past the Camuesa Connector Trail to the right. At 3.1 miles you see the Nineteen Oaks Trail to the left, just over

Nineteen Oaks

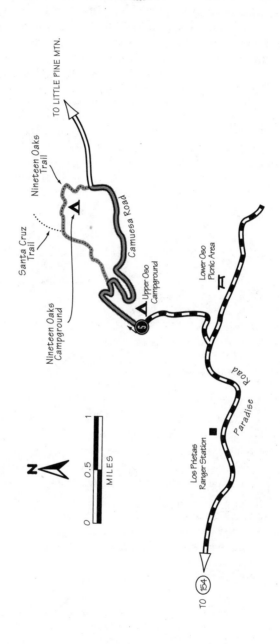

TO LITTLE PINE MTN.

Nineteen Oaks Trail

Santa Cruz Trail

Nineteen Oaks Campground

Camuesa Road

Upper Oso Campground

Lower Oso Picnic Area

Paradise Road

Los Prietas Ranger Station

N

MILES
0   0.5   1

TO 154

the berm and marked with a fence. Begin your descent down the Nineteen Oaks Trail by going around the fence. The trail quickly becomes very loose with large ruts and wash-outs. As you pass the old Nineteen Oaks Campground the trail becomes extremely steep. It then drops over a series of water bars and ends up at the Santa Cruz Trail at 4.6 miles. Turn left on the Santa Cruz Trail and follow it along the stream to 5.8 miles and veer left as the lower fork drops to the stream. Just past the fork you find yourself back at Camuesa Road. Turn right on Camuesa Road and head back to the trailhead.

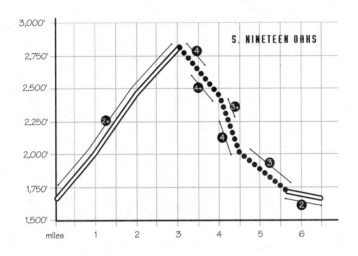

THE RIDE

0.0 Pass through the steel gate and begin to climb.
0.3 Continue on main road past a footpath to the left.
0.7 Stay on the main road as it bends to the right past the Santa Cruz Trail.
1.0 Stay on the main road as it bends to the right past a trail to the left.
1.1 Continue straight past a trail merging in from the left.
2.6 Continue straight past the Camuesa Connector Trail on the right.
3.1 Turn left onto Nineteen Oaks Trail.
4.6 Just past the water bars turn left on Santa Cruz Trail.
5.8 Veer left at the junction and then turn right onto Camuesa Road.
6.5 The end.

Camuesa Road to the Buckhorn Saddle

Location:	In the San Marcos Pass within the Los Padres National Forest.
Distance:	8.5 miles, out and back.
Time:	1 hour.
Tread:	Fireroad.
Aerobic level:	Moderate.
Technical difficulty:	2+.
Fees:	Forest Adventure Pass required.
Services:	Pit toilets in the Upper Oso Campground. All other services back near U.S. Highway 101.
Water:	Water spigots in the Upper Oso Campground.
Highlights:	Spectacular views of the Santa Ynez Mountains.
Hazards:	Dirt bikes and other off-road vehicles.
Land status:	Los Padres National Forest.
Maps:	USGS Little Pine Mountain, San Marcos Pass; Thomas Brothers, Santa Barbara County, page 366.

Access: Take California Highway 154 north from U.S. Highway 101 for approximately 10 miles and turn right on Paradise Road. Continue on Paradise Road until you reach the Lower Oso Recreation Area just after the water crossing. Turn left at the first road which is marked to Upper Oso. Toward the back of the campground, on the right, is a green-gated trail and sign that reads, "Camuesa Buckhorn OHV Route." Farther back is a little singletrack past the campsites. Don't go there.

Notes on the trail: After you pass through the gate at the trailhead begin to climb along the well-maintained, moderate dirt road. After 0.7 mile, as the road bends to the right, you see the Santa Cruz Trail straight ahead. Continue on the main road, ride past two trails merging from the left at approximately 1 mile. At 2.6 miles continue past the Camuesa Connector Trail to the right and then past the Nineteen Oaks Trail to the left another one-half mile up. From here begin the final ascent to the Buckhorn Saddle at 4.2 miles, just after passing a picnic area on the left. At the saddle the Little Pine Road veers to the left as the Camuesa Trail drops to the right. After a short break turn around and enjoy the fast descent to the bottom.

Camuesa Road to the Buckhorn Saddle

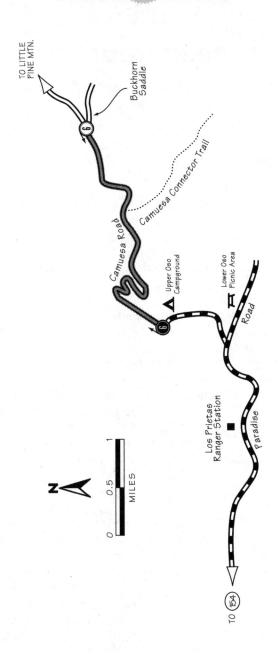

TO LITTLE PINE MTN.

Buckhorn Saddle

Camuesa Connector Trail

Camuesa Road

Upper Oso Campground

Lower Oso Picnic Area

Road

Los Prietas Ranger Station

Paradise

TO 154

N

0   0.5   1
MILES

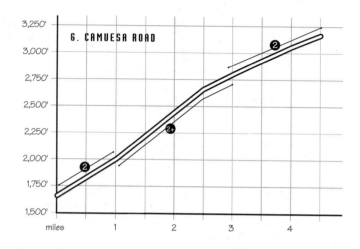

6. CAMUESA ROAD

THE RIDE

0.0 Pass through the steel gate and begin to climb.
0.3 Continue on main road past a footpath to the left.
0.7 Stay on the main road as it bends to the right past the Santa Cruz Trail.
1.0 Stay on the main road as it bends to the right past a trail to the left.
1.1 Continue straight past a trail merging in from the left.
2.6 Continue straight past the Camuesa Connector Trail on the right.
3.1 Continue straight past the Nineteen Oaks Trail on the left.
4.1 Continue straight past the footpath to the left leading to a picnic table.
4.2 Atop the Buckhorn Saddle. Turn around and enjoy the fast descent.
8.5 The end.

Arroyo Burro Loop

Location:	East Santa Barbara County.
Distance:	9-mile loop.
Time:	1.5 hours.
Tread:	The first half of the ride is on a well-maintained fireroad. The second half is on singletrack.
Aerobic level:	Strenuous.
Technical difficulty:	The first half is a Level 2. The second half is a Level 4-.
Fees:	$4.00 for parking or an Adventure Pass.
Services:	Bathrooms and camping are available in the Lower Oso area and full services are available back near U.S. Highway 101.
Water:	Water is available when you enter the park area.
Highlights:	This is a fun ride. It is especially interesting because the first half is up a very steep fireroad and the second section is a very technical downhill. When you get to the bottom you will be glad you did not go up this section.

Arroyo Burro Road.

Arroyo Burro Loop

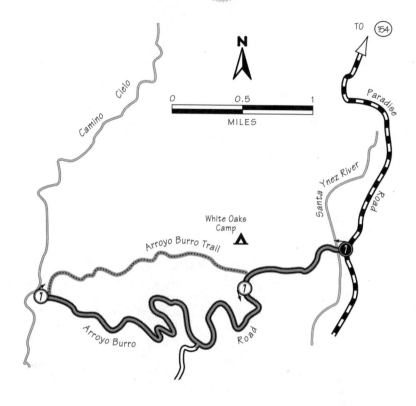

Hazards:	Be careful on the downhill as there are some gnarly sections. Depending on the time of year you may encounter hunters; we saw a few (don't wear camouflage).
Land status:	Los Padres National Forest.
Maps:	USGS Little Pine Mountain, San Marcos Pass; Thomas Brothers, Santa Barbara County, page 366.

Access: From U.S. Highway 101 exit heading north on California Highway 154. Drive for 10.3 miles to Paradise Road where you turn right. Drive 5.7 miles to the ranger kiosk and continue for another mile to a fork in the road. You veer right (or down) into the river bed. Park here on the rocks. It does not look like much of a parking lot, but you are allowed to park here.

Notes on the trail: The trail is easy to follow once you find it. From the trailhead begin to climb the very steep fireroad with amazing views. When you are almost at the top you turn right onto the Arroyo Burro Trail. From here you venture down a fun technical singletrack. The trail is rich with vegetation and running streams. Enjoy it.

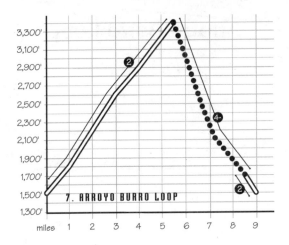

7. ARROYO BURRO LOOP

THE RIDE

0.0 Once you park, follow the road you drove in on to the beginning of the fireroad. Be prepared to cross the Santa Ynez River (it can be deep).

1.0 Continue straight on the main road past the Arroyo Burro Trail on the right.

5.5 Just before you reach Camino Cielo Road you come to a small trailhead. Make a right and ride down a short hill where you encounter a metal sign confirming that you are on Arroyo Burro Trail.

7.9 Stay to the right past the fork with a sign that reads, "Designated."

8.0 After you cross a stream you begin to climb a short hill and pass through a gate. You will see a large green water tower on your right. This is the trail you passed in the beginning of the ride.

9.0 The end.

Romero Canyon

Location:	Montecito, located a few exits south of Santa Barbara.
Distance:	13 miles, out and back.
Time:	2.5 hours.
Tread:	Combination of singletrack and fireroad.
Aerobic level:	Moderate to strenuous.
Technical difficulty:	3+.
Fees:	None.
Services:	None.
Water:	None.
Highlights:	This happens to be one of our favorite trails, primarily because one of us proposed to his wife while standing on the bluffs overlooking the beautiful Pacific Ocean. The trail has rainforest-like qualities and majestic views looking over Santa Barbara.
Hazards:	On your way down, beware of up-hill riders and watch your speed over some gnarly technical sections.
Land status:	Los Padres National Forest.
Maps:	USGS Carpenteria; Thomas Brothers, Santa Barbara County, page 987.

Access: From U.S. Highway 101 exit Sheffield Drive North. Drive 1.5 miles to East Valley Road. Turn left on East Valley Road, then immediately turn right onto Romero Canyon Road. Drive 1.5 miles to Bella Vista Road and turn right. Drive approximately one-quarter of a mile to a big locked fire gate. This is the trailhead. Park along Bella Vista Road.

Notes on the trail: This is an easy trail to travel. There are not many places to turn off. After passing through the gate at the trailhead, begin the steep ascent to a saddle at 2 miles. Continue past the trail to the right as the road turns into singletrack. Continue to ride along the trail through the lush vegetation for 4.5 miles until you reach a saddle marked by a small water tower. Turn around and enjoy an awesome fast downhill.

Romero Canyon

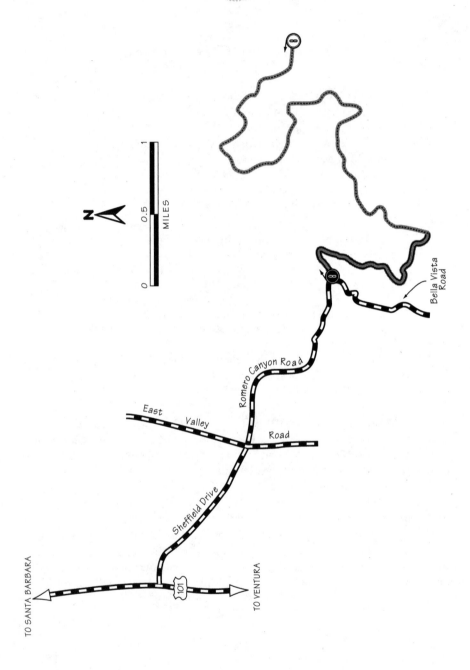

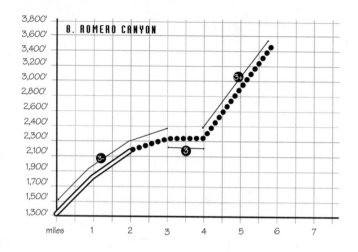

THE RIDE

0.0 Pass through the gate at the trailhead and begin your climb.

0.3 Turn right at the fork.

2.0 Continue straight past locked fire gate on your right.

4.2 Continue straight on the main road past Bella Vista Road on the left.

6.5 You will come to a steel water tower on your right. This is also a little plateau that has some trails continuing straight and a trail to the left. This is where you turn around and go back the way you came.

13.0 The end.

Ventura County

Wildwood Park

Location:	Ventura County, Newbury Park.
Distance:	6.2-mile loop with several other options.
Time:	1.5 hours.
Tread:	Mostly hardpacked dirt and fireroad. There are some singletrack sections.
Aerobic level:	Moderate.
Technical difficulty:	Mostly Level 3 with a Level 3+ section of switchbacks.
Fees:	None.
Services:	None. There are plenty of services back near U.S. Highway 101.
Water:	None. It gets hot so bring plenty.
Highlights:	Demanding switchbacks that test even the best riders. There are a few fun downhill sections. There is a nature center and a really awesome waterfall that is a nice spot to hang out and rest.
Hazards:	Some of the downhill sections are fairly technical so you need to be careful. If you are riding in the summer, the ride is hot; bring plenty of water.
Land status:	Wildwood Park.
Maps:	USGS Newbury Park; Thomas Brothers, Ventura County, page 526.

Access: From U.S. Highway 101 exit Lynn Road and head north for 2.5 miles. Turn left on Avenue De Los Arboles. Continue for 0.9 mile until you come to Big Sky Drive, which only goes to the right. You want to park to the left in the dirt parking lot.

Notes on the trail: You start with a short ride on the street. At 1.2 miles you see the trail off to the right through the wooden fence. Begin riding the singletrack as it gently climbs the side of the mountain and then drops into a valley. As you reach the bottom of the valley, at 1.3 miles, turn left at the junction with a sign that reads, "Conejo Recreation and Park District." You

Wildwood Park

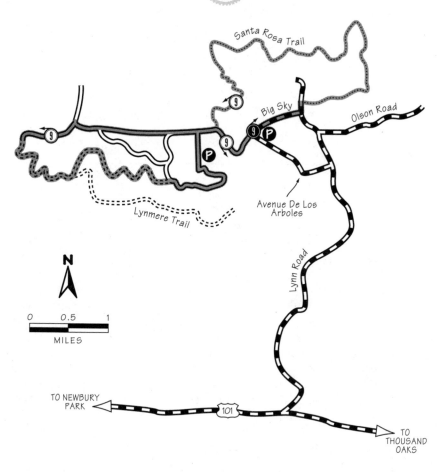

then climb some technical sections until you reach the top of the Santa Rosa Trail at 2.3 miles. At the top you begin a descent through about nine very technical switchbacks which require many riders to dismount. At the bottom of the Santa Rosa Trail (at 3 miles) turn right onto the fireroad. At 3.1 miles, continue straight at the fork with a sign that indicates Teepee Overlook Paradise Falls. Continue riding until you reach the Lizard Rock Trail on the left at 3.4 miles. At 3.9 miles, turn left and drop down into Lower Wildwood Canyon. Continue to ride straight on the main trail until you reach the picnic area at 4.9 miles and see Paradise Falls. At 5.1 miles you reach a three-way junction at the teepee and head straight, following the Meadow Cave Area sign. At 5.2 miles you reach another junction and veer left toward the Nature Center. At 5.7 miles you reach Parking Lot 1. Continue straight out of the parking lot on the dirt road until you see the Mesa Trail to the right (at 6 miles). Turn right on Mesa Trail and you quickly find yourself back at the car.

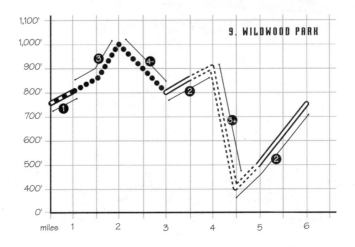

THE RIDE

0.0	From the parking lot, take Big Sky Drive to Wildwood Avenue.
0.7	Turn left on Wildwood Avenue.
1.2	After a steep climb turn right onto trailhead that is marked Santa Rosa Trail. Shortly afterwards veer right past a fork which heads down into the valley.
1.3	After short downhill, turn left as you reach a sign that reads, "Conejo Recreation and Park District."
2.3	Turn left at the sign that says, "Trail" and begin your descent through approximately nine technical rocky switchbacks.
3.0	At the bottom of the Santa Rosa Trail turn right onto the fireroad.
3.1	Continue straight at the fork with a sign that indicates Teepee Overlook Paradise Falls.
3.4	Turn left onto the Lizard Rock Trail.
3.9	Turn left and head downhill at the sign which points toward Lower Wildwood Canyon.
4.4	Continue straight at the sign which points to Lower Wildwood Canyon.
4.5	Continue straight past Skunk Hollow on the right.
4.9	At the picnic area, take the trail to the left that says, "Teepee Overlook."
5.1	At the teepee and a three-way junction, head straight following the Meadow Cave Area sign.
5.2	Veer left at another three-way junction; follow the Wildwood Canyon Trail to the Nature Center.
5.7	You get to Parking Lot 1. Continue straight out of the parking lot on the dirt road.
6.0	Turn right on the Mesa Trail toward where you parked.
6.2	The end.

Chesebro Canyon/Baleen Wall

Location:	Agoura Hills, located in Ventura County.
Distance:	12.3-mile loop.
Time:	2 hours.
Tread:	Mostly fireroad with some sections of singletrack.
Aerobic level:	Moderate to strenuous.
Technical difficulty:	3–.
Fees:	None.
Services:	A portable toilet is available in the parking area. Other services are available near the freeway.
Water:	None.
Highlights:	Chesebro is a great place to ride. There are many trails to follow that offer something for every level of rider. Some of the sections in the back of the riding area offer fun singletrack.
Hazards:	This is a very popular place for hikers and equestrians. Try and get there early; the parking lot fills up.
Land status:	Santa Monica Mountains National Recreation Area.
Maps:	USGS Simi Valley East; Thomas Brothers, Ventura County, page 558 D5.

Access: From U.S. Highway 101 exit at Chesebro. Turn north onto Palo Camado Canyon Drive and make an immediate right onto Chesebro Canyon Road. In approximately three-quarters of a mile you come to a well-marked parking area. The sign indicates Chesebro Canyon. Follow the road one-quarter mile to the second parking lot.

Notes on the trail: From the Park Service sign at the trailhead ride straight on the Chesebro Trail. At 2 miles veer left and begin the climb up to the scenic outcroppings of the Baleen Wall. As you make the 2-mile climb to the top of the Baleen Wall, you pass a few trails on your left; continue straight on the main road. At 4 miles you reach the top of the Baleen Wall and enjoy an incredible view of the valley below. At 5 miles turn left at the junction and drop down a short but fast road to Shepherd Flats. At 5.7 miles you come to a triangle-shaped junction. At the junction head straight on the moderately-technical singletrack connector to Palo Camado Canyon Trail. At 6.6 miles the singletrack ends. Turn left onto the Palo Camado Canyon Trail, which takes you down a steep hill. At 8.3 miles make a sharp left at

Chesebro Canyon/Baleen Wall

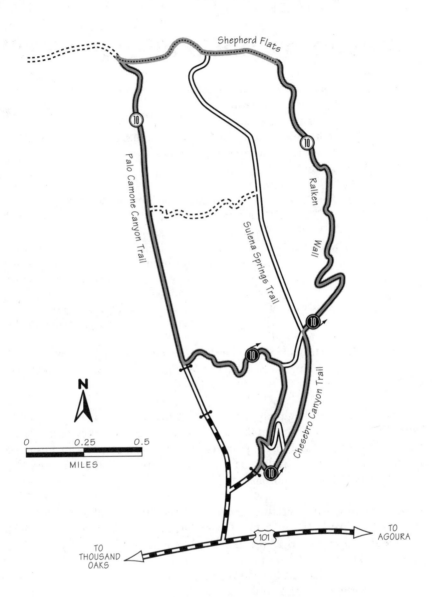

Shepherd Flats

Palo Camone Canyon Trail

Sulena Springs Trail

Ralken Wall

Chesebro Canyon Trail

N

0   0.25   0.5
MILES

101

TO AGOURA

TO THOUSAND OAKS

the sign that indicates Chesebro Canyon and begin a grueling climb to the top before you drop back down into a river crossing. After you cross the river turn right and head back to Chesebro Canyon and the beginning.

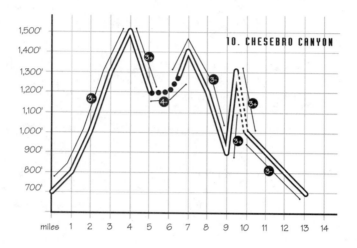

10. CHESEBRO CANYON

THE RIDE

0.0 From the trailhead at the National Park Service (NPS) information board take the Chesebro Trail straight ahead.

0.5 Continue straight past the Modello Canyon Trail on your left.

1.3 Continue straight past the Palo Camado Trail on your left.

2.0 Veer left at the fork and begin your climb up the Baleen Wall.

3.6 Continue straight past the Baleen Wall Hikers Trail on the left and then straight past the sign that reads, "No established NPS trails beyond this point."

3.7 Continue straight past the unmarked road to your left.

4.0 You reach the Baleen Wall rock outcropping. Take a minute and enjoy the view.

5.0 Turn left at the junction onto a moderately technical singletrack that leads you to Shepherd Flats.

5.7 At the triangular open area at Shepherd Flats continue straight on the singletrack connector to the Palo Camado Canyon Trail.

6.6 Turn right as the singletrack ends at the Palo Camado Canyon Trail.

8.3 Turn left at the sign that reads, "Chesebro Canyon."

11.0 Turn right after the river crossing. You are now on Sulfur Springs Trail.

12.3 The end.

Rocky Peak

Location:	Where California Highway 118 passes between the San Fernando Valley and Simi Valley.
Distance:	11.9-mile loop or 6.5 miles with car shuttle.
Time:	1.25 hours.
Tread:	Actual trail is about 60 percent fireroad and 40 percent singletrack. There are also 5.4 miles of paved road.
Aerobic level:	Strenuous.
Technical difficulty:	The climb up Rocky Peak is a Level 3 due to its steep incline. The descent down Chumash Trail is a Level 4.
Fees:	None.
Services:	No services available at trailhead but most services can be found off of the Kuehner Drive offramp to the west or Topanga Canyon Boulevard to the east.
Water:	No water at the trailhead. It gets hot so bring plenty.
Highlights:	Fun technical singletrack down the Chumash Trail. Rock formations and lookouts along Rocky Peak.
Hazards:	Rattlesnakes, mountain lions and steep cliffs off Chumash Trail.
Land status:	Santa Monica Mountains.
Maps:	USGS Simi Valley East; Thomas Brothers, Ventura County, page 499, Los Angeles County, page 499.

Access: From the San Fernando Valley, take California Highway 118 west and exit at Rocky Peak Boulevard. Turn right and you immediately dead-end at the trailhead.

From Simi Valley, take CA 118 east, exit at Kuehner Drive and turn right. In approximately 1 mile, Kuehner Drive turns into Santa Susana Pass. Continue along Santa Susana Pass until you parallel CA 118 at Rocky Peak Motorway. Turn left at Rocky Peak Motorway and cross the bridge.

To leave a shuttle car, exit CA 118 at Yosemite Avenue and drive north approximately one-quarter mile to Flanagan Street and turn right. Within three-quarters of a mile, at the end of Flanagan Street, you see the bottom of the trail.

Notes on the trail: Rocky Peak is an extremely demanding, yet fun trail. The climb to the top is quite strenuous as it quickly ascends up sections of

Rocky Peak

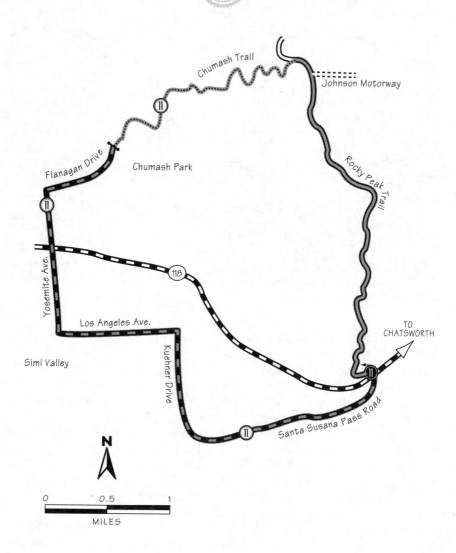

Chumash Trail

Johnson Motorway

Chumash Park

Flanagan Drive

Rocky Peak Trail

Yosemite Ave.

118

Los Angeles Ave.

Simi Valley

Kuehner Drive

TO
CHATSWORTH

Santa Susana Pass Road

N

0   0.5   1

MILES

Descending the Chumash Trail.

imbedded rock. From the trailhead climb steeply, passing footpaths on either side of you, until the trail levels off at about eight-tenths of a mile. You see the Rainbow Trail to the left but head straight on the main road. The trail once again becomes steep until a slight reprise at approximately 1.6 miles. It then steepens up again until the 2.7-mile mark where it finally levels off. At 2.7 and 3.2 miles you see dirt roads heading off to the right, which lead back down to Chatsworth. You continue straight past them. At 3.8 miles you see the marked Chumash Trail to the left. Turn left onto this singletrack and begin your descent over slate rock and ruts. At 5.5 miles you see a trail to the left; veer right. At 6 miles you come to a junction and either way you go, the two trails merge within 75 feet. At 6.5 miles you reach the bottom of the trailhead in a residential area at Flanagan Street. Ride down Flanagan Street about 1 mile and turn left on Yosemite Avenue. Pass over the freeway and at 8.5 miles go left on Los Angeles Avenue. Ride another mile and turn right on Kuehner Drive. Within 1 mile, Kuehner Drive turns into Santa Susana Pass. Climb Santa Susana Pass until you parallel California Highway 118 at Rocky Peak Motorway. Turn left at Rocky Peak Motorway, cross the bridge over the freeway, and you are back at your car.

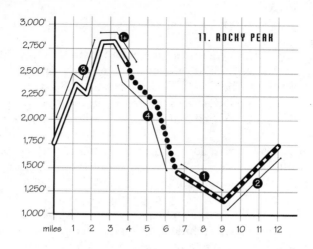

THE RIDE

0.0 Pass through trailhead and begin a steep climb.
0.2 Continue straight on main road past trail to the right.
0.5 Continue straight on main road past trail to the right.
0.8 Rainbow Trail to the left, continue straight on main road.
2.7 Continue straight past the dirt road to the right.
3.2 Continue straight past the dirt road to the right.
3.8 Turn left on Chumash Trail and begin singletrack descent.
6.0 Go either way at junction; both forks merge within 75 feet.
6.5 Bottom of trailhead at Flanagan Street. Go straight on Flanagan Street.
7.4 Turn left on Yosemite Avenue and pass over freeway.
8.5 Turn left on Los Angeles Avenue.
9.5 Turn right on Kuehner Drive. Kuehner Drive turns into Santa Susana Pass at 10 miles.
11.7 Turn left on Rocky Peak Motorway. Cross over freeway.
11.9 The end.

Point Mugu State Park

Point Mugu State Park (sometimes known as Sycamore Canyon) is located approximately 30 miles west of Interstate 405 on California Highway 1 (Pacific Coast Highway). There is a campground at the entrance and on hot days you will feel the cool breeze of the ocean, just a stone's throw from the campground. The park is populated with trees and other vegetation, such as wildflowers. After visiting this park for the first time you will be amazed that a place like this exists in Southern California. The park is home to deer, coyotes and rattlesnakes. This is a popular spot for birdwatching, as well.

This is a great place for long family rides as well as hard-core training for advanced mountain bikers. If you are looking for something easy, ride Big Sycamore Canyon and enjoy the stream crossings and shade underneath the trees. For something more technical, ride Guadalasco and enjoy the awesome singletrack. For a challenging workout you can link several loops and trails for a long 20-mile ride. Point Mugu State Park can also be accessed off U.S. Highway 101 in Ventura County.

Big Sycamore Canyon

Location:	North of Malibu in Point Mugu State Park.
Distance:	10.6-mile loop.
Time:	2 hours.
Tread:	Fireroad.
Aerobic level:	Moderate.
Technical difficulty:	3–.
Fees:	$5.00 for parking.
Services:	Bathrooms and camping.
Water:	There is a water fountain in the camping area.
Highlights:	This ride is a scenic adventure through Point Mugu State Park. This is probably one of the most scenic and relaxing rides in this book. If you are looking to warm up your legs for the season or if you want to get some peace and quiet for awhile, this is a good ride. There are many different permutations for this park. If you want to be more adventurous or desire a tougher ride, you can easily put one together.
Hazards:	Watch out for hikers and other bikers. Sometimes this section of Pacific Coast Highway is closed due to heavy rains.

Big Sycamore Canyon
Guadalasco Trail

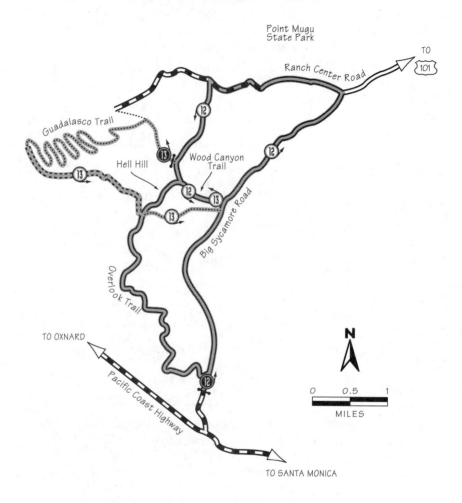

Point Mugu
State Park

Ranch Center Road

TO 101

Guadalasco Trail

Hell Hill

Wood Canyon Trail

Big Sycamore Road

Overlook Trail

TO OXNARD

Pacific Coast Highway

N

0   0.5   1
MILES

TO SANTA MONICA

Land status: Point Mugu State Park.

Maps: USGS Point Mugu State Park; Thomas Brothers, Ventura County, page 387.

Access: From Los Angeles follow Pacific Coast Highway (California Highway 1) for approximately 30 miles to Point Mugu State Park. Turn right into the park. Park in the day-parking area (follow the signs).

Notes on the trail: The trail starts at the northern most end of the campground. Follow Big Sycamore Canyon over three or four stream crossings until you get to Ranch Center Road at 4.5 miles. Here you head to the left and climb a steep hill, then descend the other side to the Ranch Center Road. You begin to descend paved road at 5.4 miles. At 5.8 miles the trail curves to the left, putting you on the Wood Canyon Trail. Continue to the junction at 7.3 miles and go straight past the junction, staying on Wood Canyon Trail. At 7.6 miles you reach Big Sycamore Canyon. Veer right and retrace your route back to the start.

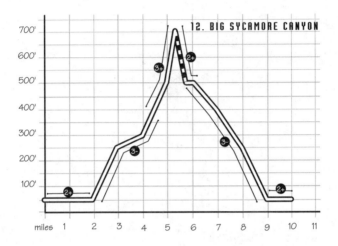

THE RIDE

0.0 From the north end of the campground ride through the locked gate.

0.8 Continue straight past the Overlook Trail, which is for hiking only.

1.0 Continue straight past Serano Canyon Trail.

3.0 Veer right at the fork past the Wood Canyon Trail on the left.

4.5 Turn left on Ranch Center Road past the continuation of Big Sycamore Canyon on the right.

5.4 You reach a paved road that shoots you down to the Ranch Center Road.

5.8 The trail curves to the left and you are on The Wood Canyon Trail.

7.1 Continue straight past the Guadalasco trail on your right.

7.3 Continue straight at the junction; stay on Wood Canyon Trail as you pass Hell Hill to the right.

7.6 Veer right at Big Sycamore Canyon and retrace your ride back to the car.

10.6 The end.

Guadalasco Trail

See Map on Page 49

Location:	Point Mugu State Park, north of Malibu.
Distance:	15-mile loop.
Time:	3 hours.
Tread:	50 percent fireroad and 50 percent singletrack.
Aerobic level:	Strenuous.
Technical difficulty:	3+.
Fees:	$5.00 for parking.
Services:	Bathrooms and camping.
Water:	There is a water fountain in the camping area.
Highlights:	Guadalasco is a fun singletrack without a lot of trail hazards to slow you down. This is a great trail to practice your singletrack skills. A couple of the climbs will also test your stamina.
Hazards:	Watch out for hikers and other bikers. Sometimes this section of the Pacific Coast Highway is closed due to heavy rains.
Land status:	Point Mugu State Park.
Maps:	USGS Point Mugu State Park; Thomas Brothers, Ventura County, page 387.

Access: From Los Angeles follow Pacific Coast Highway (California Highway 1) for approximately 30 miles to Point Mugu State Park. Turn right into the park. Park in the day-parking area (follow the signs).

Notes on the trail: The trail starts at the northern-most end of the campground. Follow Big Sycamore Canyon over three or four stream crossings until you get to Ranch Center Road at 4.5 miles. Here you head to the left and up a steep hill, then down the other side to the Ranch Center. You descend paved road at 5.4 miles. At 5.8 miles the trail curves to the left, putting you on the Wood Canyon Trail. After a series of ups and downs you come to the Guadalasco Trail on your right at 7.1 miles. Turn right and begin a fun singletrack ride to the top at 9.9 miles. You veer left and head down the Guadalasco Trail (fireroad) until it ends at the overlook trail at 11 miles. Turn left 100 feet past this junction on the Backbone Trail. This is a fast, moderately technical singletrack back to Big Sycamore Canyon at 13 miles. From here you retrace an easy ride back to the car.

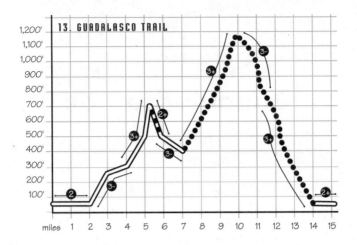

13. GUADALASCO TRAIL

THE RIDE

0.0 From the north end of the campground ride through the locked gate.

0.8 Continue straight past the Overlook Trail, which is for hiking only.

1.1 Continue straight past Serano Canyon Trail.

3.0 Veer right at the fork past the Wood Canyon Trail on the left.

4.6 Turn left on Ranch Center Road past the continuation of Big Sycamore Canyon on the right.

5.4 You reach a paved road that shoots you down to the Ranch Center.

5.8 The trail curves to the left and you are on the Wood Canyon Trail.

7.1 Make a sharp right onto the Guadalasco Trail.

9.9 Reach the top of Guadalasco Trail and head down.

11.0 Guadalasco ends at a junction. Ride straight for approximately 100 feet up a little hill. The Backbone Trail is on your left and is easy to miss.

13.0 After a fast singletrack descent toward a stream, turn right on Big Sycamore Canyon and head back to the car.

15.0 The end.

Los Robles Motorway

Location:	Newbury Park, located in Ventura County.
Distance:	11.6 miles, out and back.
Time:	1.75 hours.
Tread:	Singletrack; hardpacked dirt.
Aerobic level:	Moderate to strenuous.
Technical difficulty:	3+.
Fees:	None.
Services:	None available at the trail. All services available back at U.S. Highway 101.
Water:	At the parking area there is a water fountain by the map kiosk.
Highlights:	Fun singletrack the whole way. If you like being close to civilization this ride is for you. You are close to houses for the whole ride. There is also a great downhill called "The Switchbacks."
Hazards:	Many other bikers use this trail and can easily surprise you. This trail is also shared with many equestrians.
Land status:	This is private land. The Conejo Open Space Conservation has worked out an agreement to share the trail.
Maps:	USGS Newbury Park; Thomas Brothers, Ventura County, page 555.

Access: From U.S. Highway 101 exit Wendy Drive and head south. Drive 2.5 miles to Portero Road. Turn left on Portero Road. Continue for approximately one-half mile until you see a small parking lot on your left. There is a sign confirming that you are at the Los Robles Trail. Park in the lot. This is where you start the ride.

Notes on the trail: From the parking lot ride up a short, steep hill to the map kiosk. At 0.2 mile, cross the paved road and find yourself at a small junction. Veer left and head down a short hill. At 0.3 mile as you near a residential area, turn right onto the traversing singletrack. At 1.3 miles take a sharp right at an unmarked junction and head away from the homes. You come to a series of steep, steep hills. These hills are probably unridable. After you travel up some switchbacks and come to a junction at 2.6 miles, turn right on the Los Robles Trail. At 3.2 miles cross Ventu Park Road and head straight onto the steep singletrack. Climb to the top of the infamous

Los Robles Motorway

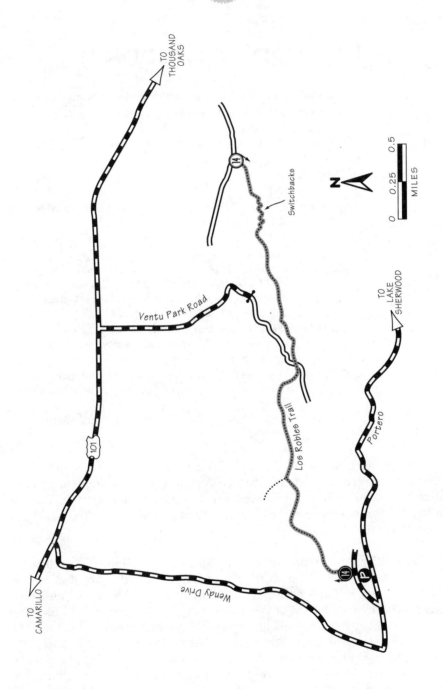

TO
THOUSAND
OAKS

Switchbacks

N

0   0.25   0.5
MILES

Ventu Park Road

TO
LAKE
SHERWOOD

101

Los Robles Trail

Portero

TO
CAMARILLO

Wendy Drive

switchbacks. After reaching the top and enjoying a great fast ride down, you reach a junction at 5.8 miles. At this point turn around and retrace your ride back to the beginning.

After fun downhill on Los Robles.

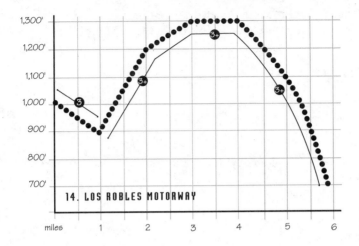

14. LOS ROBLES MOTORWAY

THE RIDE

0.0 From the parking lot, head up a short hill to the map kiosk and water fountain.

0.2 After a short climb you cross a paved road onto the trail.

0.3 Veer left at a small fork in the trail and then, shortly after, turn right onto the traversing singletrack.

1.3 Make a sharp right at the unmarked junction and head up a short but steep hill.

2.6 After a series of switchbacks turn right at the junction onto Los Robles Trail.

3.15 Continue straight across the paved Ventu Park Road and continue on the Los Robles Trail.

5.8 At the four-way intersection turn around and retrace your ride.

11.6 The end.

Los Angeles County

Will Rogers Park/ Backbone Trail

Location:	Backbone Trail starts in Will Rogers State Historic Park. It is located west of Interstate 405, off of Sunset Boulevard.
Distance:	12.4 miles, out and back.
Time:	1.75 hours.
Tread:	Singletrack and hardpacked dirt.
Aerobic level:	Moderate to strenuous (more strenuous than moderate).
Technical difficulty:	4–.
Fees:	$6.00 for parking.
Services:	Bathrooms at the parking area and a portable toilet at the top of the trail.
Water:	Water fountain at the parking area.
Highlights:	Awesome downhill with some steep sections.
Hazards:	The rains have washed out some fairly big sections. These sections can come up fast.
Land status:	Will Rogers State Historic Park.
Maps:	USGS Topanga; Thomas Brothers, Los Angeles County, page 631.

Access: Exit Interstate 405 heading west. At 4.6 miles turn right on Will Rogers Road. Continue for 1 mile until you come to the parking kiosk. After you pay for parking, park immediately. Do not pass the polo fields to your right.

Notes on the trail: From the trailhead just across from the polo fields begin a gradual climb up toward Inspiration Point. At 0.6 mile continue on the fireroad as you see another sign that reads, "Inspiration Point." At 0.7 mile, after taking a left, you come to an information board. Turn left onto

Will Rogers Park/Backbone Trail

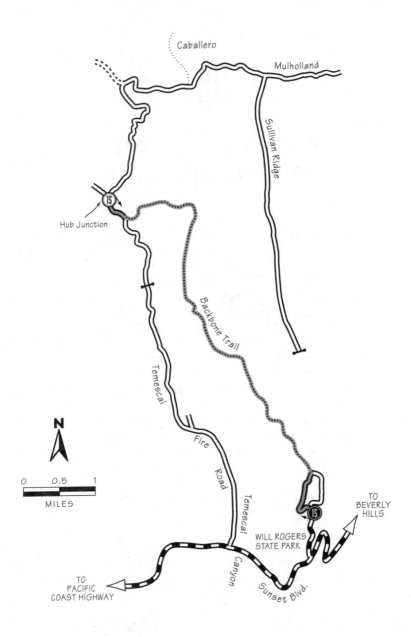

Caballero

Mulholland

Sullivan Ridge

15
Hub Junction

Backbone Trail

Temescal

Fire

Road

N

0   0.5   1
MILES

Temescal Canyon

15
TO
BEVERLY
HILLS

WILL ROGERS
STATE PARK

Sunset Blvd.

TO
PACIFIC
COAST HIGHWAY

the trail as you begin to ride the singletrack. From here, the first couple of miles climb some steep sections. The trail flattens out a little bit after that. You come to an oak tree at 2.9 miles, and after you enjoy the views of the canyon below, head left. The trail becomes almost tunnel-like with trees and bushes. You then see the ridge of Temescal Fireroad. After you climb up to the ridge at 6 miles, you can either turn around or take a right and head to the Hub Junction. At Hub Junction you can turn around, or head up to other rides such as the Eagle Rock/Eagle Spring Loop (Ride 19).

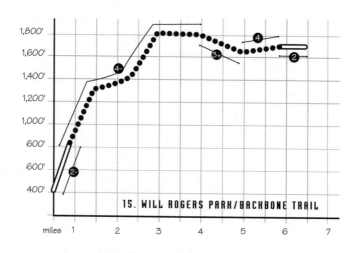

15. WILL ROGERS PARK/BACKBONE TRAIL

THE RIDE

0.0 Head up the stairs by the parking lot and turn left on fireroad.
0.6 Continue on the fireroad past another sign that indicates Inspiration Point.
0.7 Turn left down a short hill. Turn left and climb the singletrack at the information board.
1.5 Cross bridge and continue to climb.
2.9 Turn left at an oak tree.
6.0 Turn right at the Temescal Fireroad.
6.2 At the Hub Junction turn around and head back the way you came.
12.4 The end.

Caballero Canyon

Location:	Caballero Canyon is located in the San Fernando Valley off of Reseda Boulevard. The ride starts south of Ventura Boulevard just before the entrance to Braemar Country Club.
Distance:	3.2 miles, out and back.
Time:	35 minutes.
Tread:	Most of Caballero Canyon is wide singletrack with hardpacked dirt.
Aerobic level:	The first mile is easy. As the trail turns uphill the ride becomes moderate.
Technical difficulty:	The overall ride is a Level 3.
Fees:	None.
Services:	There is nothing available at the trailhead. However, on Ventura Boulevard you pass several places to purchase drinks and food.
Water:	None located at the trailhead or on the trail.
Highlights:	Caballero Canyon has a great view of the San Fernando Valley and a quick fun downhill.
Hazards:	The biggest thing to look out for is people. Caballero Canyon gets crowded, especially on the weekends.
Land status:	Santa Monica Mountains.
Maps:	USGS Topanga; Thomas Brothers, Los Angeles County, page 560.

Access: Traveling on U.S. Highway 101 (Ventura Freeway), take Reseda Boulevard Exit. Turn south toward Ventura Boulevard. Continue on Reseda Boulevard through Ventura. You come to a four-way stop (this is Wells Drive). Stay on Reseda Boulevard until you reach a three-way stop (this is Rosita Street). Continue until just past the luxury home development and you see a strip of dirt. This is where you find the trailhead and where you should park. If you get to the entrance of Braemar Country Club you have gone too far.

Notes on the trail: Caballero Canyon is a fun short trail that can be used to gain access to the vast Santa Monica Mountains or can be used as a quick ride before the sun goes down. The trail begins just before the entrance of the Braemar Country Club, starting from the left of Reseda Boulevard with a short dip into the canyon from the parking area. The trail is flat as it

Caballero Canyon
Eagle Rock/Eagle Spring Loop

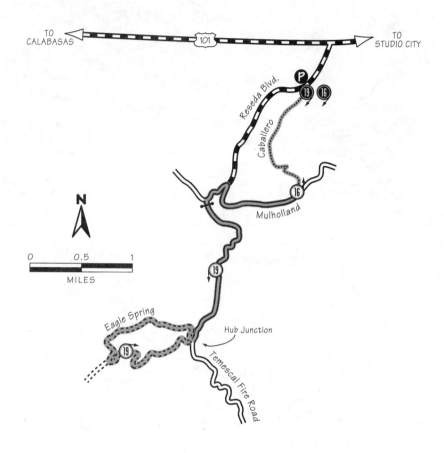

follows a dry creek. You start to climb on a wide singletrack. The trail gets steep after about 1 mile. There are no mistakes that can be made because the trail is easy to follow. Once you reach the top at 1.6 miles, you can either continue to other trails or turn around and enjoy a fun downhill back to the car. Once at dirt Mulholland you can turn left and ride to Sullivan Canyon (Ride 18) or Westridge Trail (Ride 17). A right turn takes you toward Eagle Rock/Eagle Spring Loop (Ride 19).

Brad shredding Caballero Canyon.

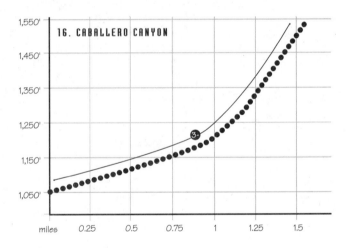

THE RIDE

0.0 From the trailhead, ride down into the canyon and then up.

0.8 Stay to the right. Head down into the dry creekbed, then back up onto the trail.

1.0 The trail starts to get steep and winds back and forth to the top.

1.6 Trail ends at Dirt Mulholland. Turn around and head back or ride along Dirt Mulholland.

3.2 The end.

Santa Monica Mountains

The Santa Monica Mountains National Recreation Area spans west of Griffith Park in Los Angeles to the east of the Oxnard Plain in Ventura County. The northern boundary is U.S. Highway 101 and the southern boundary is California Highway 1 (Pacific Coast Highway). Although the Santa Monica National Recreation Area covers quite a bit of land officially, in mountain biking lingo the area is greatly limited to the area west of the Interstate 405 (San Diego Freeway) and east of Topanga Canyon. The Santa Monica Mountains Recreation Area is a cooperative effort that joins federal, state and local agencies with private preserves and landowners to protect the resources of this area.

The Santa Monica Mountains contain a wide variety of plants and animals. It is common to see deer, coyote, rattlesnakes and occasionally a mountain lion. The Santa Monica Mountains have many beautiful canyons with running streams and dense tree and brush cover. There are many trails that you may ride where you look around, and aside from an occasional plane overhead, will not believe that you are only a few miles from a major metropolitan area.

Mountain biking opportunities in the Santa Monica Mountains are diverse. You are able to pick from a menu of rides, from relatively flat fireroads to steep technical singletrack. Another great advantage is that you can start either from the San Fernando Valley or Pacific Palisades or Brentwood. Dirt Mulholland is a dirt fireroad (a legal road frequented by cars) that acts as the nerve center for the Santa Monica Mountains. It stretches across the Santa Monica Mountains from Topanga Canyon to just west of Interstate 405. You can reach almost every ride by riding Dirt Mulholland. The Santa Monica Mountains are popular among hikers and bikers and the trails are often crowded on the weekends.

Westridge Trail

Location:	This trail is in the Santa Monica Mountains, located west of Interstate 405 and accessed off of Sunset Boulevard.
Distance:	7.2 miles, out and back.
Time:	1 hour.
Tread:	Hard-packed fireroad with optional singletrack on the ridge above.
Aerobic level:	Moderate.
Technical difficulty:	Level 2 with optional Level 3+ singletrack on ridge above.
Fees:	None.
Services:	Bathrooms and soda machine at the top of the trail.
Water:	There is no water at the beginning of the trail. However, at the top of the trail is the old Nike Missile Base, along with water fountains.
Highlights:	This is a nice, well-groomed trail that will put you at the old Nike Missile Base. Take some sandwiches and enjoy the picnic tables and the spectacular views. There are also some fun singletrack offshoots that take you along the ridge just above the main road.
Hazards:	There are not many hazards except for hikers and other riders. Bike with caution.
Land status:	Topanga State Park.
Maps:	USGS Topanga, Canoga Park; Thomas Brothers, page 597.

Access: Exit Interstate 405 on Sunset Boulevard heading west. After a couple of miles turn right on Mandeville Canyon Road. Take the first left, which is Westridge Road. Follow Westridge Road all the way to the top until the road ends. You notice a locked fire gate. This is the trailhead. You can park on the street.

Notes on the trail: Westridge Trail is an easy trail to follow. After passing through the gate begin a gradual climb along the fireroad. While the main road is easy to follow, you see singletrack that shoots off the side of the trail to the ridge above. On the way up stay on the main road. At 3.5 miles there is a trail that heads toward the left which you want to avoid. Once at the top at 3.6 miles, rest and then turn around and head back. On the way back you can venture onto the more technical singletrack offshoots that bring you back to the main road.

Westridge Trail • Sullivan Canyon Trail

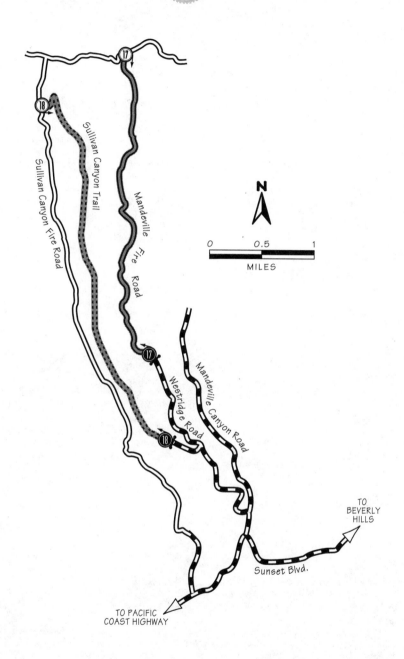

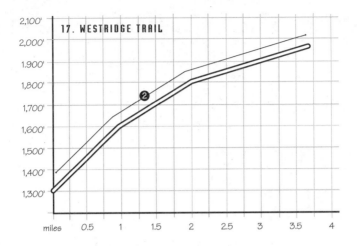

17. WESTRIDGE TRAIL

2,100'
2,000'
1,900'
1,800'
1,700'
1,600'
1,500'
1,400'
1,300'

miles   0.5   1   1.5   2   2.5   3   3.5   4

THE RIDE

0.0 Go through fire gate and head up trail.

3.5 Continue straight past the trail to the left.

3.6 Top of trail. Turn around and enjoy the downhill.

7.2 The end.

Nike Missile Tower atop Westridge Trail.

66

Sullivan Canyon Trail

See Map on Page 65

Location:	Santa Monica Mountains, west of Interstate 405 off of Sunset Boulevard, and accessed through Brentwood.
Distance:	9 miles, out and back.
Time:	1 hour.
Tread:	Almost all of the trail is doubletrack.
Aerobic level:	Moderate.
Technical difficulty:	3.
Fees:	None.
Services:	None.
Water:	None.
Highlights:	The ride is not known for its views, but once you get into the canyon would not guess that you are in the middle of Los Angeles. The trail has high canyon walls with lush foliage.
Hazards:	Water that crosses the trail.
Land status:	Topanga State Park.
Maps:	USGS Topanga, Canoga Park; Thomas Brothers, page 631.

Access: Exit Interstate 405 on Sunset Boulevard and head west (toward the beach). Take a right on Mandeville Canyon Road. Turn left on Westridge Road. You wind around until you reach Bayliss Road. Turn left on Bayliss Road. Continue for a short time and come to Queensferry Road. You notice a fire gate; this is the trailhead. Find a place to park on the street.

Notes on the trail: After passing through fire gate, you shoot down a short paved road. To the left you see the dam, to the right is the trail. Begin your gradual climb along the trail. After approximately 1 mile the trail becomes more technical as it crosses streams and traverses tree roots. As you approach the top, the trail becomes steeper before it reaches Sullivan Ridge. When you get to Sullivan Ridge you have several options. You can turn left (this takes you down the Ridge Trail and ends a distance from where you parked), you can turn right (this puts you at Dirt Mulholland), or you can turn around and enjoy a fun downhill.

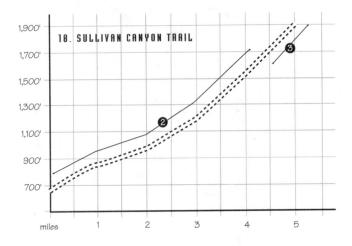

18. SULLIVAN CANYON TRAIL

❷

❸

miles   1   2   3   4   5

THE RIDE

0.0   Start down paved road through locked fire gate.

0.2   At bottom of paved road turn right and start to head up.

4.5   Reach top of Sullivan Canyon Trail. Turn around and go back the way you came.

9.0   The end.

Mark tearing up Sullivan Canyon.

Eagle Rock/Eagle Spring Loop

Location:	Santa Monica Mountains.
Distance:	11.8-mile loop.
Time:	1.5 hours.
Tread:	Mostly fireroad.
Aerobic level:	Moderate to strenuous.
Technical difficulty:	3-.
Fees:	None.
Services:	None.
Water:	None.
Highlights:	The loop is a scenic fun ride that is not too technical. It offers both fun downhill and a few challenging ascents.
Hazards:	Some of the rains have created deep ruts in the loop. They may or may not be marked, so ride with caution.
Land status:	Topanga State Park.
Maps:	USGS Topanga; Thomas Brothers, Los Angeles, page 590.

See Map on Page 61

Access: Traveling on U.S. Highway 101 (Ventura Freeway), take the Reseda Boulevard Exit. Turn south toward Ventura Boulevard. Continue on Reseda Boulevard through Ventura. You come to a four-way stop (this is Wells Drive). Stay on Reseda Boulevard until you reach a three-way stop (this is Rosita Street). Continue until just past the luxury home development and you see a strip of dirt. This is where you find the trailhead and where you should park. If you get to the entrance of Braemar Country Club you have gone too far.

Notes on the trail: There are many different ways to get to the Eagle Rock Loop. Our favorite is starting at Caballero Canyon (Ride 16) and riding that first. From the trailhead climb Caballero Canyon to Dirt Mulholland at 1.6 miles. Turn right on dirt Mulholland and rollercoaster to Temescal Fireroad at 2.3 miles where you make a left and pass through the fire gate. Temescal Fireroad climbs to the Hub Junction at 4.7 miles, a popular spot where riders convene on the weekends. From here take the Eagle Rock Trail to the far right. At 6.1 miles you reach the Eagle Springs Junction and make a sharp left. Climb back to the Hub Junction at 7.1 miles. From here, retrace your ride back to the beginning.

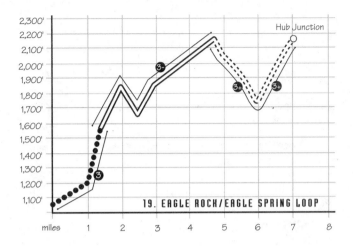

THE RIDE

- **0.0** Ride Caballero Canyon (Ride 16) to Dirt Mulholland.
- **1.6** Turn right on Dirt Mulholland.
- **2.3** Turn left at fire gate at Temescal Fireroad.
- **4.7** At the Hub Junction take the Eagle Rock Trail to the far right.
- **6.1** Make a hard left at the Eagle Springs Junction and climb back to the Hub Junction.
- **7.1** Once back at the Hub Junction, retrace your ride back to where you parked.
- **11.8** The end.

Descending Temescal Canyon on the Eagle Rock ride.

Towsley Canyon

Location:	Newhall, which is north of the San Fernando Valley on Interstate 5.
Distance:	5.5-mile loop.
Time:	1 hour.
Tread:	Singletrack.
Aerobic level:	Moderate to strenuous.
Technical difficulty:	3.
Fees:	None.
Services:	Bathrooms, pay phone and a small ranger station.
Water:	There is a water fountain up by the ranger station.
Highlights:	This is a fun singletrack that contains some fast downhill. It is right off I-5 so it is easy to get to. When you get to the park grab a map at the kiosk. The trails are very well marked.
Hazards:	Sometimes the trails are closed due to weather.
Land status:	Santa Clarita Woodlands Park. This is part of the Santa Monica Conservancy.
Maps:	USGS Oat Mountain; Thomas Brothers, Los Angeles County, page 4640.

Access: From Interstate 5 exit on Calgrove Boulevard. Turn west back under the freeway. Calgrove Boulevard curves south and become the Old Road. Follow the Old Road for one-half mile to the entrance on the right (look for signs). Turn right and follow the road for one-half mile to the Nature Center and the parking lot.

Notes on the trail: We did the trail counterclockwise. Starting at the metal post marked T16, follow the fireroad into the canyon. This takes you to the right of the Nature Center. At 1 mile you reach "The Narrows" and see a junction at T13. Veer left at the junction and begin to climb a steep fireroad until you get to T10 at 1.3 miles. At T10 make a sharp left and begin a series of switchbacks and start your singletrack ascent. At 2.3 miles you reach a peak at four big oak trees. Veer right until you start to drop. Enjoy a fun technical downhill to T6 where the trail turns to fireroad again. At 4.4 miles continue straight as you pass through the gate and then at 4.8 miles turn left on the main road and head back to where you started.

Towsley Canyon

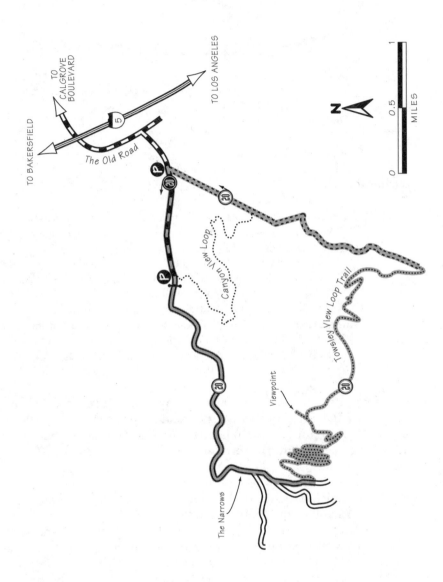

TO BAKERSFIELD

TO CALGROVE BOULEVARD

TO LOS ANGELES

5

The Old Road

P

20

20

Canyon View Loop

P

20

Towsley View Loop Trail

20

Viewpoint

The Narrows

N

0   0.5   1

MILES

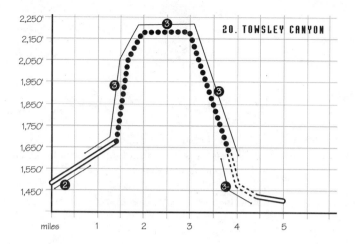

2,250'
2,150'
2,050'
1,950'
1,850'
1,750'
1,650'
1,550'
1,450'

miles   1   2   3   4   5

20. TOWSLEY CANYON

THE RIDE

0.0   Start at T16 and follow the fireroad back into the canyon.

0.3   Go through locked fire gate.

1.0   Continue straight through "The Narrows" and then veer left at the fork at T13.

1.2   Veer left at the fork at T12.

1.3   Make a sharp left at T10 and begin a series of switchbacks.

2.3   You reach a peak marked by four big oak trees. Veer to the right (this is the only way you can go). This area is a little deceiving.

4.4   Go through locked fire gate. This is where the Canyon View Loop Trail ends. Continue straight to the main road.

4.8   Turn left on main road and head back to the parking lot.

5.5   The end.

Rocky Oaks Park

Location:	Where Kanan Dume Road and Mulholland Highway intersect in the Santa Monica Mountains National Recreation Area.
Distance:	1-mile loop with optional trails for a longer ride.
Time:	The loop itself takes about 20 minutes but you can spend a few hours exploring.
Tread:	Singletrack.
Aerobic level:	Easy to moderate.
Technical difficulty:	3-.
Fees:	None.
Services:	Bathrooms and picnic areas.
Water:	There is a water fountain just beyond the trailhead.
Highlights:	This is a great ride for beginners; you can try something a little more technical than your average fireroad. All the trails are well-marked so it is almost impossible to get lost. This is a great area to ride for an hour and then picnic.
Hazards:	This is a popular spot for horses and hikers.
Land status:	Santa Monica Mountains National Recreation Area.
Maps:	USGS Point Dume; Thomas Brothers, Los Angeles County, page 587.

Access: From California Highway 1 (Pacific Coast Highway) turn east (inland) on Kanan Dume Road. Travel 6 miles until you come to Mulholland Highway. Turn left, then immediately turn right into the park.

From U.S. Highway 101 head west on Kanan Dume Road for 6 miles until you reach Mulholland Highway. Turn right on Mulholland Highway, then immediately turn right into the park. The trail begins on the opposite end. You will see a map kiosk.

Notes on the trail: Rocky Oaks Park is a great family ride. You would really have to work hard to get lost. The trails are well marked, and you can take any combination of trails and have a nice ride. From the trailhead at the map kiosk, follow the Glad Trail to Rocky Oaks Loop at 0.4 mile and turn right. Follow the Rocky Oaks Loop around the pond back to where you started.

Rocky Oaks Park

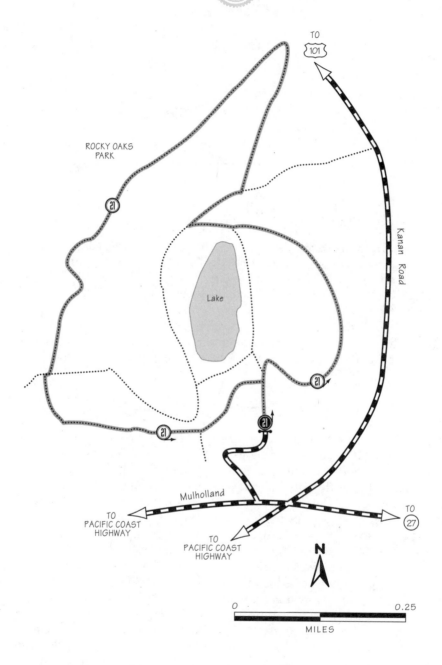

ROCKY OAKS
PARK

TO
101

Kanan Road

Lake

Mulholland

TO
PACIFIC COAST
HIGHWAY

TO
PACIFIC COAST
HIGHWAY

TO
27

N

0   0.25

MILES

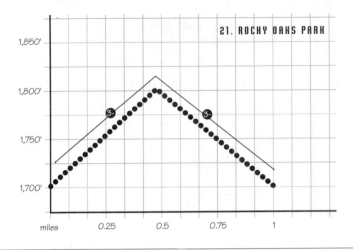

THE RIDE

0.0 Begin at the trailhead by the map kiosk. Follow the signs for Glade Trail. Stay to the right and you run into the Rocky Oaks Loop Trail.

0.4 Turn right at Rocky Oaks Loop Trail.

0.5 You see the pond. Follow trail until it lets out at opposite end of parking lot.

1.1 The end.

NOTE: There are a few ways to ride around this park. Spend a couple of hours here and decide which way you like the best.

Malibu Creek State Park

Malibu Creek State Park is located just off Las Virgenes Canyon between U.S. Highway 101 and the infamous Malibu Beach. The park consists of over 8,000 acres of mountains, streams and beautiful scenery. Although not as popular as the Getty Museum, the park is an historic landmark for Angelenos. At the turn of the century the park was a private fishing and hunting club. Twentieth Century Fox Studios purchased the land in the mid–'40s for the film industry. The park was the backdrop for many popular TV shows such as *M.A.S.H.* and *The Planet of the Apes*.

This is a great family destination for biking and hiking. If you are trying to get a youngster used to being on a mountain bike, take an easy ride over to the Visitor Center, which has a wonderful taxidermy exhibit of wildlife native to the park (open only on weekends). At any time of year there are wildflowers in bloom. A stream and a small lake offer catch-and-release fishing and add to the ambiance. If you are looking for a more challenging ride, try out the infamous Bulldog Loop. In the summer bring plenty of extra water and in the winter bring a jacket you can pack away (the mornings are cold).

Crags Road

Location:	Malibu Creek State Park, located in Malibu Canyon.
Distance:	7.6 miles, out and back.
Time:	1.5 hours.
Tread:	Mostly fireroad. There are a few sections where you ride into dried up creeks.
Aerobic level:	Easy to moderate.
Technical difficulty:	2.
Fees:	$5.00.
Services:	Bathrooms, soda machine, pay phone.
Water:	Water fountain available at lower parking area.
Highlights:	This is a nice family ride or a good place to warm up your legs at the beginning of the season. It is the set of the old television series, *M.A.S.H.*
Hazards:	This is a frequented spot for hikers and equestrians.
Land status:	Malibu Creek State Park.
Maps:	USGS Malibu Beach, Point Dume; Thomas Brothers Los Angeles County, page 588.

Access: From California Highway 1 (Pacific Coast Highway) turn east (or inland). Drive for approximately 6.5 miles until you reach the park entrance on your left. If you get to Mulholland Highway you have gone too far. From U.S. Highway 101, exit west (toward the beach) and drive approximately 4 miles to the park's entrance on your right. Drive to the bottom parking area where you find the trailhead directly across from the bathrooms.

Notes on the trail: You follow the trail across from the bathrooms at the lower parking lot and cross the concrete bridge. This easy fireroad takes you to the Visitor Center at 0.8 mile where you cross a bridge and climb up a short hill. Travel through the dry creek and cross another bridge at 1.8 miles. Try to ride through the dry, rocky creekbed. At 2.3 miles the trail curves right and turns into fireroad. You find yourself at the old *M.A.S.H.* jeep site. Head straight past a few roads until you hit the park boundary at 3.8 miles. From here turn around and head back to the start.

Crags Road • Bulldog Loop

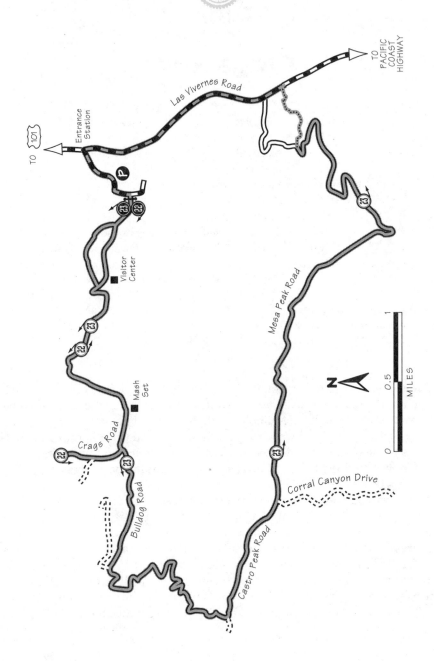

To Pacific Coast Highway

Las Vivernes Road

To 101

Entrance Station

P

Visitor Center

Mash Set

Crags Road

Bulldog Road

Castro Peak Road

Mesa Peak Road

Corral Canyon Drive

N

MILES
1
0.5
0

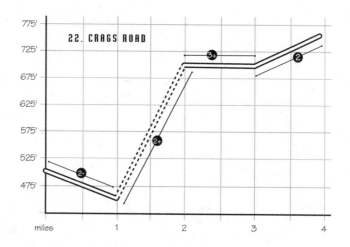

THE RIDE

0.0 Begin across from the bathrooms. You cross a concrete bridge that traverses a stream.

0.8 Reach the Visitor Center. You see a bridge on your right. Cross it and continue straight.

1.2 After a short climb and equal descent you continue onto the dry creekbed.

1.8 Cross small bridge and veer right onto the dry creekbed. This area is a little tricky and you might have to get off your bike and walk it. It almost does not seem like it could be a part of the trail, but it is.

2.3 Curve right at fireroad and come to the *M.A.S.H.* jeep site.

3.0 Continue straight past the sign that reads, "Bulldog Road Park Boundary 4.3 miles" and "Castro Peak Motorway 3.4 miles."

3.3 Stay right past a fork.

3.8 You reach a picnic table, a locked fence that crosses a dam, and a sign that indicates the park boundary. From here you turn around and retrace your path back.

7.6 The end.

Bulldog Loop

See Map
on Page 78

Location: Malibu Creek State Park, located in Malibu Canyon.

Distance: 15.3-mile loop.

Time: 3 hours.

Tread: Mostly fireroad with hardpacked dirt. The trail coming down into Tapia Park has some loose sections.

Aerobic level: Strenuous.

Technical difficulty: 3.

Fees: $5.00.

Services: Bathrooms, soda machine, pay phone.

Water: Water fountain available at lower parking area.

Highlights: Great climbing with fast, not-so-technical downhill. There are also a few sights such as small lakes and an old Army jeep which marks the location where *M.A.S.H.* was filmed.

Hazards: Loose dirt on the back section. At the end of the ride, you have to travel on the highway (Malibu Canyon), which can get busy with cars on the weekend.

Land status: Malibu Creek State Park.

Maps: USGS Malibu Beach, Point Dume; Thomas Brothers, Los Angeles County, page 588.

Access: From California Highway 1 (Pacific Coast Highway) turn east (or inland). Drive for approximately 6.5 miles until you reach the park entrance on your left. If you get to Mulholland Highway you have gone too far.

From U.S. Highway 101, exit west (toward the beach) and drive approximately 4 miles to the park entrance on your right. Drive to the bottom parking area where you find the trailhead directly across from the bathrooms.

Notes on the trail: Bulldog Loop has a lot to offer almost every rider. You follow the trail across from the bathrooms at the lower parking lot and cross the concrete bridge. This easy fireroad takes you to the Visitor Center at 0.8 mile where you cross a bridge and climb a short hill. After traveling through the dry creek, you cross another bridge at 1.8 miles and try to ride through the dry, rocky creekbed. At 2.3 miles the trail curves right onto fireroad and you find yourself at the old *M.A.S.H.* jeep site. At 3 miles veer left onto Bulldog Motorway and begin a very strenuous climb. Continue on the main fireroad until you reach the state park boundary at 6.2 miles. Continue until you reach the Castro Peak Junction (Ride 24). Turn left onto Castro Peak

Road as you begin to bomb downhill until you get to Mesa Peak Road at 7.4 miles. Turn left. Mesa Peak Road is a fireroad that has some short climbs, but is mostly downhill. At 10.2 miles you reach a water tower and veer left up a short hill, which steeply descends the other side into Tapia Park. At 12.4 miles veer right onto the singletrack. Continue until you reach Malibu Canyon Road at 13.2 miles. At Malibu Canyon Road turn left and ride along the busy canyon road until you get back to Malibu Creek State Park.

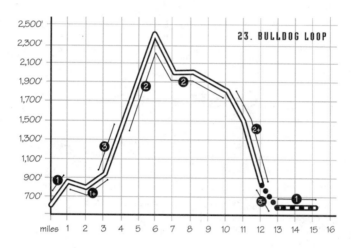

THE RIDE

0.0 Begin across from the bathrooms. You cross a concrete bridge that traverses a stream.

0.8 Reach the Visitor Center. You see a bridge on your right. Cross it and continue straight.

1.3 After a short climb and equal descent you continue onto the dry creekbed.

1.8 Cross small bridge and veer right onto the dry creekbed. This area is a little tricky and you might have to get off your bike and walk it. It almost does not seem like it could be a part of the trail, but it is.

2.3 Veer right on fireroad and come to the *M.A.S.H.* jeep site.

3.0 Veer left onto Bulldog Road and begin a steep climb.

3.8 Stay left at the fork.

4.6 Stay right at the fork.

4.8 Continue straight on Bulldog Road past the sign to the left.

6.2 At the top of Bulldog Road you see a junction marked by a fire gate and a sign that reads, "Entering State Park Boundary." Head left down Castro Peak Road.

6.7 Stay right at the fork.

7.1 Go through a locked fire gate at the top of Corral Canyon. Travel on paved road until you reach Mesa Peak Road.

7.4 Make a left turn onto Mesa Peak Motorway.

10.2 At the water tower, stay left up a short hill and down a very technical section (you might have to dismount and walk). When you reach the bottom stay left and continue into Tapia Park.

12.4 Turn right onto the singletrack to your right.

13.2 Turn left at Malibu Canyon Road and head back to where you parked at Malibu Creek State Park.

15.3 The end.

Castro Peak

Location:	The Santa Monica Mountains, north of Las Virgenes Road and accessed through Malibu.
Distance:	8.7 miles, out and back.
Time:	2 hours.
Tread:	Fireroad with hardpacked dirt.
Aerobic level:	Moderate to strenuous.
Technical difficulty:	2 + .
Fees:	None.
Services:	None.
Water:	None. Bring plenty for hot days.
Highlights:	The trail is a nice workout without testing your technical skills. When you reach the top of Castro Peak the view is amazing.
Hazards:	Some of the residences around the road are inhabited by some very colorful folks.
Land status:	Santa Monica Mountains National Recreation Area.
Maps:	USGS Point Dume; Thomas Brothers, Los Angeles County, page 628.

Access: From California Highway 1 (Pacific Coast Highway) turn north onto Corral Canyon Road. Travel approximately 5 miles to where the road ends at a locked fire gate. Park here.

Notes on the trail: You begin biking straight up on the fireroad just beyond the locked fire gate. The climb is steep until you get to the Bulldog Loop Junction at 0.9 mile. At 1.6 miles continue straight past Newton Motorway as the road levels a bit. Continue to Castro Peak just under the antennae at 1.7 miles. Enjoy a short downhill into a small residential area of trailer homes. You come to the Latigo Trail at 2.8 miles and then turn right at

Castro Peak

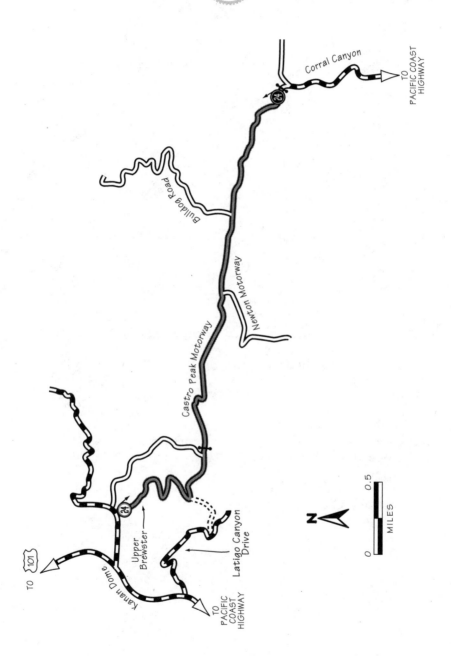

Upper Brewster Trail Junction. After heading to the right enjoy a fast descent that lets you out on Mulholland Drive at 4.4 miles. From here you turn around and head back.

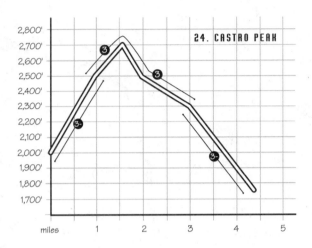

THE RIDE

0.0 From the parking area beyond the locked fire gate head straight up on the fireroad.

0.9 Continue straight toward Latigo Canyon past the junction with Bulldog Motorway (Ride 23).

1.6 Continue straight past Newton Motorway.

1.7 At the peak just below the antennae, continue straight downhill past the peak.

2.2 Continue straight past locked fire gate marked Castro Peak.

2.8 Turn right on Upper Brewster Road at the junction and head down a steep fireroad.

4.4 After a steep descent you end up on Mulholland Drive. Turn around and head back.

8.7 The end.

San Gabriel Mountains

The San Gabriel Mountains encompass the greater portion of the Angeles National Forest and are located in the northeastern portion of Los Angeles County. The area consists of countless acres of chaparral and pine-covered mountains and has a vast network of trails. The San Gabriel Mountains are most famous for their availability of outdoor recreation and for the Mount Wilson Observatory and the 150-foot solar tower. The observatory and the solar tower monitor a multitude of astronomical and astrophysical data. Due to their proximity to the city of Los Angeles, the San Gabriel Mountains have served as the playground to Angelenos since the 1800s.

Within minutes of downtown Los Angeles, the mountain range provides a break from the hustle and bustle of the city. Meandering streams and trails displace busy highways; coyotes, mountain lions and other wildlife replace businesspeople and gangbangers. When the city is 100 degrees, the mountains are 80 degrees. After a cool winter rain in the city, the mountain tops are often snow covered. Don't forget your jacket and full-fingered gloves on those winter days.

There are hundreds of miles of fireroad and singletrack within these mountains. Much of the singletrack is best left to the hikers, but mountain bikers are not without their pleasures, although trails are mostly steep and technically difficult. The Mount Wilson Toll Road is one of the steepest fireroads as it relentlessly climbs from the foothills to the Mount Wilson Observatory. The Mount Wilson Trail and the singletrack running from the Mount Lowe Railway are highly technical challenges that will have the best riders begging for mercy. All-in-all this is a great area to explore.

Brown Mountain/JPL

Location:	In the Angeles National Forest, above the foothills in Altadena.
Distance:	9.7-mile loop.
Time:	1.3 hours.
Tread:	Mostly fireroad with some singletrack sections.
Aerobic level:	Moderate.
Technical difficulty:	3–4.
Fees:	None.
Services:	There is a fast-food restaurant at the freeway exit, bathrooms at Millard Campground.
Water:	No water at the trailhead. Water is available at Millard Campground. Bring plenty of water for hot summer rides.
Highlights:	The trail starts just above NASA's Jet Propulsion Laboratory.
Hazards:	Poison oak and rattlesnakes.
Land status:	Angeles National Forest.
Maps:	USGS Pasadena, Mount Wilson; Thomas Brothers, Los Angeles County, page 535.

Access: In the city of Altadena near the Rose Bowl, exit Interstate 210 at Arroyo Boulevard and head north. A few miles up, after passing Mountain View Street on the right, you see a parking lot to the left that overlooks the Jet Propulsion Laboratories. From the parking lot, ride up Arroyo Boulevard a few hundred feet. As the road veers to the right you see a gated road straight ahead with a forest sign for Gabrieleno National Recreational Trail, 11W14.

Notes on the trail: After passing through the gate, begin a slight ascent along paved road and veer to the left as the road splits. Stay on the main road at 0.7 mile. At 0.8 mile continue straight past the bridge. Around 1.3 miles you see two roads to the left where you veer right and stay on the paved road. It turns to dirt a short way up. At 1.5 miles the trail bends to the left and you see the El Prieto Trail to the right. Stay on the main road as it switches up the hill and the grade becomes steeper. From here the real workout begins as you climb steadily up the dirt road and come to a gate at 4 miles. As you come to the saddle past the gate the road splits. If you take the left fork you top Brown Mountain within 1 mile. At the saddle take the

Brown Mountain/JPL

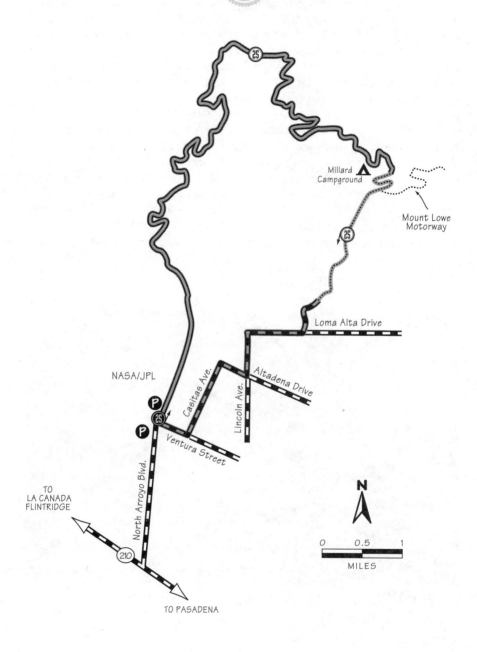

Millard Campground

Mount Lowe Motorway

25

25

Loma Alta Drive

NASA/JPL

P

25

P

Casitas Ave.

Altadena Drive

Lincoln Ave.

Ventura Street

North Arroyo Blvd.

TO LA CANADA FLINTRIDGE

210

TO PASADENA

N

0   0.5   1

MILES

right fork (2N65) which starts to drop into the canyon. After dropping into the canyon you see a singletrack to the right at 4.9 miles. You want to continue straight on the main road. At 5 miles cross the stream and veer right with the trail as you pass a trail to the left. At 5.2 miles veer left and head toward Millard Campground. At 5.9 miles veer left once again as you reach a junction near some Forest Service houses. You come to Millard Campground shortly. Just to the left of the campground, past the bathrooms, you see a little unmarked singletrack. Begin a mellow climb on this singletrack as it climbs over rocks and roots and switches up to the Mount Lowe Road. At 6.8 miles you reach the Mount Lowe Road (Ride 26). From here ride straight past the road and continue straight alongside the water treatment plant. Just after the treatment plant veer right onto the unmarked Alta Dena Crest dirt trail. This trail is extremely steep and loose. At 7.3 miles cross the paved road and continue along the dirt trail straight ahead. It becomes even steeper and looser and passes several footpaths to the left. At 8.3 miles you come to a new paved road and continue straight on it until you reach Loma Alta Drive. Go right on Loma Alta Drive and then turn left on Lincoln Avenue. At 8.8 miles turn right on Altadena Drive and then left on Casitas Avenue. At 9.4 miles turn right onto Ventura Street. This brings you back to Arroyo Boulevard and your car.

The NASA/JPL facility at the foot of Brown Mountain.

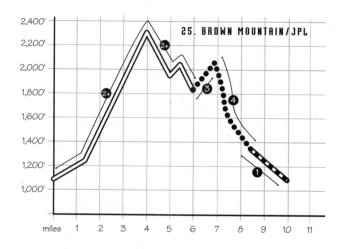

THE RIDE

0.0 Pass through the gate and begin a slight ascent along the paved road.

0.7 Veer right at fork in road; stay on paved road.

0.8 Go straight, staying on the paved road past the bridge.

1.3 Veer right at the next two junctions and then left at a third.

1.5 Veer left with the trail as you pass the El Prieto Trail on the left.

4.0 Pass through the gate and take 2N65 straight ahead; drop down into the canyon.

4.9 Continue straight past the singletrack to the right.

5.0 Cross the stream and veer right as trail bends past a trail to the left.

5.2 Veer left at the junction toward Millard Campground.

5.9 Turn left; pass the Forest Service houses and come to Millard Campground.

6.1 Take the unmarked singletrack, just past the bathrooms, to the left of Millard Campground.

6.8 Come to Mount Lowe Road near the water treatment plant. Cross the road, continue onto the paved road alongside the treatment plant.

7.1 Veer right off the pavement onto the dirt road and begin a steep, loose descent.

7.3 Cross the paved road as you see the dirt trail; continue straight ahead.

7.6 Continue straight past the trail to the left.

8.2 Continue straight past the trail to the left.

8.4 Merge with the paved street and go left.

8.5 Turn right on Loma Alta Drive.

8.6 Turn left on Lincoln Avenue.

8.8 Turn right on Altadena Road.

9.0 Turn left on Casitas Avenue.

9.4 Turn right on Ventura Street.

9.6 Ventura Street turns into Arroyo Boulevard and veers left.

9.7 The end.

Mount Lowe Railway

Location:	In the Angeles National Forest in the foothills above Sierra Madre.
Distance:	10-mile loop.
Time:	1.8 hours.
Tread:	Paved road and fireroad climb with technical singletrack descent.
Aerobic level:	Moderate to strenuous.
Technical difficulty:	The fireroad is a Level 3 due to the unrelenting steepness of the trail. The singletrack is a 3+.
Fees:	Forest Adventure Pass required.
Services:	The closest services are back in Pasadena.
Water:	There is no water on the trail. Bring plenty on hot summer days.
Highlights:	Awesome technical singletrack descent. Old hotel ruins at Echo Mountain. Historical trail markers for Old Mount Lowe Railway.
Hazards:	Steep cliffs, poison oak, lots of bugs.
Land status:	Angeles National Forest.
Maps:	USGS Mount Wilson, Pasadena; Thomas Brothers, Los Angeles County, page 505.

Access: In the city of Sierra Madre, exit Interstate 210 at Lake Avenue and head north. Turn left on Loma Alta Drive and then right on Chaney Trail. Approximately 1 mile up Chaney Trail the road makes a hairpin turn as you see a sign for Mount Lowe Motorway and Brown Mountain. Off to the left you see a gated dirt road. That is the trailhead. You can park off to the side of Chaney Trail.

Notes on the trail: Mount Lowe Railway used to be home to the Old Mount Lowe Railway, an old train used in the early 1900s. It shuttled wealthy vacationers up to the mountain resorts that used to be in the mountain range. Along the trail you come to Echo Mountain and White City where you see the remnants of one of the old hotel resorts.

After going through the gate at the trailhead you begin a steep and steady climb along paved road. You pass several singletracks on the side of the road, some of which you will be descending on. At 1.3 miles take the fork to the right as the road splits. Pass through a gate shortly afterwards. At 2 miles, just after passing the Sunset Trail (another singletrack on the left) and

Mount Lowe Railway

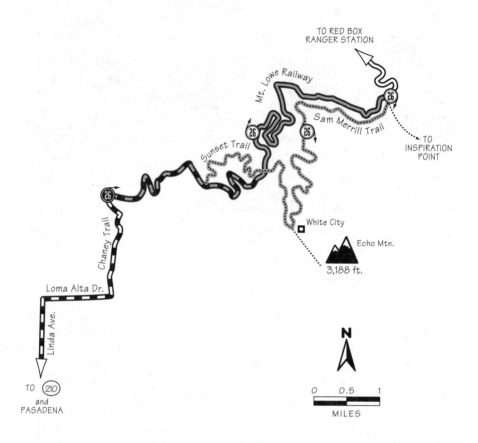

then the Echo Mount Trail (on the right), the pavement turns to dirt and the trail levels off. Continue on the main dirt road passing the Dawn Mine Trail at 2.3 miles and the trail to Mount Lowe Campground at 4 miles. At 4.1 miles you reach a saddle and see a dirt road which heads to the right toward Inspiration Point. A few feet into the Inspiration Point Road, you notice singletrack trails heading off on either side. Go to the singletrack on the right side of the Inspiration Point Road where you notice a weathered sign that reads, "Sam Merrill Trail (12W14)." Descend on this narrow, loose, technical, off-camber trail that meanders alongside a cliff. At 5.1 miles veer left at a small junction. At 6.3 miles, as you see White City hotel ruins down below, veer left and then veer right at a junction immediately below. At 6.4 miles a path to the left leads to White City atop Echo Mountain. You can

The tough ride up Mt. Lowe Motorway.

take a short rest at the hotel ruins or continue straight past the path and veer right. Veer right again at a trail marker that looks like a gravestone. After the gravestone, you begin a mild climb back to the Mount Lowe Road at 7.2 miles. Turn left down the road. About 100 feet down the road turn right onto the Sunset Trail. Descend on this technical singletrack and continue along to the right of the paved cul-de-sac at 8 miles. The trail becomes more technical as it begins to quickly switch back and forth down toward the bottom. At 8.3 miles, as the trail switches to the right, continue past the footpaths which lead off to the left. At 9.1 miles you reach a wide dirt trail and turn left. This trail gradually climbs out of a canyon until merging back with the Mount Lowe Road at 9.6 miles. Upon reaching the Mount Lowe Road, turn right and you quickly find yourself back at the trailhead.

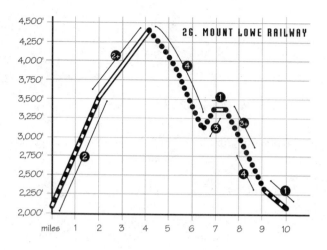

26. MOUNT LOWE RAILWAY

THE RIDE

0.0 Pass though the gate at the trailhead.

0.1 Continue straight past trails on either side of the road at the water treatment plant.

0.3 Continue straight past the Sunset Ridge Trail.

1.3 Veer right at the fork in the road.

1.5 Pass through the steel gate.

2.0 Continue straight past the Sunset Trail and another singletrack to the left. Pass the Echo Mount Trail to the right.

2.3 Continue past Dawn Mine Trail to the left.

4.0 Veer right with main road as you pass a trail to Mount Lowe Campground on the left.

4.1 At the saddle turn right onto Inspiration Point Road and immediately right on the Sam Merrill singletrack.

5.1 Veer left at the small junction.

6.3 Veer left and then veer right past another trail which heads toward hotel ruins down below.

6.4 Veer right past a trail that leads to the hotel ruins.

6.5 Veer right at the trail marker that looks like a gravestone.

7.2 Turn left at Mount Lowe Road.

7.2 Turn right onto Sunset Trail.

8.0 Stay to right on the paved cul-de-sac as the trail continues straight ahead.

8.3 Stay to the right as a few footpaths lead off to the left.

9.1 Turn left as you merge with a wide dirt trail.

9.6 Turn right on Mount Lowe Road.

9.9 The end.

Mount Wilson Toll Road

Location:	Altadena, in the Angeles National Forest.
Distance:	18 miles, out and back.
Time:	3 hours.
Tread:	Fireroad.
Aerobic level:	Strenuous.
Technical difficulty:	Although the terrain is generally Level 2, the steepness of the first 2.6 miles makes it a Level 3.
Fees:	None.
Services:	None at the trailhead. Bathrooms and picnic areas can be found at Henniger Flats and at the top.
Water:	None at the trailhead. You can find water at Henniger Flats and at the top.
Highlights:	If you are training for some type of physical fitness race, this is a good spot for you. The trail is a grueling workout, but very rewarding when you get to the top. Take in the scenery of one of the most spectacular views in California atop the Mount Wilson Observatory. Don't forget that you will have a very fast 9-mile descent.
Hazards:	For this long ride you should make sure that you have plenty of water. Be careful of hikers and equestrians. Hunting is legal at certain times of the year so do not be surprised if you see a deer carcass.
Land status:	Angeles National Forest.
Maps:	USGS Mount Wilson; Thomas Brothers, Los Angeles County, page 536.

Access: From Interstate 210, exit north (toward the mountains) on North Altadena Drive. Drive 2.7 miles to Crescent Drive and turn right. In 0.1 mile you turn right on Pinecrest Drive. The trailhead is on your right; you see a locked gate and a mailbox. This is a busy spot on weekends; you should not have any problems finding the trailhead.

Notes on the trail: Up, up, up. Mount Wilson is an easy ride to navigate. Starting at the trailhead you ride down a short paved road and, after crossing the bridge, begin your almost vertical ascent to Henniger Flats at 2.6 miles. Do not worry, the road levels after Henniger Flats. Stay on the main road past Henniger Flats as the fireroad winds in and out of dense forest

Mount Wilson Toll Road

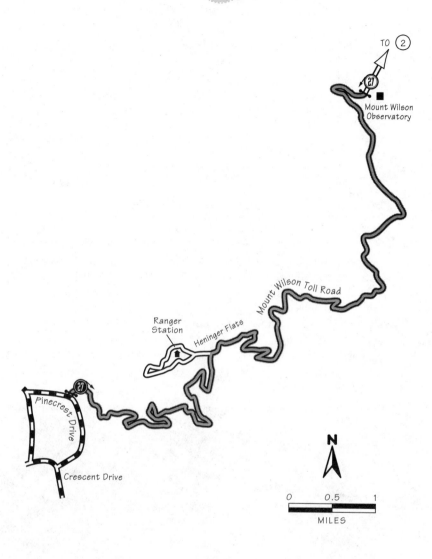

TO ②

㉗

Mount Wilson
Observatory

Mount Wilson Toll Road

Ranger
Station

Heninger Flats

㉗

Pinecrest Drive

Crescent Drive

N

0   0.5   1

MILES

until you reach the top. At 7.5 miles you see a singletrack to the right marking the Mount Wilson Trail (Ride 28). Another 1.5 miles to the top takes you to the Mount Wilson Obervatory. Turn around and be careful riding down.

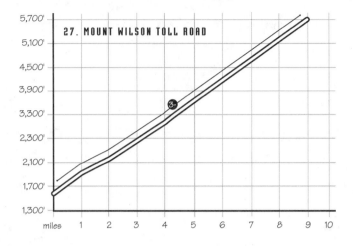

27. MOUNT WILSON TOLL ROAD

THE RIDE

0.0 From the trailhead you drop down on a short paved road and across a bridge to begin a steep climb.

2.6 At Henniger Flats continue on the road past the bathrooms and to the right of the Nature Center.

7.5 You reach a junction with a sign pointing straight to Mount Wilson Toll Road. Do not turn off road.

9.0 Reach the top of Mount Wilson. Turn around and ride the same road back to the car.

18.0 The end.

Enjoying the woodsy Mt. Wilson Trail.

Mount Wilson Trail

Location:	In the Angeles National Forest, starting near Sierra Madre.
Distance:	12 miles, out and back.
Time:	2.6 hours.
Tread:	Singletrack.
Aerobic level:	Strenuous. Requires all but the most advanced riders to do some hike-a-bike on the way up.
Technical difficulty:	4.
Fees:	None.
Services:	There are no services available on the trail. All services are available down Baldwin Boulevard off Interstate 210.
Water:	No water available on the trail.
Highlights:	Incredible downhill singletrack.
Hazards:	Lots of hikers. Poison oak.
Land status:	Angeles National Forest.
Maps:	USGS Mount Wilson; Thomas Brothers, Los Angeles County, page 537.

Access: In the city of Arcadia, exit Interstate 210 at Baldwin Boulevard and drive east toward the mountains. Turn right on Mira Monte Avenue after 1.5 miles and within 100 feet you see Mount Wilson Trail Street on the left. Park there and ride your bike up Mount Wilson Trail Street one-quarter of a mile to the trailhead.

Notes on the trail: The Mount Wilson Trail, like its neighbor the Mount Wilson Toll Road, is very strenuous. In addition to being steep, much of the terrain is over loose gravel and imbedded rock. It challenges the most advanced riders and proves disheartening to less experienced riders. Another option is to climb the Mount Wilson Toll Road (Ride 27) 7.5 miles toward the top and descend the Mount Wilson Trail. While the Mount Wilson Toll Road is also steep and strenuous, it is all fireroad and does not require the same level of technical skills as the Mount Wilson Trail does.

Close to the trailhead, there is also a paved road to the right. Both merge within one-quarter of a mile and then continue up the trail. Pass by the post at the trailhead and begin to climb as the trail winds up the woodsy hill. At 1.6 miles First Water is off to the right. Continue up the trail by veering left and climbing as the trail continues to get more difficult. At 3.6 miles you

Mount Wilson Trail

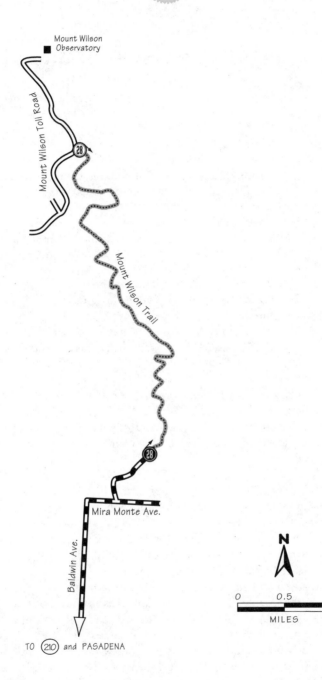

reach Orchard Camp which is the turn-around for most hikers. Since th
trail above Orchard Camp is less traveled, it soon becomes more overgrow:
and technical. After you struggle for the next few miles you reach the Man
zanita Ridge at 5.3 miles. Turn left at the ridge and ride another 0.75 mili
until you reach the Mount Wilson Toll Road at 6 miles. If you posess th
strength you can ride up the Mount Wilson Toll Road another 1.75 miles to
the top. If not, turn around and enjoy the fruits of your labor.

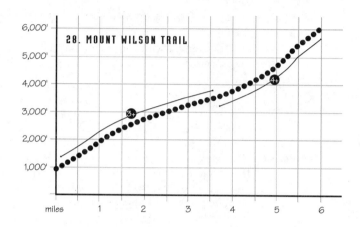

THE RIDE

0.0	Climb past the trailhead sign.
1.6	Veer left past First Water.
3.6	At Orchard Camp, trail continues off to the left.
5.3	At Manzanita Ridge turn left.
6.0	At Mount Wilson Toll Road, turn around or ride another 1.75 miles to the top.
12.0	The end.

Palos Verdes Bluffs

Location:	Palos Verdes.
Distance:	5 miles, out and back with a little loop.
Time:	1.5 hours.
Tread:	Mostly fireroad with some short sections of singletrack.
Aerobic level:	Moderate.
Technical difficulty:	3-.
Fees:	None.
Services:	None.
Water:	None.
Highlights:	You ride along the cliffs of Palos Verdes and overlook the ocean. Sometimes you see a paraglider taking off from the cliffs. You can stop and watch the surfers ride the waves off the point. In other words, the highlights are spectacular.
Hazards:	There are a few very technical sections. The whole area is under construction so some sections are blocked off. Stay away from the edge of the cliffs.
Land status:	Palos Verdes Shoreline Park.
Maps:	USGS San Pedro; Thomas Brothers, page 823.

Access: Take Interstate 110 (Harbor Freeway) south until it ends. When you get off the freeway turn left onto Gaffey Street. Continue for approximately 1.75 miles. Turn right on 25th Street. Drive 1.25 miles and turn left on Western Avenue. Turn right on South Paseo Del Mar and turn left on Stargazer Avenue. Turn right immediately on Warmouth Street and drive to the end and park anywhere around the entrance.

Notes on the trail: The whole time you have the ocean within a few hundred yards. Although there are no trail markings or signs, you will not get lost. You start following the chainlink fence to the bluff. From there you parallel the bluff until you get to a junction at 0.3 mile where you take a right and begin a 0.25 mile climb. You continue at the top of the hill to the left at 0.6 mile and follow the trail along the bluffs. From there you ride over some moderate hills and down into some deep crevices. At 1 mile you come to a fork and take the trail to the right. You see more trails cutting off to the left, but continue straight to the end of the park. At 2.3 miles wrap around the loop and head back.

Palos Verdes Bluffs

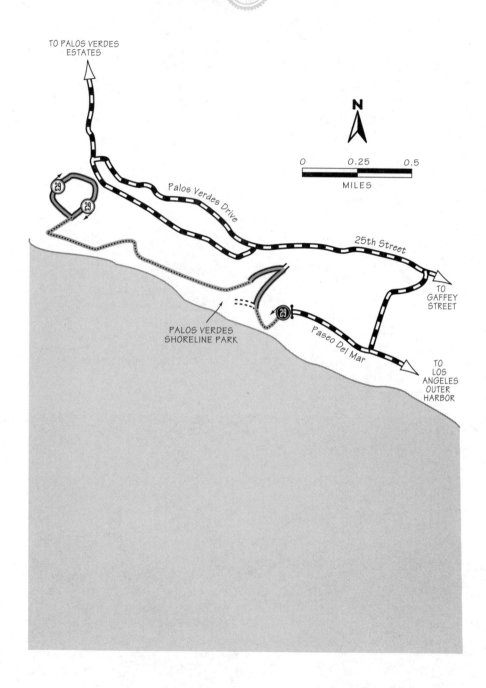

TO PALOS VERDES
ESTATES

N

0   0.25   0.5

MILES

29

29

Palos Verdes Drive

25th Street

TO
GAFFEY
STREET

PALOS VERDES
SHORELINE PARK

29

Paseo Del Mar

TO
LOS
ANGELES
OUTER
HARBOR

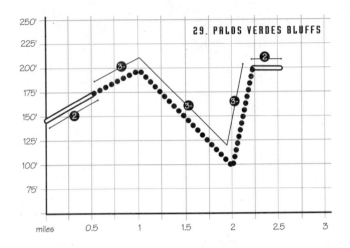

29. PALOS VERDES BLUFFS

THE RIDE

0.0 Ride through the fence about 20 yards to the bluff and turn right.

0.3 Turn right and climb hill.

0.6 Follow the trail to the left at the top of the hill.

1.0 Take the trail to the right at the fork.

1.9 Continue straight past the trails that head to the left.

2.3 You come to a fork. This is a loop so it does not matter which way you go. The trail encloses a circle of dense vegetation. After you loop around head back to where you parked.

5.0 The end.

Great view from Palos Verdes Bluffs.

Orange County

Peter's Canyon/
Lower Canyon Trail

Location:	Northern Orange County between the cities of Orange and Tustin.
Distance:	4.4 miles, out and back.
Time:	30 minutes.
Tread:	Mostly well-maintained dirt road, with a short singletrack section at the beginning.
Aerobic level:	Easy.
Technical difficulty:	2.
Fees:	$3 per vehicle.
Services:	The closest services are off Chapman Avenue approximately three-quarters of a mile north on Jamboree Road.
Water:	There is a water spigot in the parking lot next to the water trough.
Highlights:	Nice relaxing ride with options to ride around the lake.
Hazards:	Rattlesnakes and angry equestrians.
Land status:	Peter's Canyon Regional Park.
Maps:	USGS Orange; Thomas Brothers, Orange County, page 800.

Access: From the city of Orange, exit California Highway 55 at Chapman East and continue 4 miles to Jamboree Road and turn right. Approximately three-quarters of a mile down, turn right on Canyon View Avenue and see the parking lot off to the left within one-quarter mile. From Irvine, exit Interstate 5 on Jamboree Road and drive north 5 miles to Canyon View Avenue or exit Interstate 405 at Jamboree Road and drive north 9 miles to Canyon View Avenue. Turn left on Canyon View Avenue and see the parking lot off to the left within one-quarter mile. The trailhead is to the left of the far end of the parking lot marked with a sign for Lake View Loop.

Peter's Canyon/Lower Canyon Trail

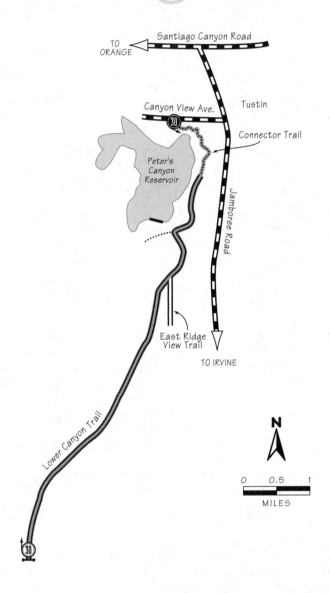

Notes on the trail: Ride along the connector trail which drops into a gully and takes you back toward the park entrance. The trail turns right as it runs parallel to Canyon View Avenue. At Jamboree Road the trail again turns right and parallels Jamboree Road before it cuts back toward the park. At 0.4 mile veer right and begin a short climb toward a building atop the hill. Turn right onto the pavement near the building and ride down as the trail turns back into dirt. At 0.8 mile continue straight past the junction that goes toward Lake View Loop on the right and East Ridge View Trail to the left. Just past the Lake View Loop Junction continue straight past the Gnatcher Trail. Stay on the main trail, passing several singletracks, until you reach a gate at the end at 2.2 miles. You can either turn around or head up the East Ridge View Trail. East Ridge View Trail is accessed through the gate to the left and climbs steeply before dropping back toward the canyon.

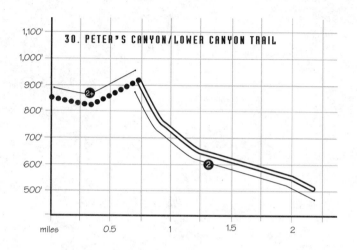

THE RIDE

0.0 Enter the connector trail marked with a sign for Lake View Loop.

0.2 Turn right, ride parallel to Jamboree Road.

0.4 Veer right at the junction onto the dirt road.

0.8 Veer right at the junction past the Lakeview Loop Trail on the right and the East Ridge View Trail to the left.

0.9 Continue straight past Gnatcher Trail on the left.

1.3 Continue straight past a narrow trail to the left.

1.4 Continue straight past a footpath to the right going down into Peters Canyon Creek.

1.7 Continue straight past as the Peter's Canyon Creek Trail comes back up from the right and the Opossum Trail heads off to the left.

2.2 Lower Canyon Trail ends at the gate. Turn around and head back to the car.

4.4 The end.

Beware of the mountain bike–eating Labrador at Peter's Canyon.

Santa Ana Mountains

The Santa Ana Mountains lie within the western area of the Cleveland National Forest, dividing Orange and Riverside Counties. The Santa Ana Mountains are accessed by several trails that all reach up from the canyons below to the Main Divide, which traverses from the city of Corona to the Ortega Highway. Most of the rides within the Santa Ana Mountains can be linked via the Main Divide to provide an entire network of intertwining trails for endless riding. Saddleback Silverado Peak, at 5,687 feet above sea level, is the highest peak within this range. This peak and its neighbor, Modjeska Peak, at 5,496 feet, are referred to as Saddleback Mountain. The winter months often bring snow to Saddleback Mountain.

A vast array of flora and fauna can be found in the Santa Ana Mountains. Chaparral-covered hills are the norm with an abundance of poison oak in the lower areas and pine trees up above. Deer, coyotes, rabbits, lizards, rattlesnakes and a variety of birds can be found in most areas and are more visible in the spring and summer months. The Santa Ana Mountains are mountain lion country. While there have been very few attacks, sightings are quite frequent.

Mountain biking in the Santa Ana Mountains is diverse and challenging. Both fireroad and singletrack reach from the canyons below to the Main

Divide. The Main Divide is a fairly wide fireroad in m
become quite steep and weathered in other parts. The Ma
to all vehicles in the summer months so be careful of negl
This range has some of the best mountain biking in the c
the infamous San Juan Trail, so often pictured in magazin

Blackstar Canyon

Location:	Northern end of the Santa Ana Mountains in the Cleveland National Forest.
Distance:	15.5 miles, out and back.
Time:	2 hours.
Tread:	Mostly well-maintained fireroad.
Aerobic level:	Moderate.
Technical difficulty:	2+.
Fees:	None.
Services:	None. Nearest services are south on Silverado Canyon or on Chapman Avenue.
Water:	None.
Highlights:	Blackstar Canyon is an excellent intermediate ride with a wide dirt road that overlooks chaparral canyons. Hidden Ranch is a cattle ranch at 5.6 miles. An old ranger area, Beeks Point, is at the top.
Hazards:	Cowpatties, rattlesnakes, mountain lions, and bike-chasing dogs.
Land status:	Cleveland National Forest.
Maps:	USGS Black Star Canyon; Thomas Brothers, Orange County, page 802.

Access: From the city of Orange exit California Highway 55 at Chapman Avenue East. After 5 miles, Chapman Avenue becomes Santiago Canyon Road. Continue another 5 miles, then turn left on Silverado Canyon Road. Within 100 yards of turning off Santiago Canyon Road to Silverado Canyon Road go left on Blackstar Canyon Road. Drive about 1 more mile until it deadends at the steel gate.

From Southern Orange County, exit Interstate 5 at El Toro Road and head east into the hills for about 7.4 miles. Here, El Toro Road ends and turns into Santiago Canyon Road to the left and Live Oak Canyon Road to the right. Go left at Santiago Canyon Road and travel north another 5 miles to

Blackstar Canyon

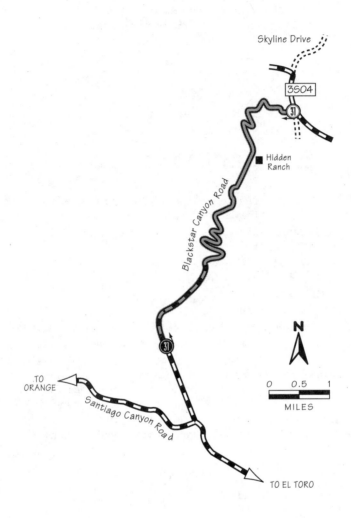

Skyline Drive

3S04

31

Hidden
Ranch

Blackstar Canyon Road

31

N

0   0.5   1
MILES

TO
ORANGE

Santiago Canyon Road

TO EL TORO

Silverado Canyon Road and turn left. Within 100 yards of turning off Santiago Canyon Road to Silverado Canyon Road go left on Blackstar Canyon Road. Drive about 1 more mile until it deadends at the steel gate.

Notes on the trail: The trailhead begins at the steel gate at the end of Blackstar Canyon Road. Pass through the gate and ride along as the trail alternates between asphalt and dirt for the first 2.5 miles with very little climbing. At 2.2 miles veer right past the private road. Here you ride past a couple of old ranches; beware of dogs that may chase. At 2.5 miles, hook a left and start your climb as the trail becomes dirt from here on out. At 4 miles you reach a little asphalt strip with a cattle crossing. Continue straight as the trail levels out and then drops into Hidden Valley. At 5.4 miles you begin your final climb to the Main Divide. At 7.6 miles you pass through steel gates. At 7.75 miles you reach the Main Divide with Beeks Point to the immediate right. This is an old ranger's house and a great place to take a rest before making the trip back. To the left within one-half mile are radio towers and the top of Skyline Drive (Ride 52).

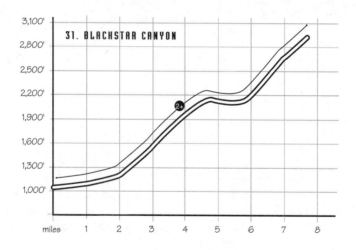

31. BLACKSTAR CANYON

THE RIDE

0.0 Trailhead begins at steel gate.
2.2 Veer right past the private road.
2.5 Asphalt ends. Begin climb.
4.0 First summit before you drop into Hidden Ranch.
5.6 Bottom of Hidden Valley. Begin final ascent.
7.6 Pass through steel gate.
7.75 Reach the Main Divide and Beeks Point. Head back the way you came.
15.5 The end.

Beeks Place atop Blackstar Canyon.

Maple Springs Trucktrail

Location:	Silverado Canyon in the Santa Ana Mountains within the Cleveland National Forest between the cities of Orange and El Toro.
Distance:	14.4 miles, out and back. Optional 1.5 miles each way to Modjeska Peak and 4 miles each way to Silverado Peak.
Time:	1.6 hours. Modjeska Peak is another 25-minute climb and Silverado Peak is another 30 minutes from there.
Tread:	The first 3 miles are old asphalt road and the rest is fireroad.
Aerobic level:	Moderate.
Technical difficulty:	3.
Fees:	National Forest Adventure Pass required.
Services:	There is a convenience store along Silverado Canyon Road.
Water:	None

Maple Springs Trucktrail

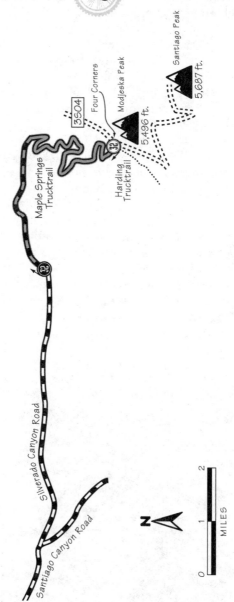

Highlights: Chaparral-covered mountains and pine trees up top. Scenic views of Orange County. Snow up above Four Corners in the winter.

Hazards: Rattlesnakes, mountain lions, motor vehicles.

Land status: Cleveland National Forest.

Maps: USGS Santiago Peak, Black Star Canyon, Corona South; Thomas Brothers, Orange County, page 802.

Access: From the city of Orange exit California Highway 55 at Chapman Avenue East. After 5 miles, Chapman Avenue becomes Santiago Canyon Road. Continue another 5 miles and then turn left on Silverado Canyon Road. Drive another 5.5 miles until you reach the steel gate.

From southern Orange County, exit Interstate 5 at El Toro Road and head east into the hills for about 7.4 miles. Here, El Toro Road ends and turns into Santiago Canyon Road to the left and Live Oak Canyon Road to the right. Go left at Santiago Canyon Road and travel north another 5 miles to Silverado Canyon Road and turn left. Drive another 5.5 miles until you reach the steel gate.

Notes on the trail: Maple Springs Trail begins with a fairly steep old paved road for the first 3 miles and then levels off as it turns to dirt. The trailhead starts at a steel gate at the end of Silverado Canyon Road. During summer months the gate is open for motorized vehicles so be careful. A few hundred yards after you start up the trail you come to a stream crossing which, during the rainy season, may require you to dismount. Just past this stream crossing, you see a singletrack trail to the left. This is the Silverado Motorway Trail, which is recommended for downhill only (Ride 33). For the next 3 miles you climb steadily along an old, beat-up asphalt road and cross several streams. At 3 miles you cross another stream and begin your ascent on dirt road. This road varies from smooth dirt to rocky, rutted-out sections. As you climb higher, the terrain looks more like a forest with pine trees shooting

Descending to the bottom of Silverado Motorway. (Ride 33)

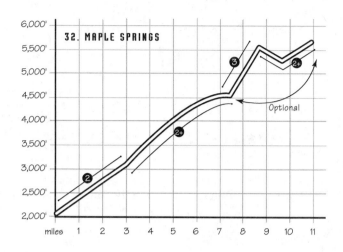

up around you. At 7.2 miles you reach Four Corners. To the immediate right is Harding Trucktrail (Ride 34) and straight ahead is the Main Divide which heads to Santiago Peak to the south and the city of Corona to the north. From here you can either turn around and ride down or continue to Santiago Peak. Santiago Peak is actually the local term for Modjeska Peak and Silverado Peak. Modjeska Peak is approximately 1.5 miles to the south at 5,496 feet and Silverado Peak is approximately 4 miles to the south at 5,687 feet. Silverado Peak is the highest peak in the Cleveland National Forest. To reach either of these peaks, ride up about 100 feet to the Main Divide and turn right. The dirt road up to Modjeska Peak is a little steeper than Maple Springs Trucktrail and has sections of loose gravel. From Modjeska Peak to Silverado Peak, the trail smoothes out. About 200 feet before the top of Silverado Peak, the trail splits. Stay on the trail to the right.

THE RIDE

- **0.0** Pass through steel gate.
- **0.3** Several stream crossings.
- **0.1** After the first stream crossing, continue straight past the singletrack on the left.
- **3.0** After last stream crossing asphalt becomes dirt road.
- **7.2** Reach top of trail at Four Corners. Head down or continue to Santiago Peak.
- **14.4** The end.

33

Maple Springs to Silverado Motorway

Location:	Silverado Canyon in the Santa Ana Mountains within the Cleveland National Forest between the cities of Orange and El Toro.
Distance:	16-mile loop.
Time:	2.5 hours.
Tread:	Mostly fireroad with a final 3-mile singletrack descent.
Aerobic level:	Moderate with one difficult section at mile 11.5.
Technical difficulty:	Mostly Level 3 with the final singletrack descent being Level 4+.
Fees:	National Forest Adventure Pass required.
Services:	There is a convenience store along Silverado Canyon Road.
Water:	None.
Highlights:	Demanding technical singletrack descent, chaparral-covered mountains, scenic views of Orange County.
Hazards:	Rattlesnakes, mountain lions, motor vehicles, loose shale rack.
Land status:	Cleveland National Forest.
Maps:	USGS Santiago Peak, Black Star Canyon, Corona South; Thomas Brothers, Orange County, page 802.

Access: From the city of Orange exit California Highway 55 at Chapman Avenue East. After 5 miles, Chapman Avenue becomes Santiago Canyon Road. Continue another 5 miles then turn left on Silverado Canyon Road. Drive another 5.5 miles until you reach the steel gate.

From southern Orange County, exit Interstate 5 at El Toro Road and head east into the hills for about 7.4 miles. Here, El Toro Road ends and turns into Santiago Canyon Road to the left and Live Oak Canyon Road to the right. Go left at Santiago Canyon Road and travel north another 5 miles to Silverado Canyon Road and turn left. Drive another 5.5 miles until you reach the steel gate.

Notes on the trail: Maple Springs Trail begins with a fairly steep old paved road for the first 3 miles and then levels off as it turns to dirt. The ride along the Main Divide is a fun rollercoaster ride with a few steep climbs. The

Maple Springs to Silverado Motorway

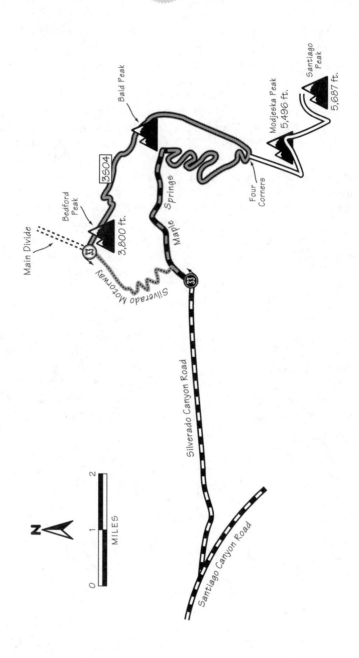

Bald Peak

Modjeska Peak
5,496 ft.

Santiago
Peak
5,687 ft.

3504

Bedford
Peak

Main Divide

3,800 ft.

33

Maple Springs

Four
Corners

Silverado Motorway

33

Silverado Canyon Road

Santiago Canyon Road

N

MILES
0   1   2

trailhead starts at a steel gate at the end of Silverado Canyon Road. During summer months the gate is open for motorized vehicles so be careful. A few hundred yards after you start up the trail you come to a stream crossing which, during the rainy season, may require you to dismount. Just past this stream crossing, you see a singletrack trail to the left. This is the bottom of Santiago Motorway where you finish your ride; it is recommended for downhill only. For the next 3 miles climb steadily along an old beat-up asphalt road while crossing several streams in the process. At 3 miles you cross another stream and begin your ascent on dirt road. This road varies from smooth dirt to rocky, rutted-out sections. As you climb higher, the terrain looks more like a forest with pine trees shooting up around you. At 7.2 miles you reach Four Corners. To the immediate right is Harding Trucktrail (Ride 34) and straight ahead is the Main Divide which heads to Santiago Peak to the south and the city of Corona to the north. Ride a few hundred feet up to the Main Divide and turn left. From here you rollercoaster for the next 6 miles. While there are still a few steep climbs, the majority of the ride is downhill. At 10.6 miles you see Bedford Canyon drop down to the right. Continue straight on the Main Divide. At 11.8 miles you see a singletrack off to the left. The sign reads, "No Vehicles." Continue straight on the Main Divide. At 13 miles you come to a big bend in the road going off to the right. There is a sign that reads, "3SO4." To the left you see wood barriers with a singletrack going up a small mountain. Here you want to go left past the wood barriers and onto the singletrack. If you continue right on the Main Divide, you reach the top of Blackstar Canyon (Ride 31) and then eventually Corona. After a short gradual climb you begin the final descent along rutted-out and rocky terrain. At 14 miles, after descending a steep rutted-out drop, you come to a three-way junction. Turn left and continue to descend. At 16 miles you reach the bottom of the singletrack and are back at the beginning of Maple Springs Trail. Turn right and ride a few hundred feet back to the car.

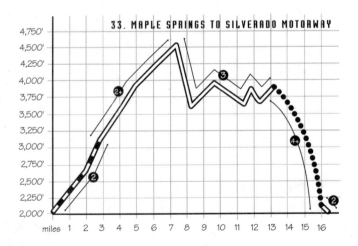

0.0	Pass through steel gate.
0.1	After the first stream crossing, continue straight past the singletrack on the left.
0.3	Several stream crossings.
3.0	After last stream crossing asphalt becomes dirt road.
7.2	Reach top of trail at Four Corners. Turn left onto the Main Divide.
10.6	Continue straight on Main Divide, past Bedford Canyon on the left.
11.8	Continue straight on Main Divide, past singletrack on the right.
13.0	Turn left onto singletrack past wood barriers as Main Divide bends to the right.
14.0	Turn left downhill at three-way junction.
16.0	Bottom of singletrack. Turn right onto Maple Springs Trail.
16.1	The end.

Harding Trucktrail

Location:	Modjeska Canyon in the Santa Ana Mountains within Cleveland National Forest between the cities of Orange and El Toro.
Distance:	18.6 miles, out and back.
Time:	3 hours.
Tread:	Fireroad that is fairly well-maintained except after a strong rain.
Aerobic level:	Moderate to strenuous.
Technical difficulty:	Although the trail is fairly well-maintained fireroad, the sheer steepness of the grade makes it a 3.
Fees:	None.
Services:	None in the immediate area.
Water:	None in the immediate area.
Highlights:	Scenic views atop the Four Corners area; access to the Main Divide and Santiago Peak. This is an excellent training ride with its steep climbs and sometimes-rutty descents.
Hazards:	Rattlesnakes and mountain lions.
Land status:	Cleveland National Forest.
Maps:	USGS Santiago Peak; Thomas Brothers, Orange County, page 802.

Harding Trucktrail

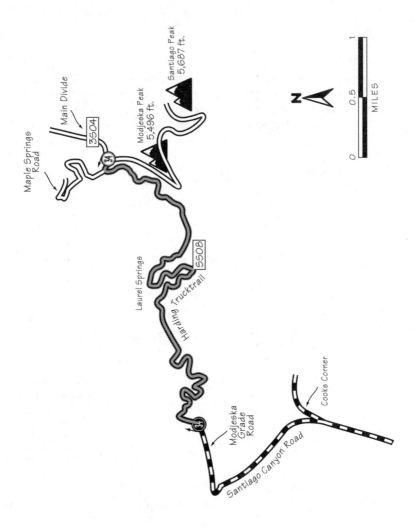

Access: From southern Orange County, exit Interstate 5 at El Toro Road and head east into the hills for about 7.4 miles. Here, El Toro Road ends and turns into Santiago Canyon Road to the left and Live Oak Canyon Road to the right. Take note of the battered old restaurant on the corner. Cooks Corner is the local hangout of mountain bike riders, roadies, and Harley riders alike. It's a great place to grab a cold one and a burger after a hard ride. Veer left onto Santiago Canyon Road and go approximately 1 mile to Modjeska Grade Road and turn right. Head up and over this road, drop into

Modjeska Canyon. At the junction turn right and head approximately three-quarters of a mile toward Tucker Wildlife Preserve. There are parking places at the loop at the end.

From northern Orange County in the city of Orange, exit California Highway 55 at Chapman Avenue East. After 5 miles, Chapman Avenue becomes Santiago Canyon Road. Continue another 10 miles, then turn left on Modjeska Grade Road. Head up and over this road and drop into Modjeska Canyon. At the junction turn right and head approximately three-quarters of a mile toward Tucker Wildlife Preserve. There are parking places at the loop at the end.

Notes on the trail: You see the trailhead at the back side of the parking loop and pass through the gate. This trail continues on steep-to-moderate fireroad for over 9 miles. It climbs to Four Corners at the top where it reaches the Main Divide. There are no side routes to get you lost. This is a great training ride but tends to get long and tiring near the end. The ride down is a blast. After 1 mile of climbing you drop about 100 feet into a small valley before beginning the rest of your climb. Most of the climb is fairly steep until you reach Laurel Springs at 4.8 miles. From there the grade decreases for the next 2 miles until it flattens out as you wrap around the other side of the mountain at the 7-mile mark. It begins a slight descent for approximately three-quarters of a mile and then begins the final climb to Four Corners. At Four Corners, you see Modjeska Peak and Silverado Peak off to the right. Toward the immediate left is the Maple Springs Trail (Ride 32) and to the middle, the Main Divide heads toward Blackstar Canyon (Ride 31) and the city of Corona. From Four Corners you have the option of going down or continuing to climb another 1.5 miles to Modjeska Peak.

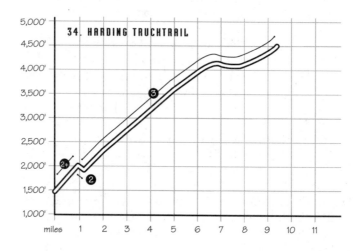

0.0   The trailhead begins on the back side of the parking loop.

1.0   Top of first climb before descent into a small valley.

4.8   Reach Laurel Springs, which is a small water spring down the side of the mountain.

7.0   Trail flattens out, then slightly descends.

9.2   Pass through forest access gate.

9.3   Reach Four Corners. Head down or continue to Modjeska Peak to the right.

18.6 The end.

Santiago Trucktrail to Old Camp

Location:	Santiago Canyon in the Santa Ana Mountains within the Cleveland National Forest between the cities of Orange and El Toro.
Distance:	15 miles, out and back.
Time:	2 hours.
Tread:	Ranges from narrow fireroad to singletrack.
Aerobic level:	Moderate.
Technical difficulty:	Overall Level 3 with a few rocky, rutty Level 4 sections near the top.
Fees:	None.
Services:	None in the immediate area.
Water:	None in the immediate area.
Highlights:	Fast, fun combination fireroad and singletrack. Old Camp at the top of the ride is rumored to have been an old Native American hunting camp.
Hazards:	Rattlesnakes and mountain lions.
Land status:	Cleveland National Forest.
Maps:	USGS Santiago Peak; Thomas Brothers, Orange County, page 802.

Access: From southern Orange County, exit Interstate 5 at El Toro Road and head east into the hills for about 7.4 miles. Here, El Toro Road ends and turns into Santiago Canyon Road to the left and Live Oak Canyon Road to the right. Take note of the battered old restaurant on the corner. Cooks Corner is the local hangout of mountain bike riders, roadies, and Harley

Santiago Trucktrail to Old Camp

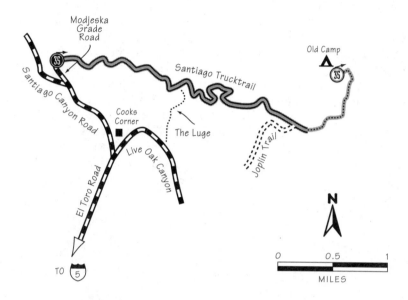

riders alike. It's a great place to grab a cold one and a burger after a hard ride. Veer left onto Santiago Canyon Road and go approximately 1 mile to Modjeska Grade Road and turn right. Approximately one-half mile up Modjeska Grade Road you see a gate to the right that marks the trailhead. Parking is available along the street a few hundred feet below.

From northern Orange County in the city of Orange, exit California Highway 55 at Chapman Avenue East. After 5 miles, Chapman Avenue becomes Santiago Canyon Road. Continue another 10 miles, then turn left on Modjeska Grade Road. Approximately one-half mile up Modjeska Grade Road you see a gate to the right which marks the trailhead. Parking is available along the street a few hundred feet below.

Notes on the trail: Pass through the steel gate and begin a moderate climb along the trail. You notice singletrack which heads up along the ridges that run above the main trail. All these trails merge back with the main trail so give them a try if you feel adventurous. Around 2 miles you ride through sections that become very overgrown and narrow during the spring and summer. At times you feel like you are tunneling through fields of giant wildflowers. Most of this is burnt or graded away by mid-fall. At 2.6 miles you begin a 0.75 mile descent down a rocky technical section before you level out and climb again. At 3.3 miles you see a singletrack trail off to the right. This trail is commonly referred to as "The Luge" by locals. The Luge is a 1-mile-long narrow, rocky, rutted-out singletrack which heads back to Live Oak Canyon Road. You can ride down "The Luge," veer right at the ranch at bottom, go left on the service road, and then go right on Live Oak Canyon Road to get back to Cooks Corner and the trailhead. After passing "The Luge" you begin a short, steep 0.3-mile climb which then levels off. At 6 miles you come to a saddle where you see the Joplin Trail that drops down to the right. The Joplin Trail ends at the Joplin Boys Prison Camp. After passing the Joplin Trail the main road narrows into singletrack as you begin the final ascent to Old Camp. The singletrack becomes more rocky and rutted-out until you reach a saddle at about 7 miles. Here you see a road that heads up to the right and deadends at some utility poles within 1 mile. Take the trail to the left which heads down to Old Camp within 0.5 mile. There is a narrow path that continues from Old Camp to the Main Divide but is not recommended. After taking a brief rest at Old Camp, turn around and enjoy the fast descent back to the car. The way down is a good time to take advantage of "The Luge".

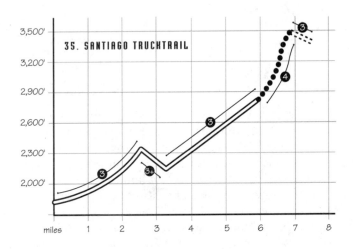

THE RIDE

0.0 Pass through gate and begin climb.

3.3 "The Luge" off to the right, continue straight.

6.0 Joplin Trail to Joplin Boys Camp to the right, continue straight.

7.0 Reach saddle above Old Camp, take trail to the left down to Old Camp.

7.5 At Old Camp, turn around and head back.

15.0 The end.

Whiting Ranch Wilderness Park

Whiting Ranch Wilderness Park is a pristine wooded area that is part of the Orange County Regional Park System. Only 7 miles from the heart of Irvine, Whiting Ranch is a wilderness away. Once in the canyon, surrounded by lumbering oaks and streams, you will not want to return. Much of the wildlife consists of birds and squirrels, although the sign at the trailhead gives the date of the last mountain lion sighting. Oak trees and chaparral surround the trail as it meanders along a stream. Extreme rains have been known to cause severe damage to this wonderful park so contact the ranger station prior to setting out on a ride after a rain.

Mustard Road to Serrano Cow Trail

Location:	Whiting Ranch is in Lake Forest in southern Orange County.
Distance:	5.6-mile loop.
Time:	Approximately 37 minutes.
Tread:	The first 1.5 miles of Borrego Springs Trail is mostly doubletrack. From the end of Borrego Springs Trail until you reach Serrano Cow Trail is fireroad. Serrano Cow Trail is singletrack followed by fireroad.
Aerobic level:	Much of the trail is easy to moderate while Emphysema Hill is strenuous.
Technical difficulty:	This trail is rated a 2+ overall with some easier fireroad climbing.
Fees:	There is a $2.00 parking fee.
Services:	At the trailhead are a grocery store, mini-mart and several fast-food restaurants. There are portable toilets at the trailhead.
Water:	There is a drinking fountain at the trailhead but none along the trail. Bottled water as well as energy replacement drinks can be purchased at the nearby mini-mart and grocery store.
Highlights:	Oak-tree-lined singletrack with several stream crossings.
Hazards:	Mountain lions. There is even a sign at the trailhead stating the last mountain lion sighting.
Land status:	Orange County Regional Park.
Maps:	USGS El Toro; Thomas Brothers, Orange County, page 862.

Mustard Road to Serrano Cow Trail

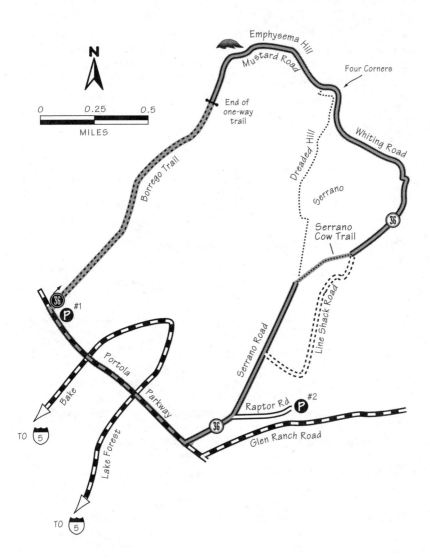

Access: Whiting Ranch is located in Lake Forest at the eastern end of Bake Parkway. From Interstate 5, just south of the El Toro Y, exit Bake Parkway and head east. After driving a little over 5 miles turn left on Portola Parkway. Drive another 100 yards and turn right on Market Place into the Ralph's Grocery parking lot. To the immediate left you see a sign for Whiting Ranch Wilderness Park. Make sure you park in the designated parking area and not the shopping center parking area. If this parking lot is full there is a second parking lot. To get there, go back to Portola Parkway and turn left. Go past Bake Parkway and Lake Forest Drive and after 1 mile turn left on Glen Ranch Road. Go up one-half mile and you come to a park sign and see a big dirt parking lot to the left.

Notes on the trail: Whiting Ranch is fun and challenging for the beginner and advanced rider alike. Although Emphysema Hill is well-deserving of its name, a beginner can struggle along and walk the mere 0.75 mile to the top in order to enjoy the rest of the loop. The first 1.5 miles of Borrego Springs Trail is one-way for bicycles and is frequented by many hikers and an occasional equestrian. Once committed, you're in for the entire trip.

To find the trailhead, go past the sculpture garden at the end of the parking lot. A sign to the left points to the bike trailhead. Descend a short asphalt road. The trailhead is just past the portable toilets. There is a sign at the trailhead listing the last mountain lion sighting.

From Parking Lot 2, go past the sign at the far end of the parking lot, pass through the gate, and head down Raptor Road. After one-quarter mile continue past the Live Oak Trail and then go left on the Serrano Road after about one-half mile. Shortly afterwards, pass though the gate and turn right on Portola Parkway. You reach Parking Lot 1 after 1.6 miles.

From the trailhead, begin a gradual ascent up Borrego Canyon, meandering along a stream and crossing it several times. The stream can be quite deep in the winter but dries up in the summer. Ride along this main trail for 1.5 miles until you come to Mustard Road. Go right at Mustard Road and pass a picnic area and a trail to Red Rock Canyon. This section of fireroad, appropriately named Emphysema Hill, gradually steepens until it reaches the 1,400-foot level at the Four Corners area after 2.2 miles. From Four Corners, take Whiting Road down the middle, which quickly dips before a fast descent that takes you from approximately 1,400 feet to 1,000 feet in less than 1 mile. Travel about 3.1 miles, and continue past Edison Road on the right. Veer right as you pass another road coming from the left. After 3.3 miles you come to Serrano Cow Trail on the right. Turn onto this short strip of singletrack which rollercoasters through a woodsy area past several stream crossings. Serrano Cow Trail ends after 3.7 miles and you reach Serrano Road. As you reach the dirt road, veer left and continue straight past several offshoots until you get to the end of the trail at 4.6 miles. Pass through the gate and turn right on Portola Parkway. Ride down paved Portola Parkway about 1 mile until you reach your car. If you parked in Parking Lot 2, turn left on Raptor Road just before the end of the trail and follow it back to your car.

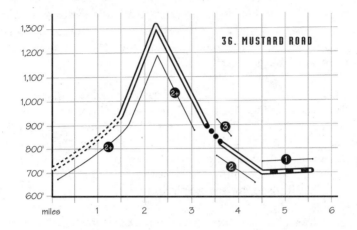

1,300'
1,200'
1,100'
1,000'
900'
800'
700'
600'

36. MUSTARD ROAD

miles   1   2   3   4   5   6

THE RIDE

0.0 At the trailhead pass though the gate and begin a gradual ascent up Borrego Canyon.

1.5 Borrego Canyon ends at Mustard Road. Go right and begin the climb up Emphysema Hill. Continue straight past Cattle Pond Loop and picnic area on the left.

1.6 Continue straight past Red Rock Canyon on the left.

2.2 Reach top of Mustard Road at Four Corners. Take the middle trail to Whiting Road.

3.1 Continue straight past Edison Road on the right. Immediately afterwards is another road on the left, veer right.

3.3 Turn right at Serrano Cow Trail.

3.7 Serrano Cow Trail ends at Serrano Road. Continue straight but veer to the left.

3.9 Continue straight past two trails which head off to the left.

4.3 Continue straight past three trails which head off to the left.

4.6 End of Serrano Road. Pass through the gate and turn right onto Portola Parkway to return to your car. If you parked in Parking Lot 2, turn left on Raptor Road just before the end and follow it back to your car.

5.6 Back at main parking lot.

Borrego Canyon in Whiting Ranch.

Cactus Loop

Location:	Whiting Ranch is in Lake Forest in southern Orange County.
Distance:	6.7-mile loop.
Time:	45 minutes.
Tread:	The first 1.5 miles of Borrego Springs Trail are mostly doubletrack. From the end of Borrego Springs Trail until you reach Serrano Cow Trail is fireroad. Serrano Cow Trail is singletrack followed by fireroad. Sage Scrub Hill is all singletrack.
Aerobic level:	Much of the trail is easy to moderate while Emphysema Hill is strenuous.
Technical difficulty:	This trail is rated a 2+ overall with some easier fireroad climbing and some Level 3 descents through Sage Scrub Hill.
Fees:	There is a $2.00 parking fee.
Services:	At the trailhead is a grocery store, mini-mart and several fast-food restaurants. There are portable toilets at the trailhead.
Water:	There is a drinking fountain at the trailhead but none along the trail. Bottled water as well as energy replacement drinks can be purchased at the nearby mini-mart and grocery store.
Highlights:	Singletrack with several stream crossings.
Hazards:	Mountain lions and cactus. There is even a sign at the trailhead stating the last mountain lion sighting.
Land status:	Orange County Regional Park.
Maps:	USGS El Toro; Thomas Brothers, Orange County, page 862.

Access: Whiting Ranch is located in Lake Forest at the eastern end of Bake Parkway. From Interstate 5, just south of the El Toro Y, exit Bake Parkway and head east. After driving a little over 5 miles, turn left on Portola Parkway. Drive another 100 yards and turn right on Market Place into the Ralph's Grocery parking lot. To the immediate left you see a sign that reads, "Whiting Ranch Wilderness Park." Make sure you park in the designated parking area and not the shopping center parking area.

If this parking lot is full there is a second parking lot. To get there, go back to Portola Parkway and turn left. Go past Bake Parkway and Lake Forest Drive and after 1 mile turn left on Glen Ranch Road. Go up one-half mile and you come to a park sign and see a big dirt parking lot to the left.

Cactus Loop

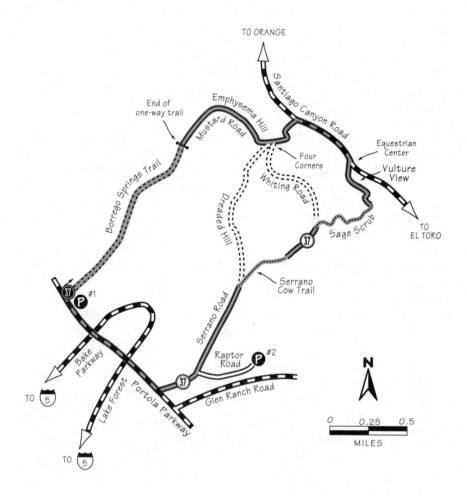

TO ORANGE

Santiago Canyon Road

Emphysema Hill

End of
one-way trail

Mustard Road

Equestrian
Center

Four
Corners

Vulture
View

Borrego Springs Trail

Whiting Road

Dreaded Hill

Sage Scrub

TO
EL TORO

37

Serrano
Cow Trail

Serrano Road

#1

37
P

Bake
Parkway

Raptor
Road

#2
P

N

TO 5

Lake Forest

Portola Parkway

37

Glen Ranch Road

0   0.25   0.5

MILES

TO 5

Notes on the trail: Whiting Ranch is fun and challenging for the beginner and advanced rider alike. Although Emphysema Hill is well-deserving of its name, a beginner can struggle along and walk the mere 0.75 mile to the top in order to enjoy the rest of the loop. The first 1.5 miles of Borrego Springs Trail is one-way for bicycles and is frequented by many hikers and an occasional equestrian. Once committed, you're in for the entire trip.

To find the trailhead, go past the sculpture garden at the end of the parking lot. A sign to the left points to the bike trailhead. Descend a short asphalt road. The trailhead is just past the portable toilets. There is a sign at the trailhead listing the last mountain lion sighting.

From Parking Lot 2, go past the sign at the far end of the parking lot, pass through the gate, and head down Raptor Road. After one-quarter mile continue past the Live Oak Trail and then go left on Serrano Road after about one-half mile. Shortly afterwards, pass though the gate and turn right on Portola Parkway. You reach Parking Lot 1 after 1.6 miles.

From the trailhead, begin a gradual ascent up Borrego Canyon, meandering along a stream and crossing it several times. The stream can be quite deep in the winter but dries up in the summer. Ride along this main trail for 1.5 miles until you come to Mustard Road. Go right at Mustard Road and pass a picnic area and a trail to Red Rock Canyon. This section of fireroad, appropriately named Emphysema Hill, gradually steepens until it reaches the 1,400-foot level at the Four Corners area after 2.2 miles. From Four Corners, take the trail to the far left and climb a short hill. Whithin one mile you descend toward Santiago Canyon Road. At 2.4 miles, continue straight past the road to the right until you reach the gate at Santiago Canyon Road. Pass through the gate and turn right on the road. Continue along the paved road until you reach the Equestrian Center at approximately 2.9 miles. As you enter the Equestrian Center, you see a dirt road to the immediate right. Take the dirt road and pass behind the old metal barn. After 3.1 miles you reach a cul-de-sac area. Take the Vulture View Trail on the left. After 3.5 miles Vulture View Trail turns into Sage Scrub Hill Trail. From this 1,300-foot level, you quickly descend some very steep and sandy singletrack. Within

The Four Corners at Whiting Ranch.

one-quarter mile you come to Cactus Hill Trail on the right which heads back to Four Corners. Continue past this trail until you get to a junction near some wire gates at the 3.9-mile mark. Veer left and shortly after veer right at a Y as you go under an oak tree and cross a stream. At 4.1 miles, merge with Whiting Ranch Road and turn left. At 4.2 miles continue straight past Edison Road and, immediately afterwards, veer right as you pass a road coming from the left. At 4.4 miles turn right onto the Serrano Cow Trail until you reach Serrano Road at 4.8 miles. As you reach the dirt road, veer left and continue straight past several offshoots until you get to the end of the trail at 5.7 miles. Pass through the gate and turn right on Portola Parkway. Ride down paved Portola Parkway about 1 mile until you reach your car. If you parked in Parking Lot 2, turn left on Raptor Road just before the end of the trail and follow that back to your car.

THE RIDE

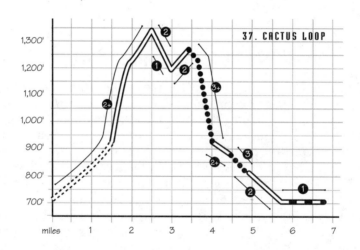

37. CACTUS LOOP

0.0 At the trailhead, pass though the gate and begin a gradual ascent up Borrego Canyon.

1.5 Borrego Canyon ends at Mustard Road. Go right and begin climb up Emphysema Hill. Continue straight past Cattle Pond Loop and picnic area on the left.

1.6 Continue straight past Red Rock Canyon on the left.

2.2 Reach top of Mustard Road at Four Corners. From Four Corners take the trail to the far left.

2.4 Continue straight past the trail on the right.

2.6 Pass through the gate and turn right on Santiago Canyon Road.

2.8 Note Modjeska Grade Road on the left, which takes you to Ride 35, Santiago Trucktrail.

2.9 Enter Equestrian Center on the right and veer right onto dirt road behind the old metal barn.

3.1 At the cul-de-sac take Vulture View Trail on the far left.

3.5 Vulture View Trail turns into Sage Scrub Hill Trail.

3.6 Continue straight past Cactus Hill on the right.

3.9 Approach wire gates, veer left and then turn right at Y and ride under oak tree and cross stream.

4.1 Merge with Whiting Ranch Road and go left.

4.2 Continue straight past Edison Road on the left. Immediately afterwards is another road on the left—veer right.

4.4 Turn right at Serrano Cow Trail.

4.8 Serrano Cow Trail ends at Serrano Road. Continue straight but veer to the left.

5.0 Continue straight past two trails which head off to the left.

5.4 Continue straight past three trails which head off to the left.

5.7 End of Serrano Road. Pass through the gate and turn right onto Portola Parkway to return to your car. If you parked in Parking Lot 2, turn left on Raptor Road just before the end and follow it back to your car.

6.7 Back at main parking lot.

O'Neill Regional Park

O'Neill Regional Park is an excellent place for the entire family to enjoy. The variety of hiking and biking trails offers recreation for the whole family. Shade in the park is provided by a blend of oak and sycamore trees. There are plenty of picnic tables and even overnight camping available. The park has abundant wildlife that ranges from squirrels and rabbits to mountain lions. From high atop the Vista Lookout you can even see the ocean.

The Arroyo Trabuco Wilderness Trail is one of two trails within O'Neill Regional Park which allows mountain bikes. This trail is a nice relaxing jaunt with very little climbing. It is an excellent trail for beginners and children. The Live Oak Trail offers a greater challenge for those with a little more skill and climbing ability. Although it is short, there is some fun singletrack.

Arroyo Trabuco Wilderness Trail

Location:	In O'Neill Regional Park in southern Orange County.
Distance:	10.6 miles, out and back.
Time:	1 hour.
Tread:	Mostly fireroad with a few narrow doubletrack sections.
Aerobic level:	Easy.
Technical difficulty:	The trail is mostly Level 1+ with two short rocky sections.
Fees:	Basic day-use fees are $2 a day during the week, $4 a day during the weekend, and $5–$10 during holidays. There are additional fees for camping and horses.
Services:	There are bathrooms with running water at the parking lot as well as picnic tables.
Water:	There are drinking fountains in the picnic area and one drinking fountain approximately 1 mile down the trail under the freeway overpass.
Highlights:	The trail is a great place for children and beginners. There is very little climbing and few technical areas and you can turn around anytime you wish.
Hazards:	This is the heart of Orange County mountain lion country. There is even a big warning sign at the trailhead.
Land status:	Orange County Regional Park.
Maps:	USGS Santiago Peak; Thomas Brothers, Orange County, pages 862, 863.

Access: From central Orange County, exit Interstate 5 at El Toro Road and head east into the hills for about 7.4 miles. Here, El Toro Road ends and turns into Santiago Canyon Road to the left and Live Oak Canyon Road to the right. Take note of the battered old restaurant on the corner. Cooks Corner is the local hangout of mountain bike riders, roadies, and Harley riders alike. It's a great place to grab a cold one and a burger after a hard ride. Head right on Live Oak Canyon Road. After 3 miles you see the entrance to the park.

Notes on the trail: From the day-use parking lot continue toward the back of the park past the loop and picnic area. You see an old mobile home to the left. To the far end of the mobile home is a forest sign and the trailhead. From the trailhead, pass through the gate and turn right. From here continue along the relatively flat fireroad which begins a very gradual ascent after

Arroyo Trabuco Wilderness Trail

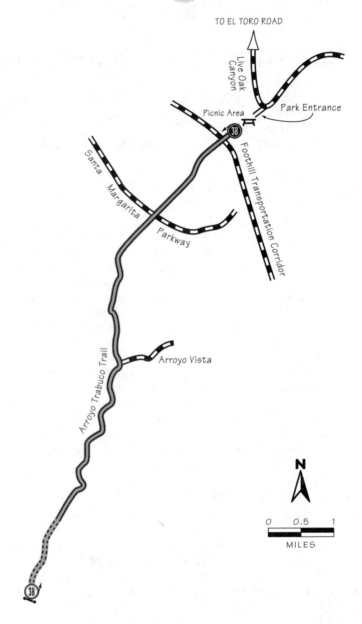

TO EL TORO ROAD

Live Oak Canyon

Park Entrance

Picnic Area

38

Santa Margarita Parkway

Foothill Transportation Corridor

Arroyo Vista

Arroyo Trabuco Trail

38

N

0   0.5   1

MILES

one-half mile. After 1 mile the trail levels off as you cross through two small streams and pass under the freeway overpass. Continue on a short gradual descent. After about 1.5 miles the trail turns into doubletrack for almost one-half mile and becomes a little rocky and sandy. After 2 miles the trail widens back to a fireroad and then begins a short climb for about one-quarter mile. After 2.2 miles you pass through a gate and come to a junction in the road. The left deadends in a residential area in Santa Margarita. Turn right and after 2.5 miles the trail travels alongside a residential street. At 2.6 miles you reach the Arroyo Vista area and continue straight past a small singletrack to the right. This singletrack is restricted from bicycle use. At 3.3 miles you come to another junction in the trail. About one-quarter mile after this, you come to a short quick downhill that drops approximately 90 feet in one-quarter mile. After passing the 4-mile mark, you pass two trails coming in from the right. Keep going straight past these trails. At 4.7 miles you cross a stream. Just after the stream, you go straight past a series of trails that come in first from the right, then the left, then the right again. At 5.2 miles you cross another stream and then reach the end at a gate at 5.3 miles. Turn around and head back.

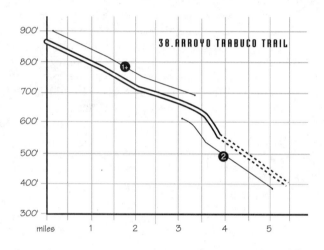

THE RIDE

0.0 At the trailhead pass though the gate and turn right.
1.0 Cross two small streams and go under the freeway overpass.
2.2 Pass through gate and turn right.
2.5 As trail travels along residential street veer right.
2.6 Continue straight past singletrack to right (restricted from bicycle use).
3.3 At junction take trail to the left and continue to the end of the trail.
3.6 Descend a one-quarter-mile short, fast downhill.
4.1 Continue straight past trail from right.
4.4 Continue straight past trail from right.
4.7 Cross river bed and continue straight past road from right.
4.9 Continue straight past trail from left.
5.0 Continue straight past trail from right.
5.3 Reach a gate at the end of the trail. Head back.
10.6 The end.

39

Live Oak Trail

Location:	In O'Neill Regional Park in southern Orange County.
Distance:	3.5-mile loop.
Time:	35 minutes.
Tread:	Mostly singletrack with some fireroad and paved sections.
Aerobic level:	Moderate.
Technical difficulty:	The trail is a combination of Levels 2 and 3.
Fees:	Basic day-use fees are $2 a day during the week, $4 a day during the weekend, and $5-$10 during holidays. There are additional fees for camping and horses.
Services:	There are bathrooms with running water at the parking lot as well as picnic tables.
Water:	There are drinking fountains in the picnic area.
Highlights:	This is a fun short ride with good singletrack.
Hazards:	This is the heart of Orange County mountain lion country.
Land status:	Orange County Regional Park.
Maps:	USGS Santiago Peak; Thomas Brothers, Orange County, pages 862, 863.

Access: From central Orange County, exit Interstate 5 at El Toro Road and head east into the hills for about 7.4 miles. Here, El Toro Road ends and turns into Santiago Canyon Road to the left and Live Oak Canyon Road to the right. Take note of the battered old restaurant on the corner. Cooks Corner is the local hangout of mountain bike riders, roadies, and Harley riders alike. It's a great place to grab a cold one and a burger after a hard ride. Head right on Live Oak Canyon Road. After 3 miles you see the entrance to the park.

Notes on the trail: From the day-use parking at the upper section of the loop you see a trailhead sign. The first four-tenths of a mile is actually a connector trail. Go through the chainlink fence and ride on the asphalt for approximately one-half mile. You then see a trail junction. Take the singletrack in the middle and start a short steep singletrack climb. At 0.2 mile you come to a T junction with a sign that reads, "Live Oak Trail." Continue straight and begin a short descent past two technical switchbacks. At the bottom, you reach an asphalt cul-de-sac and see the trail continue on the other side of the asphalt. The Live Oak Trail is to the left and you also see the Pawfoot Trail further to the right (closed to bicycles). Here you begin to climb as you

136

Live Oak Trail

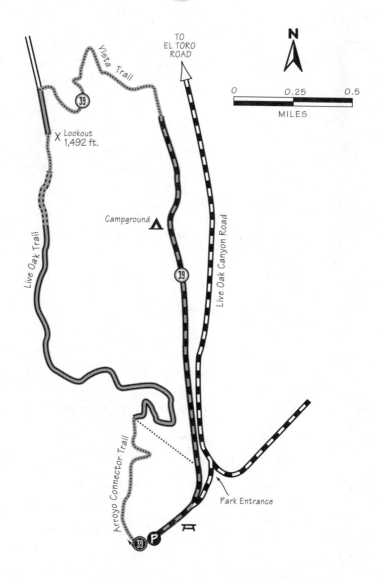

TO
EL TORO
ROAD

N

0   0.25   0.5
MILES

Vista Trail

39

X Lookout
1,492 ft.

Campground ▲

Live Oak Canyon Road

39

Live Oak Trail

Arroyo Connector Trail

Park Entrance

39 P

approach the Hoffman Homestead Trail on the right at 0.6 mile. Stay on the main road and veer to the left as the trail levels off and then begins another short climb. At 1.25 miles you begin a slight descent to a four-way junction at 1.4 miles. The trail to the left goes into a residential area and the trail to the right, Lincoln Ridge, goes back to the parking lot. Continue straight and begin a short, steep climb which may require some to hike-a-bike. At the top of the climb, at 1.6 miles, is the overlook with hitching posts and picnic tables. From the overlook continue down the trail to 1.7 miles. Here you see the Vista Trail to the right. Turn onto the Vista Trail and begin a short descent into a fun section of singletrack with five switchbacks. At 1.8 miles, at the fork in the road, veer left and continue to the bottom at 2.3 miles. Here, turn right and at 2.6 miles you merge with the paved road in the campground. As you continue on this road you see the main entrance to the left and then approach the day-use parking lot on the right.

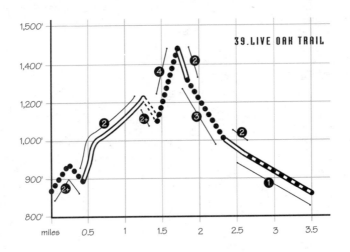

THE RIDE

0.0 At the trailhead pass though the gate and head up the asphalt until you reach the three-way junction. Turn left off the asphalt onto the middle trail.

0.2 After short climb veer left past sign onto the Live Oak Trail before you descend.

0.4 Approach asphalt cul-de-sac and see trail continue to the left. Don't take Pawfoot Trail on the right.

0.6 As you climb, veer left past Hoffman Homestead Trail on the right.

1.4 As you descend, reach four-way junction and go straight.

1.6 Reach overlook and continue down other side.

1.7 As you descend look for sharp right onto Vista Trail. Turn right and begin singletrack.

1.8 Veer left at fork.

2.3 Reach bottom of singletrack and turn right.

2.6 Merge onto paved road and continue past park entrance to your car.

3.5 The end.

Holy Jim Trail

Location:	In the Santa Ana Mountains within the Cleveland National Forest in southern Orange County.
Distance:	10 miles, out and back. An excursion to the top of Santiago Peak is another 3 miles in each direction.
Time:	2 hours.
Tread:	All singletrack.
Aerobic level:	Moderate with some difficult sections.
Technical difficulty:	Although much of the trail itself is in decent condition and would otherwise be rated a 3+, the combination of overgrown trees and rutted-out switchbacks makes it a 4+.
Fees:	Forest Adventure Pass required.
Services:	None. The closest services are back at Cooks Corner where El Toro Road turns into Live Oak Canyon Road.
Water:	There is no water along the trail so bring plenty.
Highlights:	Incredible singletrack, over 15 rutted-out, hairpin switchbacks.
Hazards:	100-foot cliffs, poison sumac, and poison oak.
Land status:	Cleveland National Forest.
Maps:	USGS Alberhill, Santiago Peak; Thomas Brothers, Orange County, page 864.

Access: From central Orange County, exit Interstate 5 at El Toro Road and head east into the hills for about 7.4 miles. Here, El Toro Road ends and turns into Santiago Canyon Road to the left and Live Oak Canyon Road to the right. Take note of the battered old restaurant on the corner. Cooks Corner is the local hangout of mountain bike riders, roadies, and Harley riders alike. It's a great place to grab a cold one and a burger after a hard ride. Head right on Live Oak Canyon Road. After another 4 miles you see a dry creekbed and dirt road on the left which is Trabuco Creek Road. Turn left onto Trabuco Creek Road, and drive down the dirt road for approximately 4.5 miles. You then come to the Holy Jim Canyon Firehouse. There is an open area for parking immediately thereafter. Here you see a forest sign with a map of the Santa Ana Mountains.

Notes on the trail: The Holy Jim Trail is singletrack at its best. The ride begins with a gradual ascent along the floor of Holy Jim Canyon. After it crosses several streams, the trail begins a relentless climb along the edge of

Holy Jim Trail

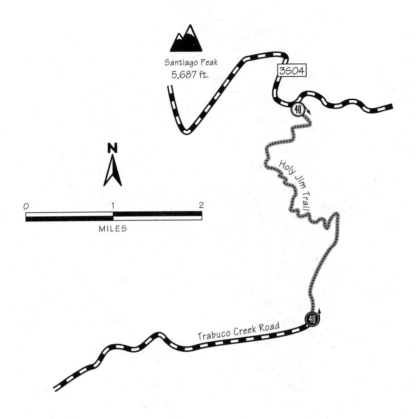

100-foot cliffs, past several switchbacks to the Main Divide.

From the parking area you see two dirt roads that head into Holy Jim Canyon. Take the road to the right, which starts near the forest sign and begins with a slight climb. Do not continue on Trabuco Creek Road. After approximately one-half mile you pass the houses of volunteer firefighters and reach the Holy Jim Trailhead sign. At the trailhead you immediately dismount and carry your bike across the stream. Begin the gradual ascent past the trailhead as you come to several streams which requires you to dismount and carry your bike. At approximately 1.4 miles you come to a series of crosses in the trail. Go left at the first one, right at the second one, and left at the third one just before the stream crossing. Shortly after you see a small, 2-foot waterfall you see the trail head up the hill to the left. Cross the waterfall and hike up the trail for approximately 50 feet. The trail goes in two directions. The right deadends within 1 mile at Holy Jim Falls. Take the left trail which heads up the mountain. From here you begin a long ascent which takes you from 2,000 feet to 4,000 feet within 3.5 miles at the Main Divide. Although it seems that you are heading back to the mouth of the canyon, you climb up toward the Main Divide as you begin a series of approximately 16 switchbacks which start at 1.7 miles and continue until mile 3. Much of the trail from here is extremely overgrown with off-camber sections that overlook hundreds of feet of cliff. After 5 miles of relentless climbing you come to a short 4x4 post in the ground where a sign used to be. The post is followed by a 100-foot, steep hike-a-bike which takes you to the Main Divide. Here you can either turn around and enjoy the trip down, or you can turn left on the Main Divide and climb 3 more miles to Santiago Peak. This last mile to Santiago Peak is some of the steepest and roughest fireroad to be found. Here you climb from 4,000 feet to 5,687 feet, the highest point in the Santa Ana Mountains. You can also turn right on the Main Divide and ride approximately 8 miles to the top of Trabuco Canyon Trail (Ride 41) and take it back down to the bottom of Holy Jim Canyon. Whether you continue to Santiago Peak or head down, be careful on the way down.

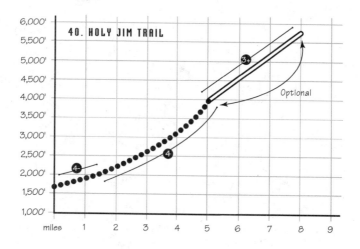

THE RIDE

0.0 Parking area.

0.5 Pass though gate at Holy Jim Trailhead and cross stream.

1.4 You come to a series of three trail diversions. Continue straight past all three of these diversions. You then see a small waterfall which you need to cross, followed by a 50-foot hike-a-bike. Once the trail levels out head left.

1.7 Approach first of approximately 16 switchbacks.

5.0 End of trail. Hike-a-bike 100 feet up to Main Divide. Go left to Santiago Peak if desired.

10.0 The end.

Hammerin' the chaparral hillsides of Holy Jim.

Trabuco Canyon Trail

Location:	In the Santa Ana Mountains within the Cleveland National Forest in southern Orange County.
Distance:	9.2 miles, out and back.
Time:	1.75 hours.
Tread:	Technical singletrack.
Aerobic level:	Moderate.
Technical difficulty:	3+ to 4+.
Fees:	Forest Adventure Pass required.
Services:	No services are available near the trail. The closest are back at Cooks Corner.
Water:	There is no water on the trail.
Highlights:	Technical singletrack that rises from the rocky creekbed to the Los Pinos Saddle.
Hazards:	Loose shale rock on trail, poison oak, rattlesnakes, and bugs.
Land status:	Cleveland National Forest.
Maps:	USGS Alberhill, Santiago Peak; Thomas Brothers, Orange County, page 864.

Trabuco Canyon Trail

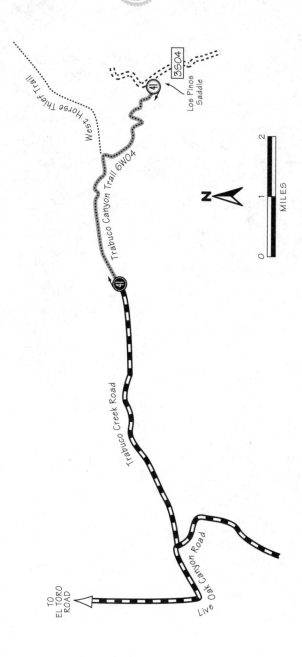

West Horse Thief Trail

3S04

Los Pinos Saddle

Trabuco Canyon Trail 6W04

N

MILES

0 1 2

Trabuco Creek Road

Live Oak Canyon Road

TO
EL TORO
ROAD

One of Trabuco Canyon Trail's more friendly sections.

Access: From central Orange County, exit Interstate 5 at El Toro Road and head east into the hills for about 7.4 miles. Here, El Toro Road ends and turns into Santiago Canyon Road to the left and Live Oak Canyon Road to the right. Take note of the battered old restaurant on the corner. Cooks Corner is the local hangout of mountain bike riders, roadies, and Harley riders alike. It's a great place to grab a cold one and a burger after a hard ride. Head right on Live Oak Canyon Road. After another 4 miles you see a dry creekbed and dirt road on the left which is Trabuco Creek Road. Turn left onto Trabuco Creek Road and drive down the dirt road. Pass Holy Jim Canyon at approximately 4.5 miles. Pass a series of houses past Holy Jim Canyon and park at the end of the road as it deadends.

Notes on the trail: Begin by riding through the gate and up the rocky canyon as you cross a series of dry creekbeds. These often require a short portage. At 0.7 mile continue past a trail to the right and after crossing the stream at 1 mile, you see the trail continue toward the left. At 1.5 miles go straight past a trail to the right. At 1.7 miles you see a dry creekbed and boulder garden to the right. A trail marker shows the West Horse Thief Trail that continues straight ahead. Carry your bike approximately 100 feet across the boulder garden to the right and you see the Trabuco Trail continue past the boulders. The trail becomes steeper as it traverses up the side of the mountain and climbs over sections of loose shale rock. At 3 miles you cross a little creek and the trail levels off and becomes less rocky. From here the tree-covered trail climbs into the lush woodlands of the national forest. At 3.5 miles continue straight past the small saddle as you see footpaths go off in either direction. At 4.6 miles you reach the top as the trail merges with the Main Divide at the Los Pinos Saddle. You can enjoy the awesome, technical ride down or turn left at the Main Divide and ride approximately 8 miles to the top of the Holy Jim Trail (Ride 40) which heads back into Trabuco Canyon.

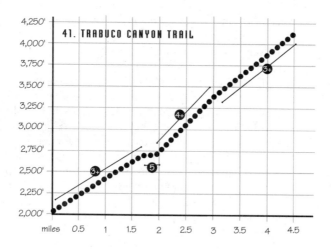

0.0 Pass through the gate at the trailhead and begin your rocky ascent into the canyon.

0.7 Continue straight past a trail to the right.

1.0 Cross the stream, continue on the trail to the left.

1.5 Continue straight past a trail to the right.

1.7 Reach junction of West Horse Thief Trail and Trabuco Canyon Trail. Carry your bike over the dry creekbed and boulder garden to the right as you see the Trabuco Canyon Trail continue to the right.

3.5 Continue straight past trails on either side.

4.6 Reach the Main Divide Trail at top. Either enjoy the quick, technical descent back down the way you came, or turn left to the Holy Jim Trail.

9.2 The end.

San Juan Trail

Location:	San Juan Capistrano in the Santa Ana Mountains east of Interstate 5.
Distance:	21.2 miles, out and back.
Time:	4 hours.
Tread:	Singletrack.
Aerobic level:	Strenuous.
Technical difficulty:	4+.
Fees:	Forest Adventure Wilderness Pass.
Services:	Bathrooms in the lower parking lot and at Blue Jay Campground at the top.
Water:	None at bottom. There is a water faucet at Blue Jay Campground at the top.
Highlights:	San Juan Trail is regarded as one of the best singletracks in California. If you are a strong biker with good technical skills, you will love this ride.
Hazards:	Take your pick. Exposed roots, large rocks, steep drops next to the trail. Do not do this ride unprepared. There is no food or water, and you are far from any help. Many Southern California professional racers use this as a downhill training course.
Land status:	Cleveland National Forest.
Maps:	USGS Canada Gobernadora, Alberhill; Thomas Brothers, Orange County, page 924.

San Juan Trail

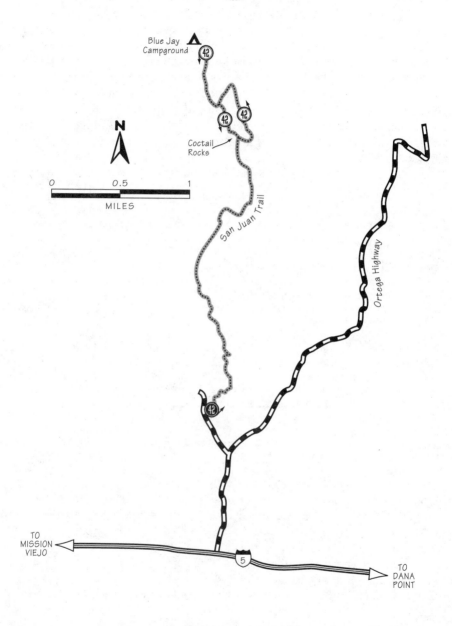

Blue Jay Campground

Coctail Rocks

San Juan Trail

Ortega Highway

N

| 0 | 0.5 | 1 |

MILES

TO MISSION VIEJO

TO DANA POINT

5

Access: Exit Interstate 5 on California Highway 74 (Ortega Highway); go east for 12.5 miles. You come to San Juan Fire Station on your left. Turn left off the main highway at the fire station. Follow dirt road behind the station for 1 mile. Park in dirt lot that surrounds the bathroom.

Notes on the trail: San Juan Trail is not for the novice biker. It is awesome technical singletrack at its best. As you start up the trail you immediately enter a series of over 12 steep technical switchbacks. After a few miles the trail flattens out a little. You navigate plenty of technical rocky sections the whole way. There are several sections where you have to get off your bike and maneuver some scary drops. At 5.5 miles you reach a junction at Cocktail Rocks. Turn right and the trail becomes even rockier and more technical. Stay on the main trail and at 8.7 miles you pass the Viejo Tie Trail on the right. At 9.3 miles ride past the Chiquita Trail on the right and then past a beaten dirt road that crosses the trail. You travel up through lush forest and cross the merge with the top of the beaten dirt road at 10.1 miles. Continue straight on the main trail and at 10.3 miles veer left into Blue Jay Campground.

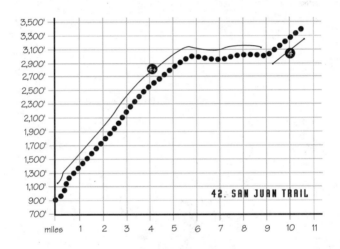

THE RIDE

0.0   Start directly across from the where you see a sign that marks the beginning of the trail. You start your ascent on about 12 steep switchbacks.
5.5   Take the right fork at Cocktail Rocks.
6.2   Stay right at the fork in the trail.
8.7   Continue straight past the Viejo Tie Trail.
9.3   Continue straight past the Chiquita Trail.
9.4   Continue straight past the beaten dirt road that crosses the trail.
10.1   Veer to the left at the fork and continue up.
10.3   Veer left at the fork into Blue Jay Campground.
10.6   Reach campground. Turn around and enjoy a well-deserved downhill.
21.2   The end.

The notorious switchbacks of San Juan Trail.

Moro Canyon

Moro Canyon is the epitome of Southern California mountain bike riding. The parking area is located along Pacific Coast Highway and the upper ridges of the park overlook the Pacific Ocean. On a clear day you can see Laguna Beach to the south and Catalina Island out across the ocean. This 3,000-acre mountain bike mecca is part of Crystal Cove State Park, an approximately 2-mile stretch of undeveloped beach. On a hot day, a dip in the cool Pacific Ocean is only one-quarter mile away from the trails. There is an abundance of wildlife at Moro Canyon. Throughout the year, coyote and bobcats can be found. Rabbits come out in the springtime and are abundant until fall. Rattlesnakes come out of hibernation in mid-to-early March and can be seen until August, although they are most prevalent until May. During the spring and early summer artichoke thistles bloom and mustard plants grow over six feet tall, sometimes impairing trail visibility. Although "it never rains in Southern California," winter rains cause severe destruction to Moro Canyon and the rangers are quick to close the park for a few days after severe rains.

Moro Canyon combines moderate-to-difficult riding through a myriad of trails that link the lower Moro Canyon Trail with Ridge Trail to the east and No Name Ridge and Red Tail Ridge to the west. The convergence of both fireroad and singletrack provides challenging riding for both novice and experienced riders. For these reasons, Moro Canyon is a favorite among coastal residents.

Moro Ridge Trail to Red Tail Ridge Loop

Location:	Adjacent to Pacific Coast Highway between Laguna Beach and Newport Beach.
Distance:	9.85-mile loop.
Time:	1 hour.
Tread:	Most of the climbing is done on doubletrack and fireroad, and most of the descents are singletrack.
Aerobic level:	Moderate.
Technical difficulty:	This trail is rated Level 3 overall with some easier fireroad climbing and a Level 4 descent along Red Tail Ridge.
Fees:	There is a parking fee of $5 and no parking is allowed along Pacific Coast Highway for several miles in each direction.
Services:	Visitor Center is next to the parking lot and offers maps and other materials on the natural habitat. The rangers also organize guided hikes through the park and in the tide pools at the beach sections of the park. Bathrooms are available at the parking lot and are also scattered along the trails.
Water:	There is a drinking fountain in the parking lot and a bottled water vending machine.
Highlights:	Fun singletrack. The bottom of Moro Canyon is home to thousands of rabbits throughout the spring and summer. The picnic area on the Ridge Trail is an excellent place to take a rest (there is also a restroom). On a clear day you can see Catalina Island out across the ocean.
Hazards:	Kamikaze rabbits that run out in front of you. Rattlesnakes can often be found sunning on the trail during spring and summer months. The lower section of Red Tail Ridge drops quickly over a series of rock shelves. This section may require some riders to take a walk in lieu of flying over the handlebars.
Land status:	Crystal Cove State Park.
Maps:	USGS Laguna Beach; Thomas Brothers, Orange County, page 920.

Moro Ridge Trail to Red Tail Ridge Loop

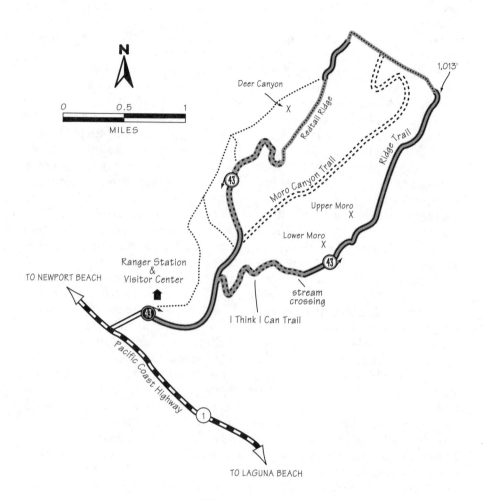

Access: From Newport Beach at Macarthur Boulevard, drive approximately 4 miles southeast to the Crystal Cove area. From Laguna Beach at Laguna Canyon Road, drive approximately 3 miles north to the Crystal Cove area. The entrance to the park is adjacent to El Moro School. Once in the parking lot ride south toward the park entrance. Just behind the ranger kiosk turn left onto the dirt road through the gate.

Notes on the trail: While the park contains various trails that make up many miles of riding, this loop provides an excellent sample of the best trails at Moro Canyon. Most of the climbing is gradual with a few steep sections. A combination of fireroad climbs and singletrack descents provides many challenging obstacles that demand good bike-handling skills. Pass behind the kiosk, ride a short ways down, and quickly drop down into Moro Canyon. You quickly come to a trail to the right which is the first cutacross to Ridge Trail. Proceed past this trail along a slight grade and ride about 1.5 miles until you come to I Think I Can trail on the right. Pass over the culvert and begin your ascent as you steadily climb about 500 feet within 1 mile. After riding approximately 2.5 miles you see a Y in the trail. Veer to the left and you shortly reach the top of I Think I Can trail and Ridge Trail. At the top, turn left and begin to climb an old washed-out asphalt road to a picnic area at the end of the asphalt. From here you take the dirt road to the right and rollercoaster up and down until you ride approximately 4.5 miles. You see a little singletrack which veers off to the left. Take this singletrack and climb until you reach the top at 1,013 feet above sea level. If you miss the singletrack, Ridge Trail will shortly deadend at a gate. After a short rest, continue on the singletrack and descend through rocky and rutted-out areas that require close attention to the trail. This is where it gets fun! After about one-half mile of singletrack the trail turns into doubletrack and you see another trail to the left. Continue past this trail until you reach a gate at approximately 5 miles. At the gate, go left along the barbed-wire trail for a few hundred feet. At the fork in the trail turn right and climb to the hub. To the right you see another gate with a singletrack just to the left of it. Head to this singletrack which takes you along a barbed-wire fenceline for less than one-half mile. You come to two forks in the trail which end up in the same place. At 5.5 miles you reach Red Tail Ridge. Go left on this section of fireroad which quickly descends until you reach a Y in the trail, a little over one-quarter mile down. Go left at the Y; the trail turns into singletrack. This part of the trail drops and climbs over large rocks and rutts until you make a short climb to the 6.75-mile mark. Here at Slant Peak you begin a quick descent over gnarly singletrack. At just over 7 miles you see a fork in the road just below a huge electrical pole. The left trail deadends at the pole. Turn right and quickly drop another two hundred feet on a fireroad. (During the spring months this section is overgrown and there is barely a singletrack.) At 7.9 miles you see another fork in the road. Head left back down into Moro Canyon. Here again you quickly descend until you hit the bottom of the canyon at the 8.4-mile mark. At the bottom, turn right and enjoy the easy ride back down the canyon to the parking lot.

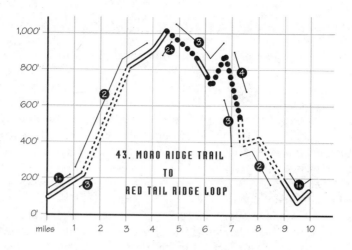

THE RIDE

0.0 From the singletrack behind the ranger kiosk, head down to Moro Canyon.

1.4 Turn right at Cut-Across 2 (I Think I Can) and climb for 1.25 miles.

2.5 Veer left at Y.

2.6 Turn left at top of I Think I Can trail and climb up asphalt to picnic area.

3.0 At picnic area turn right onto fireroad.

4.4 Veer left off fireroad onto singletrack.

4.5 Highest point of Moro Canyon. Continue on singletrack.

4.9 Continue right, past road that heads down.

5.0 Turn left at gate along barbed wire. At end of short singletrack section turn right and head up hill.

5.1 At hub turn right toward gate and once at gate turn left onto singletrack.

5.5 Turn left on Red Tail Ridge.

5.9 At Y in road, take left fork to singletrack.

7.2 At end of rocky singletrack, go right at electrical pole.

7.9 After gradual climb turn left back down to Moro Canyon.

8.4 After fast descent turn right at bottom of canyon. Head back to car.

9.8 The end.

Aliso/Wood Canyons (Top of the World)

Aliso/Wood Canyons are high in the hills in the Laguna Beach Greenbelt. Appropriately named "Top of the World" by locals, Aliso/Wood Canyons look over Laguna Beach and across the Pacific Ocean. The upper West Ridge Trail overlooks Laguna Canyon Drive to the west. Lower Wood Canyon is owned by the county of Orange, while the upper areas are city property. The park is home to rattlesnakes throughout the spring and early summer, while the lower canyon areas are abundant with poison oak throughout the warmer months.

Like its neighbor, Moro Canyon, the upper ridges of Aliso/Wood Canyons benefit from the cool ocean breeze on hot summer days. Top of the World hosts a series of trails in over 5,000 acres of parkland. The upper West Ridge Trail is linked to Wood Canyon through four trails that vary in length and difficulty. A multitude of loops can be derived by combining the various connector trails.

Rock-It/Cholla Loop

Location:	Aliso/Wood Canyons, Laguna Beach.
Distance:	6.5-mile loop.
Time:	45 minutes.
Tread:	Mostly singletrack with some fireroad.
Aerobic level:	Moderate with one strenuous climb.
Technical difficulty:	3.
Fees:	None.
Services:	At the Alta Laguna Park there are restrooms with running water and a playground as well as tennis courts for those with plenty of energy left over. The city of Laguna Beach offers services of all kinds.
Water:	There is a drinking fountain at Alta Laguna Park.
Highlights:	Singletrack descent with rock-shelf drop down Rock-It Trail. Views above Laguna Beach overlook the Pacific Ocean.
Hazards:	Rattlesnakes.
Land status:	Aliso/Wood Canyons Regional Park. Combined city and county parks.
Maps:	USGS Laguna Beach, San Juan Capistrano; Thomas Brothers, Orange County, page 951.

Rock-It/Cholla Loop

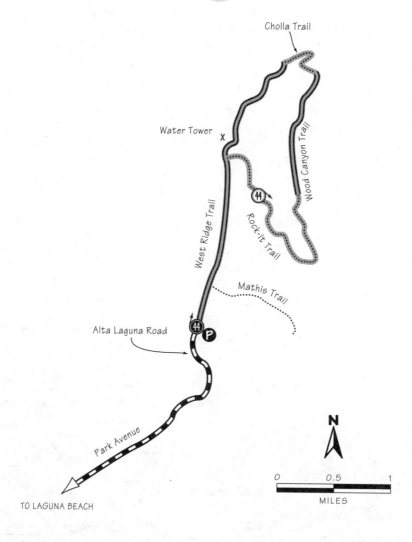

Cholla Trail

Water Tower   X

Wood Canyon Trail

West Ridge Trail

Rock-It Trail

Mathis Trail

Alta Laguna Road

Park Avenue

TO LAGUNA BEACH

N

0   0.5   1

MILES

Access: From the city of Laguna Beach on Pacific Coast Highway, approximately one-quarter mile east of Laguna Canyon Road, turn north on Legion Street. Go up approximately one-quarter mile and Legion Street turns into Park Avenue as you continue up. After about 1.85 miles go left on Alta Laguna Boulevard and park at end of cul-de-sac or in Alta Laguna Park parking lot. At the end of the cul-de-sac you see a picnic area. This is where the trail starts.

Notes on the trail: From the picnic tables you see a sign for Laguna Heights. You see a level trail to the left of the sign and another trail to the right that heads toward the canyon. This is West Ridge Trail. Head toward the right but do not take the next immediate right or you end up in the parking lot. Within a few hundred yards, you quickly drop 300 feet before you climb up another 50 feet to the top of Mathis Trail at approximately one-half mile. Continue on West Ridge Trail and you quickly drop another 120 feet immediately after passing Mathis Trail. From here you rollercoaster for another mile until you see a water tank on the left. To the right of the water tank is the top of Rock-It Trail at 680 feet. Turn right on Rock-It Trail. Rock-It Trail quickly turns into singletrack as it meanders through chaparral and past cactus. You see a wide road to the left of the trail after about 1.85 miles. This road deadends at a utility pole. After about 2.25 miles you reach the section of trail that is Rock-It Trail's namesake. Here you drop 80 feet over the distance of less than one-quarter mile. You travel over imbedded rock shelves that make your forearms scream for mercy. A local biker who braved the climb up Rock-It Trail stated, "Climbing up this kicks your ass!" Continue down the trail to the bottom of Rock-It Trail at 2.8 miles where the elevation is at a low 180 feet. Turn left and continue straight past the trail to the right and the trail to the left immediately after. After about 3 miles there is a small stream crossing where some may need to dismount. After the stream crossing, you reach Wood Canyon and go left. After about 3.5 miles you see two trails to the left. The first one deadends within one-half mile and the second one is the Lynx Trail that climbs up to West Ridge Trail. Continue along Wood Canyon where you begin a short climb just before 4 miles. Within a few hundred feet you reach the Cholla Trail. Climb the Cholla

Descending the Rock-It Trail.

Trail as it ascends from 360 feet to 635 feet within less than one-half mile. Not only is the Cholla Trail steep, it is sandy and rutted-out. At the top of Cholla Trail turn left on West Ridge Trail and head back to your car. As you climb back up West Ridge Trail there are a few diversions to the right that climb up on a short ridge and merge back to the main trail. To the left of the main road you see the Lynx Trail, Rock-It Trail, and Mathis Trail as you make the 2-mile climb back to your car.

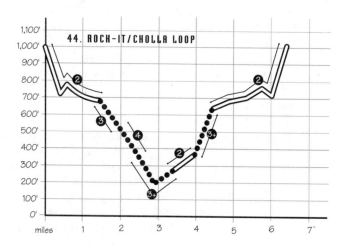

THE RIDE

0.0 From the Laguna Heights sign near the picnic tables take the trail to the right which heads down West Ridge Trail.

0.5 Mathis Trail to the right. Continue straight on West Ridge Trail.

1.5 Come to water tank and see Rock-It Trail to the right. Turn right on Rock-It Trail.

1.8 Pass utility road on left and continue straight.

2.2 Reach top of rocky technical section.

2.8 Reach bottom of Rock-It Trail and go left. Continue straight past first trail to the right and then one to the left.

3.0 Stream crossing where most people have to dismount. Immediately after, you reach Wood Canyon Road and turn left.

3.5 Continue past two trails to the left. First trail deadends at utility pole. Second trail is Lynx Trail and heads back to West Ridge Trail.

3.9 Reach Cholla Trail to the left and climb up this steep technical trail to West Ridge Trail.

4.3 At West Ridge Trail turn left and return to the top of Alta Laguna Park.

4.5 Continue straight past Lynx Trail on the left.

4.8 Continue straight past Rock-It Trail on the left.

5.8 Continue straight past Mathis Trail on the left.

6.3 The end.

Lynx/Mathis Loop

Location:	Aliso/Wood Canyons, Laguna Beach.
Distance:	5.5-mile loop.
Time:	Less than 40 minutes.
Tread:	Mostly singletrack with some fireroads.
Aerobic level:	Mostly moderate with a strenuous climb up Mathis Trail.
Technical difficulty:	3+.
Fees:	None.
Services:	At the Alta Laguna Park there are restrooms with running water and a playground as well as tennis courts for those with plenty of energy left over. The city of Laguna Beach offers services of all kinds.
Water:	There is a drinking fountain at Alta Laguna Park.
Highlights:	Singletrack descent with rock chutes down Lynx Trail. Views above Laguna Beach overlook the Pacific Ocean.
Hazards:	Rattlesnakes.
Land status:	Aliso/Wood Canyons Regional Park. Combined city and county parks.
Maps:	USGS Laguna Beach, San Juan Capistrano; Thomas Brothers, Orange County, page 951.

Access: From the city of Laguna Beach on Pacific Coast Highway, approximately one-quarter mile east of Laguna Canyon Road, turn north on Legion Street. Approximately one-quarter mile after you turn, Legion Street turns into Park Avenue. After about 1.85 miles go left on Alta Laguna Boulevard and park at end of cul-de-sac or in Alta Laguna Park parking lot. At the end of the cul-de-sac you see a picnic area. This is were the trail starts.

Notes on the trail: From the picnic tables you see a sign for Laguna Heights. You see a level trail to the left of the sign and another trail to the right that heads toward the canyon. This is West Ridge Trail. Head toward the right but do not take the next immediate right or you end up in the parking lot. Within a few hundred yards, you quickly drop 300 feet before climbing up another 50 feet to the top of Mathis Trail at approximately one-half mile. From here you rollercoaster for another mile until you see a water tank on the left and pass Rock-It Trail on the right. Continue another quarter of a mile until you come to the Lynx Trail on the right after 1.8 miles. Turn right

Lynx/Mathis Loop

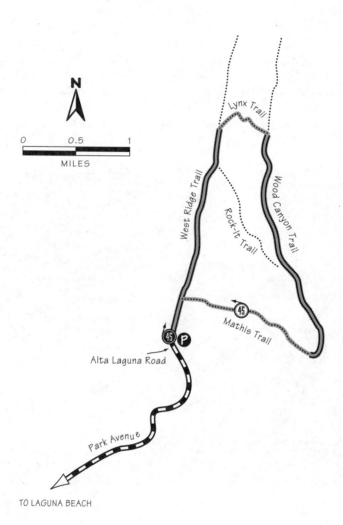

onto the Lynx Trail. Lynx Trail quickly descends from over 300 feet in less than one-half mile as you drop down narrow shoots and past large ruts. You reach the bottom at the 2.2-mile mark. Turn right at the bottom of Wood Canyon Road and continue along this smooth dirt road for 1.5 miles until you see the river drain after 3.6 miles. Turn right, pass through the river and continue straight until you see the bottom of the Mathis Trail at 3.9 miles. Mathis Trail quickly climbs approximately 600 feet as it begins an extremely steep 100-yard dash. It then levels out a bit but becomes more technical as it climbs over rocks and through ruts. After 4.3 miles you pass a small marker which is the city/county border. Continue until you reach the top after 5 miles. Once at the top, turn left and head back to your car.

Doc conquering the Lynx Trail.

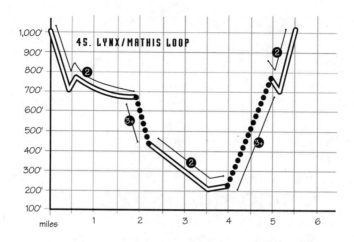

THE RIDE

0.0 From the Laguna Heights sign near the picnic tables take the trail to the right which heads down West Ridge Trail.

0.5 Mathis Trail to the right. Continue straight on West Ridge Trail.

1.5 Come to water tank and see Rock-It Trail to the right.

1.8 Turn right on the Lynx Trail.

2.2 At the bottom of the Lynx Trail, turn right on Wood Canyon Road.

2.7 Continue past the trail to the right.

3.6 Turn right at the man-made stream crossing.

3.9 Bottom of Mathis Trail.

4.3 Cross the city/county line.

5.0 Reach the top of Mathis Trail and turn left.

5.5 Back at the Top of the World.

Chino Hills State Park

Location:	In Carbon Canyon near the city of Brea.
Distance:	17 miles.
Time:	1.6 hours.
Tread:	Mostly doubletrack and fireroad with 3 miles of singletrack.
Aerobic level:	Moderate.
Technical difficulty:	3.
Fees:	Parking at the west entrance at Carbon Canyon Park is $4. Parking at the east entrance through the Chino Hills State Park is $5.
Services:	Bathrooms in the parking lot and at the far end of the ride in the Chino Hills State Park parking lot. All major services near the freeway.
Water:	Water in the parking lot and at the far end of the ride in the Chino Hills State Park parking lot. But bring plenty of water for the trail.
Highlights:	Awesome singletrack on Raptor Ridge.
Hazards:	Climbing the Three Bitches. Rattlesnakes, bobcats, and mountain lions.
Land status:	Chino Hills State Park.
Maps:	USGS Prado Dam, Yorba Linda; Thomas Brothers, Orange County, pages 709,710, San Bernardino County, page 711.

Access: To access the park from the west side in the city of Brea, exit California Highway 57 at Lambert Road. Head east on Lambert Road which turns into Carbon Canyon Road as you cross Valencia Avenue. Three miles down the road you see Carbon Canyon Regional Park to the right. Park here. To access the park from the east side rom the city of Yorba Linda (near the Prado Dam) exit California Highway 91 to California 71 Highway north.

Chino Hills State Park

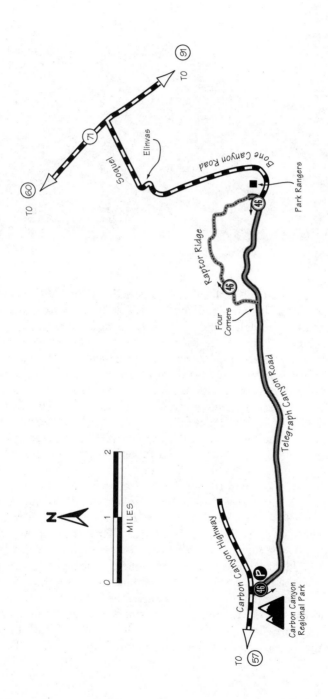

N

MILES

0   1   2

TO 91

TO 60

71

Soquel

Elinvas

Bone Canyon Road

Park Rangers

46

Raptor Ridge

46

Four Corners

Telegraph Canyon Road

Carbon Canyon Highway

46 P

Carbon Canyon Regional Park

TO 57

The grassy hills of Chino Hills State Park.

Notes on the trail: From Carbon Canyon Regional Park, ride out of the park onto Carbon Canyon Road and head east. Within one-quarter mile you see a dirt road to the right that heads down toward a wash. Pass through the gate and head past the wash to the trailhead. From the east entrance within Chino Hills State Park, follow the directions starting at 8.7 miles.

On the west side, as you pass through the trailhead you see Northridge Trail to the immediate left and Telegraph Canyon Road straight ahead. Begin a gradual climb along Telegraph Canyon Road. You pass a few trails on either side. Continue straight until you reach the Four Corners area at 5.7 miles where you find picnic tables. From Four Corners you see several trails. To the immediate left of the trail you just came from, you see a dead-end fireroad that heads to telephone poles. To its right you see a beaten unmarked singletrack called Raptor Ridge Trail. To the right of Raptor Ridge Trail is the continuation of Telegraph Canyon Road. To the right of Telegraph Canyon Road is a singletrack heading up to Southridge Trail. Turn onto Raptor Ridge Trail and begin a gradual quarter-mile climb before starting to rollercoaster through the grassy hills. At 6.6 miles you pass under a large electrical tower and shortly after come to a sharp left turn. At 7.6 and 7.8 miles you see trails coming in from the left; veer right. At 8.7 miles you come to a paved road and the parking area for the east entrance within the Chino Hills State Park. You see a ranger's house to the left and a picnic area and barn to the right. There is a water spigot near the parking area. Continue on the paved road for one-quarter mile and you see the Telegraph

Canyon Trailhead to the right. As you climb back up Telegraph Canyon you hit the first of the Three Bitches at 10.1 miles. Climb 300 feet within one-half mile. At 10.9 miles turn right onto Telegraph Road as the trail to the left goes to Southridge Trail. At 11.4 miles you find yourself back at Four Corners. From here, head down Telegraph Canyon Road back to your car.

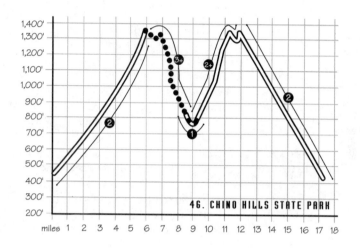

46. CHINO HILLS STATE PARK

THE RIDE

0.0 Pass through the trailhead and go straight; begin a gradual climb up Telegraph Canyon Road. Continue straight past two dirt roads and a singletrack which climb off to the right.

5.7 Come to Four Corners where you find a picnic table with socializing bike riders. To the immediate left is a dirt road and right next to that is the Raptor Ridge Trail singletrack where you want to continue riding.

6.7 Just past the electrical tower, make a sharp left turn onto the singletrack.

7.6 Veer right past the trail to the left.

7.8 Veer right past the trail to the left.

8.7 Reach a paved road at the east end of Chino Hills State Park. Continue on the paved road.

9.0 Turn right onto Telegraph Canyon Road.

10.1 First of Three Bitches.

10.9 Turn left; continue on Telegraph Canyon Road.

11.4 Back at Four Corners. Head back down Telegraph Canyon Road to your car.

17.1 The end.

Pilot Rock/Miller Canyon Road

Location:	In the San Bernardino National Forest near Silverwood Lake and about 20 miles west of Lake Arrowhead.
Distance:	11.2-mile loop.
Time:	1.3 hours.
Tread:	Fireroad. Most of the climbing is a well-maintained fireroad and a lot of the descent is on heavily-eroded fireroad.
Aerobic level:	Moderate.
Technical difficulty:	3 overall, with a few rougher sections.
Fees:	Forest Adventure Pass required.
Services:	The only immediate services are a drinking fountain and bathrooms in the day-use area. Most other services can be found further up California Highway 138.
Water:	There is a drinking fountain in the day-use area but bring plenty of your own water.
Highlights:	Magnificent views to the east of Miller Canyon Road. Pine trees in a mountain setting.
Hazards:	Eroded, rocky downhill.
Land status:	San Bernardino National Forest.
Maps:	USGS Silverwood Lake, Lake Arrowhead; Thomas Brothers, San Bernardino County, page 92.

Access: From San Bernardino, take California Highway 18 approximately 18 miles north to Crestline. From Crestline continue north on California Highway 138 approximately 7 miles to the Miller Canyon Picnic Area. Turn right at the Miller Canyon Day-Use Area. Within 100 feet turn right onto to the dirt road over the cattle crossing. Park off to the side of the road.

Notes on the trail: After parking off the side of the dirt road, turn left onto the road you came in on. At 0.7 mile you come to a junction with a sign for Pilot Rock 2N36. Here you turn left, veer right past another small junction, and begin your climb. At 0.9 mile you see a trail come in from the right. Veer left and continue your climb on the main road. At 2.7 miles you reach the top and merge with 2N33. Make two right turns and ride straight on the main road. You see several singletrack offshoots head up the upper ridge of the road. You can either venture onto those trails which merge back with the main road or just stay on the main road. At 3.9 miles you see 2N17X to

Pilot Rock/Miller Canyon Road

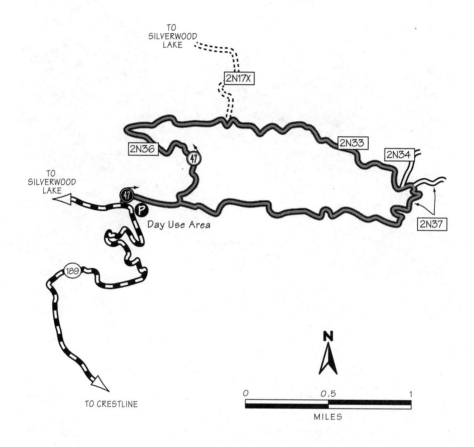

TO
SILVERWOOD
LAKE

2N17X

2N36

2N33

2N34

47

TO
SILVERWOOD
LAKE

47

P

Day Use Area

2N37

189

TO CRESTLINE

N

0   0.5   1

MILES

the left which goes to Silverwood Lake. Ride straight on the main road and eventually follow the fenceline until you get to a three-way junction at 6.4 miles. Here, turn right toward 2N34, Miller Canyon. At 7 miles turn right onto 2N37 and begin a loose section of steep downhill. At 8.4 miles veer right past the trail that comes from the left. At 8.5 miles the trail levels off and then begins a final descent at 9 miles. At 9.3 miles continue straight past the trail to the right. At 9.9 miles veer left at the junction and at 10.4 miles veer right as the trail merges with 2N38. At 10.5 miles you come back to 2N36 to the right. Continue straight past 2N36 and back to your car.

Down to Miller Canyon.

THE RIDE

0.0	Turn left onto dirt road.
0.7	Turn left at 2N36 toward Pilot Rock. A few feet up is another junction; veer right.
1.0	Veer left past road coming from right.
2.7	Reach top of 2N36. Make two rights onto 2N33.
2.9	Continue on main road past the steep trail that heads up the ridge.
3.9	Continue straight past 2N17X which goes to Silverwood Lake.
5.7	Continue straight past trail coming from the left.
6.4	Turn right at the three-way junction toward Miller Canyon.
7.0	Turn right onto 2N37.
8.4	Continue straight past trail to left.
9.3	Continue straight past trail to right.
9.9	Veer left at junction.
10.4	Veer right as trail merges with 2N38.
10.5	Continue straight past 2N36 on right; head back to your car.
11.2	The end.

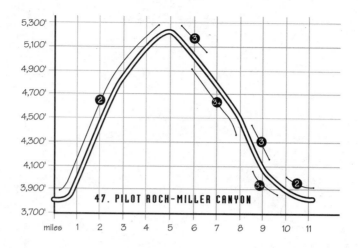

47. PILOT ROCK-MILLER CANYON

Butler Peak

Location:	San Bernardino National Forest at Big Bear Lake near Fawnskin.
Distance:	12 miles, out and back.
Time:	1.75 hours.
Tread:	Mostly well-maintained fireroad with some rocky sections near the top.
Aerobic level:	Moderate.
Technical difficulty:	3.
Fees:	Forest Adventure Pass required.
Services:	There is a town store, restaurant, and hotel near the trailhead.
Water:	There is no water on the trail.
Highlights:	The Butler Peak Lookout Tower used by the forest service to spot fires. Balcony open to the public.
Hazards:	Four-wheel drive vehicles and dirt bikes.
Land status:	San Bernardino National Forest.
Maps:	USGS Butler Peak, Fawnskin; Thomas Brothers, San Bernardino County, page 97.

Butler Peak

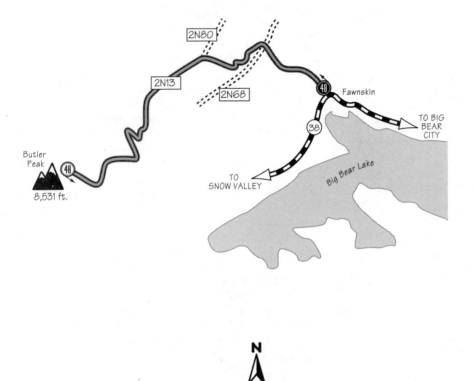

Access: From San Bernardino, take California Highway 330 to California Highway 18 and head east toward Big Bear Lake. Where California Highways 38 and 18 split, take CA 38 toward Fawnskin. Once in the town of Fawnskin turn left on Rim of the World Highway and park near the fire station. You see a sign with the Butler Peak Tower on it.

Notes on the trail: From the Fawnskin fire station continue on Rim of the World Highway (3N14), as it turns to dirt after 0.4 mile. At 1.3 miles turn left on 2N13 where you see another sign for Butler Peak. At 1.6 miles you come to a junction with 2N80. Continue on 2N13; veer left. Be cautious of another unnamed road to the far left of the junction. Pass a few trails to either side of you until you get to the junction with 2N70 at 2.3 miles. Continue on 2N13; veer right. Around 3.3 miles the trail becomes steeper and more technical as you begin to climb rapidly along the washed-out, rocky road. At 3.4 miles turn left on 2N13C as you get to a T junction and once again see the Butler Peak sign. Around 5.6 miles you begin your final ascent along a narrow ridge with the Butler Peak Tower in view. Once at the foot of the tower, you can take a walk to the top and overlook the valley below from the 8,400-foot lookout.

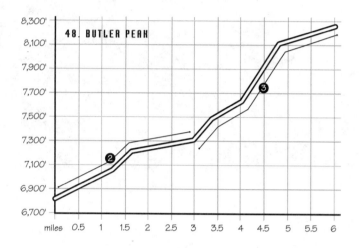

THE RIDE

0.0 From the fire station ride up Rim of the World Highway (3N14) as it turns to dirt at 0.4 mile.
0.8 Go straight past a trail to the left.
1.3 Turn left onto 2N13.
1.6 Veer left past 2N80, continue on 2N13. Avoid the trail off to the far left.
1.9 Continue straight past the road to the left.
2.1 Continue straight past the footpath to the right.
2.3 Veer left past 2N70.
3.0 Veer right past the road to the left.
3.4 Turn left onto 2N13C.
5.9 Continue straight toward the Butler Peak Tower past a trail to the right.
6.0 Top of the trail. Take a hike up to the top of the lookout tower. Head back.
12.0 The end.

The last stretch to Butler Peak.

Champion Lodgepole

Location:	San Bernardino National Forest at Big Bear Lake.
Distance:	10.4 miles, out and back.
Time:	1.25 hours.
Tread:	Mostly well-maintained fireroad. One-mile easy singletrack spur.
Aerobic level:	Easy to moderate.
Technical difficulty:	2+.
Fees:	Forest Adventure Pass required.
Services:	There are bathrooms at the Aspen Glen Park and full services off California Highway 18. Bear Valley Bicycles at the corner of California Highway 18 and Mill Creek Road.
Water:	Water is available at Aspen Glen Park.
Highlights:	The Champion Lodgepole is the largest living lodgepole pine tree in the San Bernardino National Forest.

Champion Lodgepole

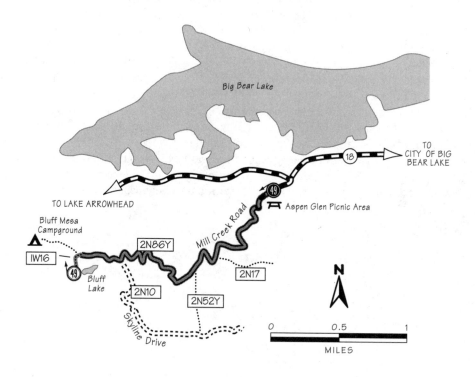

Hazards:	Four-wheel drive vehicles and dirt bikes.
Land status:	San Bernardino National Forest.
Maps:	USGS Big Bear Lake; Thomas Brothers, San Bernardino County, page 98.

Access: From San Bernardino, take California Highway 330 to California Highway 18 and head east toward Big Bear Lake. Where California Highways 38 and 18 split, take CA 18 toward Big Bear Lake. Once in the town of Big Bear Lake turn right onto Mill Creek Road and drive another one-quarter mile to Aspen Glen Park.

Notes on the trail: The Champion Lodgepole ride is a fairly moderate ride and fun for riders of all levels. It gradually climbs a wide Forest Service road until it gets to a short singletrack, which takes you to the Champion Lodgepole. From Aspen Glen Park, continue on Mill Creek Road 100 yards to the junction of Mill Creek Road and Tulip Road adjacent to the Oak Knot Lodge. Turn left onto Mill Creek Road. Continue on Mill Creek Road as it becomes

2N10 passing several dirt paths until it turns to dirt at 0.8 mile. After the road turns to dirt you pass several more roads on the left side as you continue to climb. The trail levels off at around 1.3 miles. At 2.4 miles you see 2N52Y to the left and then 2N10B to the right shortly afterwards. 2N52Y is the turnoff for the Pine Knot Trail (Ride 50). Continue straight on 2N10. Pass these two roads and several other dirt roads until you reach 2N86 at 3.9 miles. Turn right on 2N86 and then veer left on 2N86A. At 4 miles is a small junction; veer left. The right fork takes you to the Castle Rock Trail. Keep riding along 2N86A as you pass several small trails to the left. You come to a big Y junction at 4.6 miles. Veer left at this junction and continue straight. The left fork begins a slight descent. You quickly see two trails to the left as you ride toward the Bluff Mesa Campground. The second trail is marked "Bluff Mesa Trail to Champion Lodgepole (1W16)." Turn left on this singletrack, veer right past a couple of junctions, then go right after crossing the bridge at 5.1 miles. Shortly after the bridge you will see the Champion Lodgepole. Loop around the wooden railing and head back.

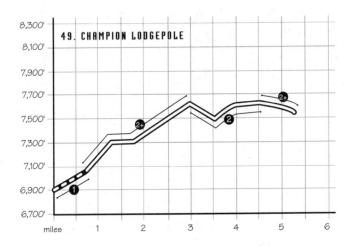

THE RIDE

0.0 From Aspen Glen Park turn left on Mill Creek Road.

0.1 Left on Mill Creek Road at the junction with Tulip Road.

0.2 Continue straight past trail to the left.

0.7 Continue straight past trail to the left.

0.8 Paved road ends. Veer left at junction. Continue straight past several little trails to the left.

1.6 Continue straight past the road to right.

1.7 Continue straight past 2N17 to left.

1.9 Continue straight past a private road to left.

2.4 Continue straight past 2N52Y to the left. This is the turnoff for the Pine Knot Trail (Ride 50). Just past 2N52Y veer left past 2N10B to the right.

2.9 Reach saddle and go straight past footpaths on either side.

3.9 At Y junction go right on 2N86, then left on 2N86A.

4.0 Veer left at the junction. Trail to the right goes to Castle Rock Trail.

4.1 Continue straight past two trails to the left.

4.4 Continue straight past two trails to the left.

4.6 At Y junction veer left.

4.7 Continue straight past trail to the left.

4.8 Turn left at Bluff Mesa Trail to the Champion Lodgepole Pine (1W16).

5.0 Veer right past two trails to the left and then cross the bridge.

5.1 Turn right immediately after the bridge.

5.2 Reach the Champion Lodgepole with wooden railing around it. Loop around and head back.

10.4 The end.

Pine Knot Trail via Skyline Drive

Location:	San Bernardino National Forest at Big Bear Lake.
Distance:	8-mile loop.
Time:	1 hour.
Tread:	Combination fireroad and singletrack climb with singletrack descent.
Aerobic level:	Moderate.
Technical difficulty:	3.
Fees:	Forest Adventure Pass required.
Services:	There are bathrooms at the Aspen Glen Park and full services off California Highway 18. Bear Valley Bicycles at the corner of CA 18 and Mill Creek Road.
Water:	Water is available at Aspen Glen Park.
Highlights:	The Pine Knot Trail is an extremely fun singletrack that winds around lodgepole pines with an occasional technical section.
Hazards:	Four-wheel drive vehicles and dirt bikes on the Forest Service roads and hikers along Pine Knot Trail.
Land status:	San Bernardino National Forest.
Maps:	USGS Big Bear Lake; Thomas Brothers, San Bernardino County, page 98.

Pine Knot Trail via Skyline Drive

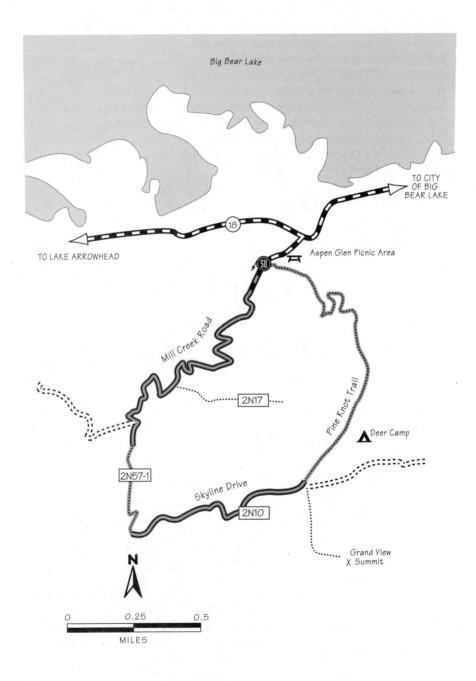

Big Bear Lake

TO CITY
OF BIG
BEAR LAKE

18

TO LAKE ARROWHEAD

50

Aspen Glen Picnic Area

Mill Creek Road

2N17

Pine Knot Trail

Deer Camp

2N57-1

Skyline Drive

2N10

Grand View
X Summit

N

0   0.25   0.5

MILES

Access: From San Bernardino, take California Highway 330 to California Highway 18 and head east toward Big Bear Lake. Where California Highways 38 and 18 split, take CA 18 toward Big Bear Lake. Once in the town of Big Bear Lake turn right onto Mill Creek Road and drive another one-quarter mile to Aspen Glen Park.

Notes on the trail: The Pine Knot Trail combines fun, windy singletrack with mostly gradual fireroad ascent. It is an excellent trail for intermediate climbers to find good singletrack. From Aspen Glen Park, continue on Mill Creek Road 100 yards to the junction of Mill Creek Road and Tulip Road, adjacent to the Oak Knot Lodge. Turn left onto Mill Creek Road. Continue on Mill Creek Road as it becomes 2N10; pass several dirt paths until it turns to dirt at 0.8 mile. After the road turns to dirt you pass several more roads on the left side as you continue to climb. The trail levels off at around 1.3 miles. At 2.4 miles you come to 2N52Y to the left. Turn onto 2N52Y and continue a gradual fireroad climb until you reach a camping-area loop at 2.7 miles. Off to the far left end of the loop you see the trail continue over a berm. After riding over the berm, the trail turns to singletrack as you cross a deep stream. The rest of the trail meanders up along a creek. At 3.4 miles you reach Skyline Drive (2N10) and turn left. Continue a gradual climb until the road finally levels off at 4.3 miles and begins a gentle descent. At 5.2 miles you reach a junction area and see 2N08 to the left. Just past 2N08 you see a forest sign marking the Pine Knot Trail (1E01) to the left. To the

Mark descending from the Grandview Summit above Skyline Drive.

right is a 0.25-mile climb to the Grandview Summit, a nice place to take a rest before starting down the hill. Turn left on the Pine Knot Trail as you begin your final singletrack descent. At 5.5 miles the trail levels off as you pass 2N08 to the left. At 6 miles you see 2N08 again to the left. Continue straight as you ride through Deer Camp and see the trail contine off to the left. Shortly after Deer Camp you cross a road as you see the singletrack straight ahead. From here the trail becomes more technical as you cross over rocks and tree roots that extend across the trail. At 7.2 miles you pass a trail to the right with a sign that reads, "NO TRESPASSING." At 7.5 miles veer right at the junction and then continue straight as you see two more trails that come in from either direction. At 8 miles you ride through a rocky section and continue straight past a trail from the left. At 8.1 miles you find yourself at the end of the trail and back on Mill Creek Road. Turn left. You immediately see the Aspen Glen Park.

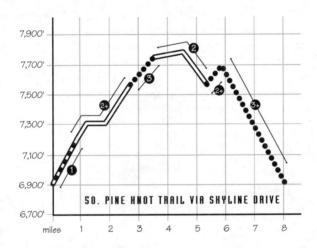

50. PINE KNOT TRAIL VIA SKYLINE DRIVE

THE RIDE

0.0   From Aspen Glen Park turn left on Mill Creek Road.

0.1   Turn left on Mill Creek Road at the junction with Tulip Road.

0.2   Continue straight past trail to the left.

0.7   Continue straight past trail to the left.

0.8   Paved road ends. Veer left at junction. Continue straight past several little trails to the left.

1.6   Continue straight past the road to right.

1.7   Continue straight past 2N17 to left.

1.9   Continue straight past a private road to left.

2.4   See two small trails to the left, then turn left onto 2N52Y.

2.7   Reach end of dirt road and see singletrack continue off to the left over dirt berm.

2.9 Stream crossing.

3.4 Turn left on Skyline Drive (2N10).

3.9 Continue straight past trail to the right.

5.2 Reach junction area and turn left on Pine Knot Trail after passing 2N08.

5.5 Veer right as the trail parallels 2N08.

6.0 Pass 2N08 as it comes in from the left and ride through Deer Camp.

6.1 Cross dirt road as singletrack continues straight across.

7.2 Continue straight past trail to the right with "NO TRESPASSING" sign.

7.5 Veer right at the junction.

7.6 Continue straight past two trails that come from either direction.

8.0 Go straight through rocky sections, past trail from left.

8.1 Back at Mill Creek Road. Turn right and see Aspen Glen Park.

Santa Ana River Trail

Location:	In the San Bernardino National Forest in the town of Angelus Oaks.
Distance:	9.6-mile loop. Over 11 miles of singletrack are available with a car shuttle or longer loop.
Time:	1.3 hours.
Tread:	5.4 miles of singletrack and 4.2 miles of paved road and fireroad.
Aerobic level:	Moderate.
Technical difficulty:	3+.
Fees:	None.
Services:	Most services are available in the town of Angelus Oaks.
Water:	Water is available in town but bring water with you.
Highlights:	Awesome singletrack without tons of climbing. The 5.4 miles of singletrack are part of a much longer 11-mile incredible singletrack.
Hazards:	Narrow trails overlooking cliffs. Lots of bugs.
Land status:	San Bernardino National Forest.
Maps:	USGS Big Bear Lake, Moonridge; Thomas Brothers, San Bernardino County, pages 55–57.

Santa Ana River Trail

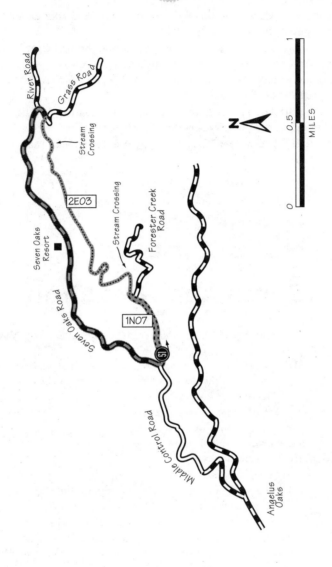

River Road

Grass Road

Stream Crossing

2E03

Stream Crossing

Forester Creek Road

Seven Oaks Resort

Seven Oaks Road

1N07

Middle Control Road

Angelus Oaks

N

MILES

1

0.5

0

Access: In the city of Redlands, exit Interstate 10 onto California Highway 38 heading north. Drive approximately 18 miles to Angelus Oaks. Turn onto Middle Control Road and park at the junction of Seven Oaks Road and Middle Control Road.

To shuttle the 11-mile trail, leave one car at the corner of Middle Control Road and Seven Oaks Road. Drive the other car approximately 10 miles up CA 38 to where the road crosses the Santa Ana River near the South Fork Campground. Park here and ride the singletrack back to the other car.

Notes on the trail: From the junction of Seven Oaks Road and Middle Control Road, begin a gradual climb up Middle Control Road heading south. At 0.9 mile turn left onto the dirt road (1N07) past the gate. At 2.7 miles stay right past the trail to the left that deadends at an overlook. At 2.9 miles you reach the Santa Ana River Trail (2E03) and veer right. The trail crosses Forsee Creek, which becomes quite high during wet months. At 3.2 miles you see Seven Oaks Resort to the left. You then ride through two stream crossings before you get to Glass Road at 5.4 miles. Turn left onto Glass Road and left again onto Seven Oaks Road. Take Seven Oaks Road back to your car.

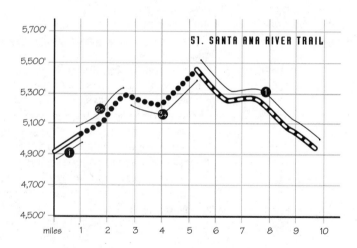

THE RIDE

0.0 Begin gradual climb up Middle Control Road.
0.9 Turn right onto 1N07 and pass through gate.
2.7 Veer right past trail to the left.
2.9 Veer right onto Santa Ana River Trail (2E03).
5.4 Turn left onto Glass Road.
5.5 Turn left onto Seven Oaks Road. Head back down to car.
9.6 The end.

Riverside County

Skyline Drive

Location:	Northeastern section of the Santa Ana Mountains within the Cleveland National Forest in Riverside County.
Distance:	9.8 miles, out and back, with optional 3 miles to Sierra Peak in each direction.
Time:	1.3 hours. The excursion to Sierra Peak adds another 50 minutes.
Tread:	Well-maintained fireroad.
Aerobic level:	Moderate to strenuous.
Technical difficulty:	While the well-maintained aspect of the trail would make it a 2, the steepness of the climb makes it a 3.
Fees:	None at the bottom. The trail can be driven during the summer months and a Forest Adventure Pass is required past the 4-mile mark.
Services:	There are full services along Lincoln Avenue including fast-food, supermarkets, and gas stations.
Water:	None at the trailhead. Bring plenty of water on warm days since this ride is very exposed to the sun.
Highlights:	Views of Corona and the San Bernardino Mountains.
Hazards:	Rattlesnakes. The road is open to motor vehicles.
Land status:	Cleveland National Forest.
Maps:	USGS Corona South; Thomas Brothers, Riverside County, page 773.

Access: In the city of Corona, exit California Highway 91 at Lincoln Avenue. Turn south toward the Santa Ana Mountains. About 2.5 miles after the freeway, veer right on Lincoln Avenue as the left fork becomes Foothill Parkway. Make an immediate right on Chase Drive and drive another one-half mile to Skyline Drive. Turn left just after crossing the wash. One-quarter mile after turning onto Skyline Drive, the street deadends at the steel gates where you park. If the wash is too deep to drive through, you need to park on Chase Drive and find another way to cross the wash.

Skyline Drive

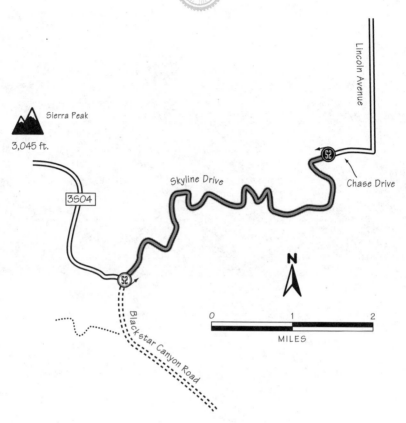

Notes on the trail: The trail begins as you pass through the steel gates at the end of Skyline Drive. The trail starts off flat as it travels along a riverbed off to the right. At 0.3 mile veer right as the road to the left is private property. At 1 mile the road takes a quick right and begins its steady climb to the top. You also see a footpath which goes straight. As you climb this steep fireroad you notice an occasional singletrack offshoot throughout the trail. While some of these merge back to the trail and are fun little detours, others go off in unknown directions; be careful. The trail continues to wind along at a strenuous pace until you reach the 4-mile mark and come to a forest sign. The trail then levels off and gently drops for the next one-half mile before starting a short climb to the top. At 4.9 miles you come to a four-way junction at the Main Divide where a sign reads "NMain3S04." Straight ahead are radio towers. To the left, the Main Divide heads south to Blackstar Canyon (Ride 31), and eventually Santiago Peak. To the right is Sierra Peak. You can either head back down or continue right to Sierra Peak. To go to Sierra Peak, turn right and gently climb 400 feet over 3 miles to the radio towers.

Looking down the windy Skyline Drive.

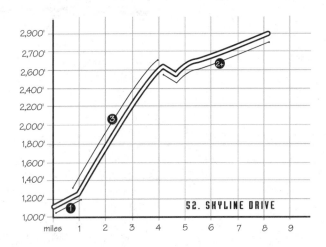

THE RIDE

0.0   Trailhead begins at steel gates.

0.3   Turn right as private road goes straight.

1.0   Turn right past the footpath straight ahead.

4.0   Enter Cleveland National Forest.

4.9   Reach Main Divide. Turn back or turn right to Sierra Peak.

9.8   The end.

Sycamore Canyon Park

Location:	Riverside County near Moreno Park.
Distance:	4-mile loop.
Time:	30 minutes.
Tread:	Mostly singletrack with some wide fireroad.
Aerobic level:	Easy.
Technical difficulty:	3.
Fees:	None.
Services:	There is a gas station and convenience store near the offramp at Allesandro Boulevard.
Water:	None on the trail. Bring plenty for hot summer rides.
Highlights:	Fun rollercoastering singletrack similar to cross-country race conditions. Wide variety of other trails to explore.
Hazards:	Ticks and severe summer heat.
Land status:	Riverside City Park.
Maps:	USGS Riverside East; Thomas Brothers, Riverside County, page 716.

Access: In the city of Riverside near Moreno Valley, exit Interstate 215 at Allesandro Boulevard and head west. Turn right on Sycamore Canyon Boulevard and make another left at Eastridge Avenue. Just past the Pepsi Plant turn left at the stop sign and park at the dead end. You see the trailhead to the right of the fence.

Notes on the trail: As you pass around the fence, ride toward your right and begin a mellow rollercoaster along the wide dirt road. Continue along the dirt road until you climb a short steep hill and see a trail marker to the left at 0.7 mile. Turn left here and then veer left just afterwards as the trail splits. The trail then becomes narrow and windy as it rollercoasters through the grassy hills. At 1.2 miles veer left past a junction and continue to roll through the hills until you reach Sycamore Canyon Boulevard at 1.9 miles. Turn right onto the dirt path that runs parallel to the street and at 2 miles turn right and head back toward the park. You ride through an area that looks like a dumpyard. Ride straight past a trail off to the right. At 2.2 miles turn right at the road and ride to a where the trail splits at 2.3 miles. Turn left (this takes you back into the rolling hills). At 2.7 miles continue straight past the trail merging in from the right. At 3.2 miles you find yourself back at the main road. From here you can do some further exploration or turn right and head back to the car.

Sycamore Canyon Park

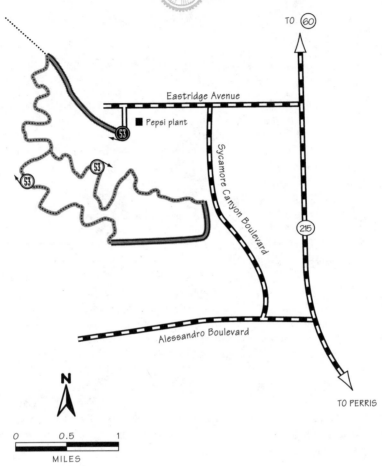

TO ⑥⓪

Eastridge Avenue

■ Pepsi plant

Sycamore Canyon Boulevard

②①⑤

Alessandro Boulevard

TO PERRIS

N

0   0.5   1

MILES

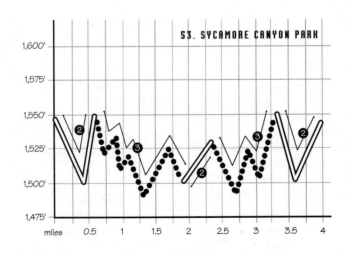

53. SYCAMORE CANYON PARK

1,600'
1,575'
1,550'
1,525'
1,500'
1,475'

miles   0.5   1   1.5   2   2.5   3   3.5   4

0.0	Pass around the side of the gate and turn right onto the dirt road.
0.4	Continue straight past the trail to left.
0.6	Continue straight past the trail to right.
0.7	At the top of the short climb turn left at the trail marker and then veer left as the trail splits shortly after.
1.2	Veer left at the junction.
1.9	Turn right on the dirt path that runs parallel to Sycamore Canyon Boulevard.
2.0	Turn right on dirt road.
2.1	Pass through dumping-ground and go straight past the trail to right.
2.2	Turn right at the dirt road.
2.3	Veer left as the trail splits.
2.7	Continue straight past the trail merging from the right.
3.2	Back at the main road. Turn right or venture on.
3.9	The end.

Box Springs Mountain Park

Location:	In Riverside County in the mountain range between the city of Grand Terrace and Moreno Valley.
Distance:	9-mile loop.
Time:	1.3 hours.
Tread:	Fireroad climb with a fast technical singletrack descent and paved road back to the trailhead.
Aerobic level:	Moderate.
Technical difficulty:	The fireroad climb is Level 2 to 2+ with the singletrack reaching Level 4.
Fees:	$2 per person.
Services:	Portable toilets at the trailhead. More services back at the freeway.
Water:	None at the trailhead. Bring plenty for hot summer rides.
Highlights:	Fun, technical singletrack descent. Views of Riverside from atop the radio tower lookouts.
Hazards:	Extreme heat in the summer. The sign in the parking lot warns of bears, mountain lions, rattlesnakes, and poison oak.
Land status:	Riverside County Park.
Maps:	USGS Riverside East; Thomas Brothers, Riverside County, page 686.

Box Springs Mountain Park

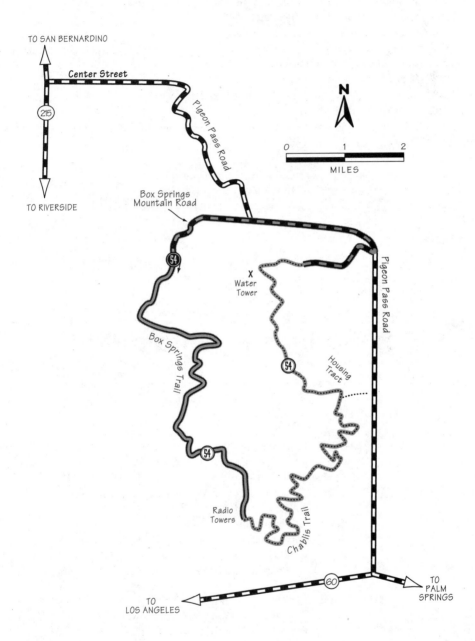

TO SAN BERNARDINO

Center Street

215

TO RIVERSIDE

Pigeon Pass Road

N

0   1   2

MILES

Box Springs
Mountain Road

54

X
Water
Tower

Box Springs Trail

54

Pigeon Pass Road

Housing
Tract

54

Radio
Towers

Chablis Trail

60

TO
LOS ANGELES

TO
PALM
SPRINGS

The grassy hills of Box Springs Mountain Park.

Access: From Interstate 215 in the city of Grand Terrace, exit at Center Street/Highgrove. Drive east on Center Street and at Mount Vernon Avenue turn right. At the junction of Mount Vernon Avenue and Pigeon Pass Road, veer right toward Pigeon Pass Road. Approximately 1.5 miles after the junction, Pigeon Pass Road turns to well-graded dirt road and then turns back to paved road. (Note that construction was going on during the publication of this book and the entire road may be paved at a later date.) Continue on Pigeon Pass Road until you reach Box Springs Mountain Road. Turn right. One-half mile up you enter the park and continue on the dirt road to the parking lot. You see the trailhead past the gate directly in front of you.

From California Highway 60 in Moreno Valley, exit east at Pigeon Pass Road and drive up 4 miles until Pigeon Pass veers off to the right. Take Box Springs Mountain Road as it continues straight. Continue straight 1 mile as you enter the park; drive a short ways to the parking lot.

Notes on the trail: As you pass through the gate at the trailhead begin a gradual ascent to a junction at 0.5 mile. Veer left. After this junction the road begins to climb more steeply and at 1 mile, as you go right around a bend, you see a footpath off to the left. Continue on the main road around the bend. At 1.6 miles continue straight past the road to the right which goes up to the radio towers. At 2 miles veer left as the road deadends at the radio towers. At 2.1 miles the main road ends. Off to the left you see a singletrack marked with a sign that reads, "Chablis Mountain." Here you begin your descent over rocky, rutted-out, overgrown terrain with switchbacks. At 3.4 miles continue straight past the trail from the right. At 4.1 miles you reach the bottom of the Chablis Trail at the foot of the mountain. You come to a dirt road that runs across the trail and see a housing tract straight ahead. Turn right onto the dirt road that narrows out as it loops around the housing tract at the foot of the mountain. At 4.8 and 5 miles are trails to the right which lead toward the houses. Continue straight past these trails and at 5.1 miles veer right into a gully. The left fork takes you back to the mountain. At 5.9 miles you reach a paved road and see a camouflaged water tower to the left. Turn right here and at 6.2 miles go around the fence onto Green Ridge Drive in the housing tract. Continue to Hidden Springs Drive at 6.4 miles and turn left. At 6.8 miles turn left on Pigeon Pass Road. At 7.8 miles continue straight as Pigeon Pass Road turns into Box Springs Mountain Road. Begin the final climb back to the trailhead.

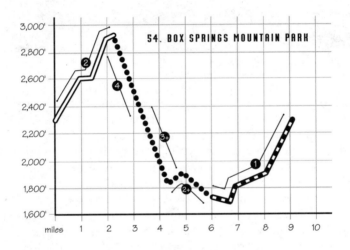

THE RIDE

0.0 Pass through the gate and begin to climb.

0.5 Veer left at the junction.

1.0 Veer right around the bend as you see a footpath to left.

1.6 Continue straight past the road to the right that goes to the radio towers.

2.0 Turn left as the road heading straight goes to radio towers.

2.1 As the main trail ends, turn left onto the singletrack marked with a sign that reads, "Chablis Mountain."

3.4 Continue straight past the trail to the right.

4.1 Reach the bottom of the singletrack and turn left on the road which leads around the foot of the mountain.

4.8 Continue straight past the trail to the right.

5.0   Continue straight past the trail to the right.

5.1   Veer right at the junction; drop into a little gully.

5.9   At the paved road turn right.

6.2   Go around the fence at Green Ridge Drive and head straight.

6.4   Turn left on Hidden Springs Drive.

6.8   Turn left on Pigeon Pass Road.

7.8   Continue straight as Pigeon Pass Road veers right and Box Spring Mountain Road goes straight.

9.0   The end.

Ramona Trail/ Thomas Mountain Road

Location:	In the western region of the San Bernardino National Forest near Lake Hemet.
Distance:	16.9-mile loop.
Time:	2.25 hours.
Tread:	Fireroad climb and singletrack descent.
Aerobic level:	Moderate.
Technical difficulty:	3+.
Fees:	Forest Adventure Pass required.
Services:	Convenience store 1 mile west on California Highway 74 at Lake Hemet. More services available at Mountain Center approximately 4 miles west on CA 74.
Water:	None available on trail.
Highlights:	Incredibly fun, technical singletrack. Great view of Lake Hemet. Cooler temperatures than the desert cities below.
Hazards:	Lots of bugs, off-road vehicles, hunters. This author experienced a cattle stampede atop Thomas Mountain.
Land status:	San Bernardino National Forest.
Maps:	USGS Anza; Thomas Brothers, Riverside County, pages 844, 904.

Ramona Trail/Thomas Mountain Road

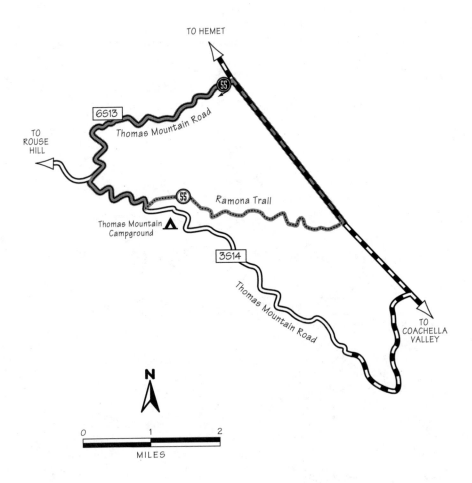

TO HEMET

6S13

Thomas Mountain Road

TO ROUSE HILL

Ramona Trail

Thomas Mountain Campground

3S14

Thomas Mountain Road

TO COACHELLA VALLEY

N

0   1   2
MILES

Access: From California Highways 111 and 74 in Palm Desert drive south on CA 74 into the mountains. After 27 miles you pass the eastern end of Thomas Mountain Road. After 31.5 miles turn left on the western end of Thomas Mountain Road, just 1 mile before Lake Hemet. Drive in about one-quarter mile and park in the turnout under the trees.

Notes on the trail: Ride up Thomas Mountain Road (6S13) as it gently climbs fireroad above Lake Hemet. At 1.6 miles continue straight past a gated road to the right and at 3.4 miles veer left as the trail splits. At 4.3 miles veer left toward Thomas Mountain as the road splits and goes to Rouse Hill to the right. Climb the main road as you go past smaller trails. Around 5.5 miles you near the top. At 7.2 miles turn left on a narrow unnamed singletrack with a multi-use trail marker. (If you go too far on the main road you level off and then begin to descend as you pass campgrounds toward the left.) As you begin to descend on the singletrack you pass several trail markers as the trail rollercoasters and winds through the trees. At 7.5 miles you see two trails going up the grassy hill to the left. Ride straight past these trails. Then ride straight as another trail cuts across. At 9.3 miles you come back to the main road. Cross the main road as trail continues straight across. At 9.6 miles you reach the Ramona Trail (3E26) and go left. From here the trail becomes more technical. It is sandy at first but then rides over small boulders and red clay soil as it switches down the mountain. At 13.3 miles you reach the bottom of the Ramona Trail and turn right, heading toward California Highway 74 at 13.5 miles. Turn left on CA 74 and then left again at Thomas Mountain Road at 16.6 miles. Continue until you reach your car shortly after.

Enjoying the Ramona Trail.

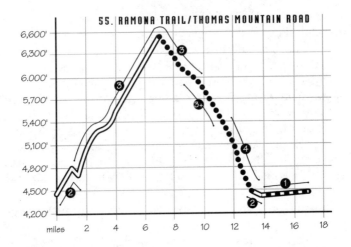

THE RIDE

0.0   From your car begin to climb Thomas Mountain Road.

1.6   Continue straight past a gated road to the right.

3.4   Veer left at the junction.

4.3   Veer left toward Thomas Mountain as the right fork goes to Rouse Hill.

5.6   Continue straight past the jeep road which crosses the main road.

5.8   Continue straight past a road to the right.

7.2   Turn left on unnamed trail to the left with a trail marker.

7.5   Continue straight past two trails that veer to the right.

7.7   Continue straight as another trail cuts across the trail.

9.3   Reach the main road and continue to ride straight as the trail continues on the other side of the road.

9.6   Turn left at the junction with Ramona Trail.

13.3 Reach the bottom and turn right toward California Highway 74.

13.5 Turn left on CA 74.

16.6 Turn left on Thomas Mountain Road.

16.9 The end.

Dunn Road

Location:	In the Santa Rosa Mountain Range above Palm Desert.
Distance:	20.5 miles, one way with a car shuttle.
Time:	1.4 hours.
Tread:	Dirt road.
Aerobic level:	Easy.
Technical difficulty:	Average Level 2 with some steep sandy Level 3 sections.
Fees:	None.
Services:	There are portable toilets about 13 miles down the trail. The Sugarloaf Café is 1 mile east of the upper trailhead and plenty of services are available near the bottom.
Water:	None available on the trail.
Highlights:	Mostly fast downhill with speeds approaching 40 miles per hour in sections. Good downhill training.
Hazards:	Fast dirt road with sandy sections. Jeep tours.
Land status:	Bureau of Land Management, San Bernardino National Forest.
Maps:	USGS Cathedral City, Rancho Mirage, Toro Peak; Thomas Brothers, Riverside County, pages 817, 907.

Access: To park your first car, drive east on California Highway 111 from Palm Springs to the corner of CA 111 and Cathedral Canyon Drive. There are several commercial parking lots and side streets to park there.

Drive your second car approximately 6.5 miles to California Highway 74 and turn right. Drive up CA 74 approximately 16 miles and turn right onto Palm Canyon Drive. Park off to the side of the road.

Notes on the trail: From California Highway 74 and Palm Canyon Drive begin to rollercoaster down the dirt road and pass several smaller dirt roads on either side of the road. At 2.8 miles go around the gate and continue to another gate at 3.8 miles, which marks the entrance to the San Bernardino National Forest. Continue past the gate and quickly drop as the road narrows and becomes steeper and rockier. At 4.9 miles ride along the grove of trees to the right and continue to follow the fenceline. At 5.4 miles the main road veers sharply to the right as an old beaten-up trail goes straight ahead. Veer right with the main road as it continues to follow the fenceline and

Dunn Road

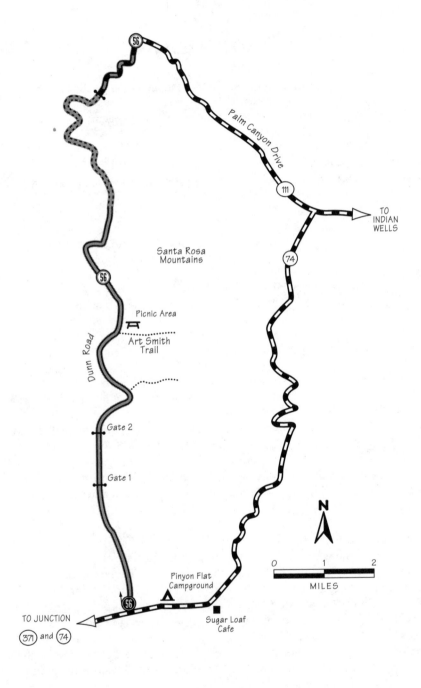

56

Palm Canyon Drive

111

TO
INDIAN
WELLS

74

Santa Rosa
Mountains

56

Picnic Area

Art Smith
Trail

Dunn Road

Gate 2

Gate 1

N

0   1   2

MILES

Pinyon Flat
Campground

56

TO JUNCTION

371 and 74

Sugar Loaf
Cafe

Descending Dunn Road into Coachella Valley.

begins to climb. The road becomes more sandy and climbs for the next mile. At 6.6 miles you reach a wide junction and veer left. The trail levels off for about one-half mile. The trail then begins to drop quickly as you reach speeds in excess of 30 miles per hour. At 8.5 miles you see two trails that cut off to the left and then two trails that cut off to the right shortly after. Continue straight past all these trails and stay on the main road. At 13.1 miles you see the Art Smith Trail to the right along with picnic tables and portable toilets. Continue straight past the Art Smith Trail as the road begins to get steep again. At 15.4 miles you pass a trail to the left and then the trail begins to get extremely windy as hairpin turns take you down the hill. At 17 miles you pass through a big gnarly Gothem City-looking steel gate. Continue to 18.4 miles to the last gate that takes you to a residential area. After coming out the trail at the corner of Carrol Drive and Channel Drive, ride straight down Carrol Drive and turn left on Elna Way. One-half mile up Elna Way, veer right onto Grandview Avenue and then turn left on Vista Drive. Turn right on Terrace Road and then left on Cathedral Canyon Drive. Continue on Cathedral Canyon Drive until you reach California Highway 111 at 20.5 miles.

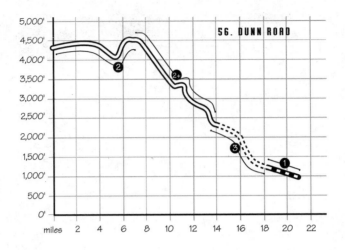

56. DUNN ROAD

THE RIDE

0.0 From the corner of California Highway 74 and Palm Canyon Drive, ride down Palm Canyon Drive. Pass several dirt roads and houses on either side.

2.8 Pass through gate and continue on main road; pass dirt roads on either side.

3.8 Pass through another gate and begin descent.

4.9 As you approach the fenced-in tree grove, continue straight past the road to the right.

5.4 Veer right with main road and fenceline as a beaten-up road goes straight ahead.

6.6 Reach wide junction and turn left as the trail levels off.

8.5 Continue straight past a series of two trails to the left and then two trails to the right.

10.8 Continue straight past a trail to the right.

12.3 Continue straight past a trail to the left.

12.5 Continue straight past a trail to the left that merges with the one you just passed.

13.1 After short climb come to the Art Smith Trail to the right. Continue straight.

15.4 Continue straight past a trail to the left.

17.0 Pass through a big gnarly steel gate.

18.4 Pass through the final gate onto paved street. Go straight on Carrol Drive.

18.5 Go left on Elna Way.

18.9 Elna Way veers right onto Grandview Avenue.

19.2 Turn left on Vista Drive.

19.5 Turn right on Terrace Road.

19.8 Turn left on Cathedral Canyon Drive.

20.5 Back at the corner of Cathedral Canyon Drive and California Highway 111. The end.

San Diego County

Lake Hodges

Location:	Lake Hodges in northern San Diego County near Escondido.
Distance:	6.8 miles, out and back.
Time:	43 minutes round-trip.
Tread:	The first 2.5 miles are singletrack followed by doubletrack and fireroad.
Aerobic level:	The trail is easy as it gently rollercoasters along the lake.
Technical difficulty:	Most of the trail is Level 2 singletrack with one short hike-a-bike.
Fees:	None.
Services:	As you turn left into the parking lot there is a service road leading to the back of the lake. If you continue in that direction you find a little store with cold drinks and snacks. Full services are available back near the freeway.
Water:	There is no water at the parking lot but bottled water may be purchased at the lake store.
Highlights:	This trail is fun easy singletrack which runs along the south side of the lake.
Hazards:	Summer heat, gnats, and ticks.
Land status:	City of San Diego Water Utilities Department.
Maps:	USGS Rancho Santa Fe; Thomas Brothers, San Diego County, page 27.

Access: From Interstate 15 in northern San Diego County, exit at Via Rancho Parkway and head west. After 3 miles turn left on Lake Drive and within 1 mile you see a parking lot off to the left.

Notes on the trail: The trailhead can be seen at the far end of the parking lot directly across from the entryway. As you enter the trailhead you pass a sign that reads, "Off road vehicle activity prohibited." Ride through the oak grove and within one-quarter mile you rollercoaster up and down some fun

Lake Hodges

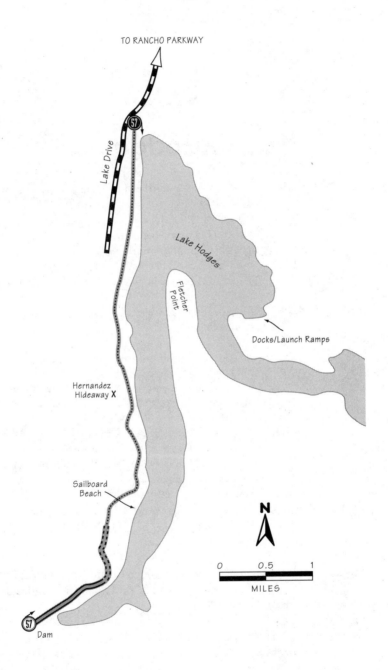

TO RANCHO PARKWAY

Lake Drive

57

Lake Hodges

Fletcher Point

Docks/Launch Ramps

Hernandez
Hideaway **X**

Sailboard
Beach

N

0   0.5   1
MILES

57
Dam

The shores of Lake Hodges.

singletrack as you meander along the side of the lake. You see several little offshoots which either head up to the road or down to the lake. Use your best judgment as you approach each offshoot, since most lead back to the main trail. The worst that can happen is that you will deadend after 100 feet. At 1.1 miles you reach a concrete cul-de-sac area where you find some benches and a portable toilet. Up to the right, on the other side of the road, you see Hernandez' Hideaway Restaurant. Ride to the other side of the cul-de-sac and you quickly see the trail that continues on the other side. You continue on the same type of terrain to the 2.0-mile mark and reach a beach area with a rental shack. Continue straight past the beach area as you see two dirt roads coming in from the main road. At 2.1 miles you begin a moderate climb and at the 2.2-mile mark veer left on the singletrack as you approach the road. At 2.5 miles, the trail seems to disappear and you need to crawl under a bamboo tunnel for approximately 10 feet. Just after the tunnel, hike-a-bike up a 10-foot cliff where you reach a dirt road. At the dirt road, turn left and begin a gradual descent until you ride alongside the lake. You then begin to climb to the 2.9-mile mark where you see a road that comes in from the right. Veer left and continue past the sign that says, "Road Closed." You then begin a mellow descent toward the dam. At the 3.4-mile mark veer left as the road splits and then left again at another split in the road. At the 3.5-mile mark you reach the dam. Turn around and venture back to the car.

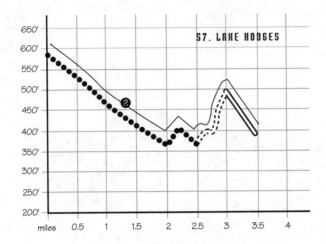

57. LAKE HODGES

THE RIDE

0.0 Enter trailhead at far end of parking lot.

1.1 Come to concrete cul-de-sac and continue on trail on other side.

2.0 At water continue straight past dirt road that comes in from right. As you come around the beach area continue straight, past the second dirt road.

2.2 Veer left on singletrack.

2.5 Crawl under the bamboo tunnel to the right followed by a 50-foot hike-a-bike. At the doubletrack go left.

2.9 Climb to top of little hill, veer left on fireroad.

3.3 Veer left as the road splits twice.

3.4 Reach the dam and return the same way you came.

6.8 The end.

Los Penasquitos

Location:	San Diego near where Interstates 5 and 805 meet.
Distance:	7.3 miles, out and back.
Time:	50 minutes.
Tread:	Fireroad.
Aerobic level:	This trail is easy with some moderate climbs as you ride through the rolling valley.
Technical difficulty:	2.
Fees:	None.
Services:	There is a portable toilet in the parking lot. There is a liquor store as you exit the freeway.
Water:	No water is available in the park.
Highlights:	Waterfall.
Hazards:	Several trails closed to mountain bikers. Many violators can be found.
Land status:	San Diego City Park.
Maps:	USGS Del Mar, Poway; Thomas Brothers, San Diego, pages 38,39.

Access: From Interstate 5, exit Sorrento Valley Road and head east on Sorrento Valley Boulevard for 1.5 miles. After driving through an industrial area you see Los Penasquitos Canyon Reserve on the right.

Notes on the trail: Pass through the trailhead at the end of the parking lot and quickly drop approximately 25 feet before reaching an intersection marked by a park sign. Turn left at this point and head under the bridge. You then make a short climb as you pass a narrow singletrack on the left which heads toward a residential area. After one-half mile and a slight descent continue straight past a trail that comes from the left. After 1.2 miles and some more rollercoastering you reach a Y in the road where both trails end up in the same place. As you pass the 2-mile mark there are two trails that come off from the left which are closed to mountain bikes. At 2.7 miles you make a short climb atop the waterfall vista. There are bike racks and hitching posts so you can take a short break and hike about 100 feet down to the waterfalls. As you begin to ride again, you come to a sign after 3.5 miles that directs you to turn left at Carson Crossing. Ride through this little meadow and over the bridge; turn right at the fork. Ride another hundred feet to a junction; turn right and head back to your car.

Los Penasquitos

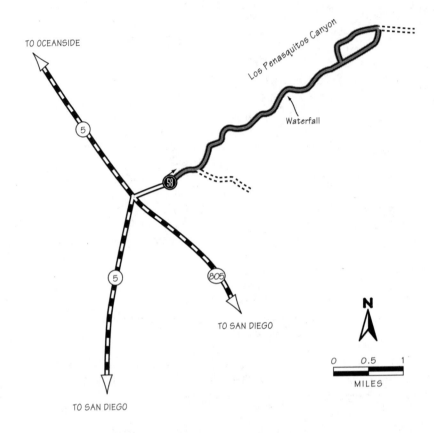

THE RIDE

0.0	Trailhead begins at far end of parking lot.
0.1	Turn left toward the bridge when you reach the junction with the park sign.
0.2	Continue past all singletrack which heads toward the residential area.
0.5	Continue straight past the trail from left.
1.2	Trail splits but merges again.
2.0	Don't take trail to left—closed to mountain bikes.
2.2	Don't take trail to left—closed to mountain bikes.
2.7	Waterfall viewpoint.
3.5	Turn left at the fork at Carson Crossing Road. Go through meadow and over bridge.
3.6	Go right at the fork.
3.7	Turn right at the junction and head back to the car.
7.3	The end.

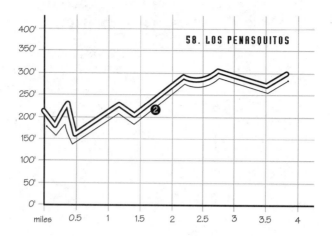

58. LOS PENASQUITOS

59

San Clemente Canyon

Location:	In San Diego, southeast of La Jolla.
Distance:	7.2 miles, out and back.
Time:	55 minutes.
Tread:	Doubletrack with singletrack offshoots.
Aerobic level:	Easy.
Technical difficulty:	2.
Fees:	None.
Services:	There are picnic tables and bathrooms at the park.
Water:	Available in the bathrooms.
Highlights:	This is very mellow singletrack and a great place for beginners to develop some bike-handling skills.
Hazards:	Watch out for all the hikers and joggers.
Land status:	Marian R. Bear Natural Park, San Diego City Park.
Maps:	USGS La Jolla; Thomas Brothers, San Diego County, page 44.

Access: From Interstate 5 near La Jolla, take California Highway 52 east and exit at Claremont Mesa Boulevard. Head south and within a few hundred feet you see a sign for the park. You can enter the park from either side of Claremont Mesa Boulevard.

San Clemente Canyon

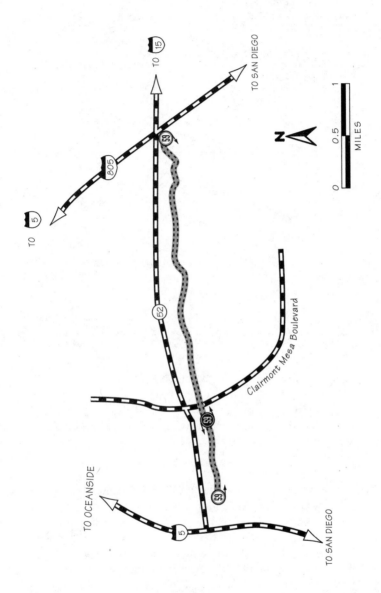

Notes on the trail: This is an all-around fun place. There are little singletrack offshoots for the first 2.5 miles that rollercoaster back and forth along the main trail. Most of these offshoots merge back into the main path and should be explored. However, a few of the offshoots lead up into the nearby residential areas. This is a very wooded area and gets extremely wet in the winter. You see the trail merge into the parking lot at several points. Head east onto the trail. If you start in the far west parking lot, you pass under a bridge along pavement. As you come into the next parking lot, you see the trail head off again to the left. At 1.3 miles you pass under a bridge. At 2.6 miles you come to the Interstate 805 Underpass. This is where you turn around and head back since the land past I-805 is part of the U.S. Miramar Naval Base. On your way back ride past your car. The trail deadends at the stream about 1 mile to the west. From there turn around and head back to your car.

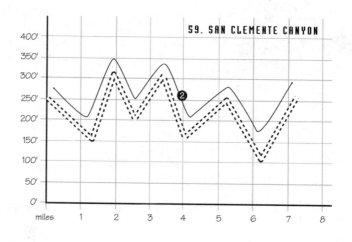

THE RIDE

0.0   See trail off to left of parking lot.
1.3   Pass under bridge.
2.6   Approach Interstate 805 Underpass and turn around.
5.2   Back at the beginning. Ride to the west end of the trail.
6.2   At the stream turn around and head back to your car.
7.2   The end.

Friendly singletrack at San Clemente Canyon.

Mission Trails Regional Park

Location:	Central San Diego County in the city of Tierra Santa.
Distance:	7.2-mile loop.
Time:	1.2 hours.
Tread:	Mostly fireroad.
Aerobic level:	Moderate with a strenuous climb up "The Alley."
Technical difficulty:	3.
Fees:	None.
Services:	Portable toilets are available at the parking lot and real restrooms are available at the Visitor Center.
Water:	Water is available at the parking lot and the Visitor Center. Bring plenty of water on the trails.
Highlights:	Fun trails not far from the heart of San Diego. Lots more trails to explore.
Hazards:	Very hot in the summer. Rattlesnakes.
Land status:	Mission Trails Regional Park.
Maps:	USGS La Mesa; Thomas Brothers, San Diego County, page 1230.

Mission Trails Regional Park

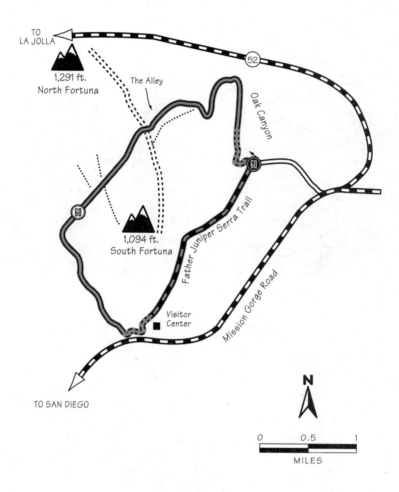

TO
LA JOLLA

1,291 ft.
North Fortuna

The Alley

Oak Canyon

52

60

1,094 ft.
South Fortuna

Father Juniper Serra Trail

60

Visitor
Center

Mission Gorge Road

TO SAN DIEGO

N

0   0.5   1

MILES

Access: In Tierra Santa, exit California Highway 52 at Mission Gorge Road and go right 1.5 miles to Father Juniper Serra Trail. Turn right on Father Juniper Serra Trail. As you approach the gate, you see a parking lot off to the right. If you were to travel up Mission Gorge Road another 4 miles you would reach the other end of Father Juniper Serra Trail, which leads to the Visitor Center and then back down to the parking lot.

Notes on the trail: From the parking lot ride along the well-maintained walking path past the benches. The trail then travels over cobblestones. Ride over the bridge and then across the sandy, dry creekbed. At 0.4 mile turn left at the junction on Oak Canyon Trail and dismount as you cross the stream. At 0.6 mile veer right to Oak Canyon/Fortuna Mountain and then

Looking down from Mt. Fortuna.

veer left as the trail splits two more times. At 0.9 mile continue straight past two more roads coming in from the right. After 1 mile you begin to climb and then veer left past another road as you pass under the electrical towers. At 1.3 miles continue straight past the trail to the right, which leads to Oak Canyon. At 1.4 miles you reach the top of the hill and continue to ride on the main road as you see an arrow pointing to Oak Canyon/Fortuna Mountain. Pass one trail to the left and two utility roads to the right. You then drop down a loose fireroad and at 1.5 miles continue straight past two trails to the right. At 1.7 miles you reach the bottom of the hill; continue straight past a trail to the right. You then begin to climb a steep, rocky fireroad and pass Oak Canyon Trail on the right. At 1.9 miles you reach "The Alley." While both forks at the junction go to the same place, the trail straight ahead is more tolerable, although quite demanding. The road climbs steeply to the Fortuna Saddle and gets steeper and looser the higher you go. You finally reach the saddle at 2.4 miles and see North Fortuna to the right and South Fortuna to the left. While North Fortuna has ridable trails to explore, South Fortuna ends at a narrow staircase-type footpath that this author accidentally went down. From the saddle continue straight as you drop to the valley below and pass a trail on the right. Stay to the right of the powerlines and continue on the main road. After you begin to climb, turn left at 3.1 miles. Continue to climb and then ride past the singletrack to the left at 3.4 miles. At 3.6 miles you reach a five-way junction and take the wider trail to the left. As you continue, ride past two singletracks on the left and quickly drop to the San Diego River. At 4.4 miles you cross the San Diego River, which can be very deep in the winter. After crossing the river, take the left fork toward Father Juniper Serra Trail. At 4.6 miles the fireroad turns to doubletrack; at 4.8 miles go right as the trail splits. Go right again at 4.9 miles. At 5.1 miles take the right fork and find yourself atop Father Juniper Serra Trail just above. At Father Juniper Serra Trail turn left and cruise just over 2 miles down the paved road back to your car.

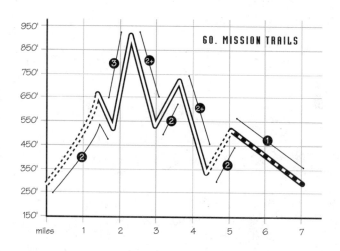

THE RIDE

0.0   From the parking lot, ride out the trail, travel over the bridge, and cross the sandy, dry creekbed.

0.4   Turn left at the junction with Oak Canyon Trail.

0.6   Veer right to Oak Canyon/Fortuna Mountain Trail.

0.7   Veer left as a dirt road merges from the right.

0.8   Veer left as a dirt road merges from the right.

0.9   Veer left as two roads come in from the right.

1.1   Veer left under the electrical towers, past a road coming from the right.

1.3   Veer left toward Fortuna Mountain.

1.4   At top of hill continue straight past one trail to the left and two utility roads to the right.

1.5   Continue straight past two trails to the right.

1.7   Continue straight past a trail to the right.

1.9   Ride straight up "The Alley" passing a trail on the left.

2.4   Atop Fortuna Saddle; ride down straight ahead. Pass North Fortuna to the right and South Fortuna to the left.

2.6   Continue straight past a trail on the right.

3.0   Continue straight past a trail merging in from the right.

3.1 Continue straight past a trail merging in from the left and then turn left on another trail just after you begin to climb.

3.4 Continue straight past the singletrack to the left.

3.6 Reach a five-way junction and take the wider trail to the left.

3.8 Ride past two singletracks on the left.

4.4 Cross the San Diego River and take the left fork.

4.8 Turn right as the trail splits.

4.9 Turn right as the trail splits.

5.1 Veer right as the trail splits and then turn left on Father Juniper Serra Trail just above.

7.2 The end.

Noble Canyon

Location:	Pine Valley, about 40 miles east of San Diego.
Distance:	19-mile loop.
Time:	2.6 hours.
Tread:	8.25-mile ascent on paved road and 10.75-mile singletrack descent.
Aerobic level:	Moderate.
Technical difficulty:	3+ overall with some Level 4 and Level 5 sections. Much of the lower sections are extremely technical and require excellent bike-handling skills.
Fees:	Forest Adventure Pass required.
Services:	All services are available at the freeway exit. Water and bathrooms are available at the second parking area.
Water:	Water is available at the second parking area and at the Laguna Mountain Recreation Area Campground at the top.
Highlights:	There is some incredible singletrack within this woodsy forest setting. Ecological Reserve near Laguna Mountain Recreation Area.
Hazards:	Rattlesnakes. Hikers near the Laguna Mountain Recreation Area.
Land status:	Cleveland National Forest.
Maps:	USGS Descanso; Thomas Brothers, San Diego County, 51W.

Noble Canyon

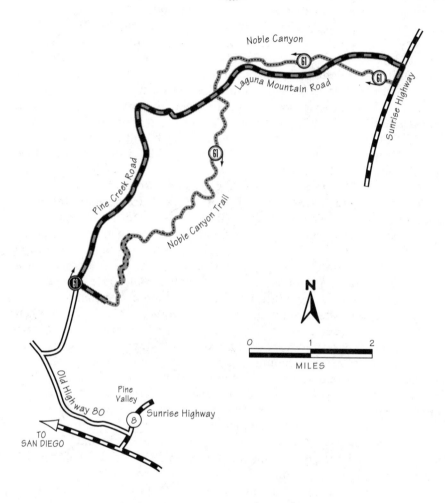

Access: From San Diego, where Interstates 805 and 8 meet at Qualcomm Stadium, drive 40 miles east on I-8 and exit at Pine Valley. Then go left. Drive approximately one-half mile and at California Highway 80 turn left toward Julian. You see the Pine Valley County Park. Drive one more mile and make a sharp right at Pine Creek Road, just after crossing the bridge. After one more mile you see a sign for Cleveland National Forest, Noble Canyon. To the right you see a dirt parking area. Additional parking can be found by turning right at this parking lot and driving another 200 yards.

This trail can also be shuttled. Leave one car at the above parking lot and drive the other car back to I-8. Take the Sunrise Highway Exit to Penny Pines Recreational Area.

Notes on the trail: This is an incredibly fun and technical trail. From the parking lot continue to ride your bike on Pine Creek Road. After one-quarter mile you cross a deep stream. After 0.5 mile you get to a junction with a dirt road. Veer left and stay on the paved road. You stay on the paved road and pass dirt roads and trails that branch off to each side. At 2.9 miles, after a steady climb, you cross a cattle crossing and get to a junction. Here you want to turn right and continue to ride up the paved road. The paved road also continues straight into a valley but don't go there. Climb steadily up the paved road and after it levels off around 5.5 miles you pass several dirt trails on either side of the road, some being the Noble Canyon Trail. Continue on the paved road through the Laguna Mountain Recreation Area at 6.5 miles and onto Sunrise Highway at 7.6 miles. Turn right onto Sunrise Highway, and at 8.3 miles you see cars parked on either side of the highway at the Penny Pines Recreational Area. To the right you see the Noble Canyon Trail (5E02). Turn right onto the trail and begin a slight ascent on what begins as mellow, non-technical singletrack. About 100 yards from the trailhead you come to a junction. The Big Laguna Trail heads off to the left and Noble Canyon Trail goes straight. At 9.4 and 9.5 miles you come to the paved road. Cross the road and continue on the singletrack on the other side. At 10.4 miles you come to a three-way junction with a sign. Turn left, staying on Noble Canyon Trail. A right takes you to Cayamuca State Park. At 11.2 miles you cross the road for the last time while the terrain becomes more technical. At 11.6 miles pass through the gate. Don't forget to close it behind you. You then get into four gnarly switchbacks and cross a stream. At 12.7 miles you travel over rock-strewn sections for about one-quarter mile, which may require some riders to dismount. After crossing the pond at 13 miles you begin another extremely technical short section. After you cross another stream at 14 miles you see a trail to the right. Keep veering left. At 14.5 miles you descend a short rocky section and come to a cave on the left. At 15.8 miles you get to a three-way junction; turn left and head toward Pine Valley. Immediately after you see another junction veer right and head down into the creek. Just after climbing out of the creekbed, veer left past the trail that comes in from the right. At 17 miles a trail comes in from the left. Continue to ride straight. At 17.5 miles go straight past the trail that comes in from the left. At 18.7 miles you reach a gate at the end of the trail. You are now at the second parking area. Turn right and head back to your car.

THE RIDE

0.0 Ride out parking lot and continue on Pine Creek Road.
0.2 Cross deep creekbed.
0.5 Four-way junction, veer left and stay on pavement.
1.1 Stay on main road past dirt road to left.
1.2 Stay on main road past dirt road to right.
2.5 Stay on main road past dirt road to right.

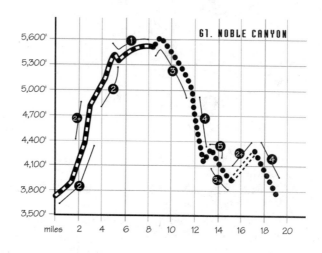

2.6 Miner's Trail to the left, continue straight.

3.7 Stay on main road past dirt trail to right.

2.9 Pass over cattle crossing and reach sign for Pine Creek Road. Turn right.

4.3 Stay on main road past dirt road to left.

4.5 Stay on main road past dirt road to right.

4.8 Turnout to right heading back into canyon. Stay on main road.

5.3 Stay on main road past dirt road to left.

5.5 Stay on main road past dirt road to right.

5.7 Stay on main road past dirt road to right.

6.1 Stay on main road past dirt road to right.

6.3 Noble Canyon Trail singletrack crosses road. Stay on road.

6.5 Pass Laguna Mountain Recreation Area sign. See Noble Canyon Trail singletrack to right but stay on road.

7.6 Reach Sunrise Highway. Go through gate and turn right.

8.3 Reach Penny Pines area. See Noble Canyon Trailhead on both sides. Take trail to right.

8.3 Reach three-way junction with sign pointing straight for Noble Canyon Trail.

9.4 Cross the paved road and continue on the singletrack on the other side.

9.5 Cross the paved road and continue on the singletrack on the other side.

10.4 Three-way junction with a sign. Turn left, staying on Noble Canyon Trail.

11.2 Cross the road for the last time. The terrain becomes more technical.

11.6 Pass through gate and don't forget to close it behind you. Enter four gnarly switchbacks.

14.5 Descend a short rocky section and come to a cave on the left.

15.8 Three-way junction, turn left and head toward Pine Valley. You see another junction and veer right to head down into the creek. Just after you climb out of the creekbed, veer left past the trail that comes in from the right.

17.0 Continue straight past the trail from the left.

17.5 Continue straight past the trail from the left.

18.7 Reach a gate at the end of the trail. You are now at the second parking area. Turn right and head back to your car.

19.0 Back at car.

Stonewall Mine

Location:	East San Diego County.
Distance:	9.1-mile loop.
Time:	2 hours.
Tread:	Fireroad with mostly hardpacked dirt and some rocky sections.
Aerobic level:	Moderate with some strenuous sections.
Technical difficulty:	3.
Fees:	$5.00 for parking or a State Park day-use pass.
Services:	Bathroom, phone and Visitor Center.
Water:	There is a water fountain next to the small museum.
Highlights:	The trail offers beautiful pine and oak forests, wonderful meadows, and running streams. There are some great technical sections and some fun downhills. You will enjoy being out in the wilderness while only being 40 miles east of San Diego.
Hazards:	There is one gnarly uphill section that is really technical. Other than that the trail is fairly nice.
Land status:	Cleveland National Forest.
Maps:	USGS Cuyamaca Peak; Thomas Brothers, San Diego County, page 405.

Access: From San Diego, take Interstate 8 east to California Highway 79. Follow CA 79 north for 11 miles to the park headquarters on the right side of the highway. Turn onto the entrance road and park in the parking lot across from the bathrooms. The trailhead is located next to the museum.

Notes on the trail: This is a fun trail. When you leave you feel like you got a good workout and practiced your technical riding skills. You start right next to the museum. Ride down a short dirt road and head left. At 1.4 miles veer left past the sign for Los Vaqueros Recreational Area. The first few miles are flat with a couple of stream crossings. At 2.9 miles take the beaten trail straight ahead—otherwise you end up on paved highway. The trail gets into the dense forest and you travel over several ups and downs. At 3.8 miles veer left past a trail that goes off to the right. At 5.4 miles turn left on Stonewall Creek Fireroad and then at 5.5 miles turn left on Soapstone Road. As you turn onto Soapstone Road you begin to climb a steep technical section. After you level out you have an incredible view of Lake Cuyamaca to your right. Veer left, staying on Soapstone Road as it begins a slightly technical descent back toward the bottom and the car.

Stonewall Mine

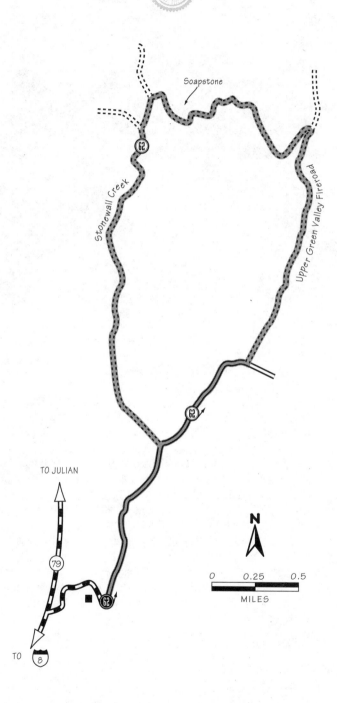

Soapstone

62

Stonewall Creek

Upper Green Valley Fireroad

62

TO JULIAN

79

62

TO 8

N

0   0.25   0.5

MILES

The rough road to Stonewall Mine.

THE RIDE

0.0 Follow road marked "Bike Trail" parallel to museum. Head left at the sign. Travel down a short paved road where you make an immediate left.

0.5 Pass through the fire gate with a sign for Stonewall Creek and Harvey Moore Trail.

1.4 Veer right at the fork with a sign for Los Vaqueros Recreational Area.

2.9 Veer left toward the more beaten trail as the main trail turns into paved highway within 50 feet.

3.8 Follow the arrows to the left at a junction with a sign that indicates Park Boundary Upper Green Valley Fireroad.

5.4 Turn left at a junction with a sign that indicates Stonewall Creek Fireroad to Los Vaqueros.

5.5 Stay left on Stonewall Fireroad past Los Vaqueros Trail on the right.

7.8 You have finished the loop and are at the first junction that you came to at the beginning of the ride. Stay to the right and follow the road back to the parking lot.

9.1 The end.

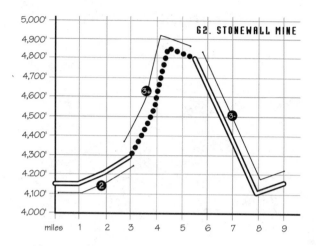

Corral Canyon

Location:	Near Lake Morena, approximately 60 miles east of San Diego.
Distance:	16-mile loop.
Time:	2 hours.
Tread:	Mostly rough fireroad with some seriously eroded sections on Espinosa Trail.
Aerobic level:	Moderate to strenuous.
Technical difficulty:	3.
Fees:	Forest Adventure Pass required.
Services:	There is a pit toilet at Four Corners.
Water:	None. It gets very hot so bring plenty of water.
Highlights:	Good hardcore fireroads.
Hazards:	Off-road vehicles, motorcycles, rattlesnakes, and severe heat.
Land status:	Cleveland National Forest.
Maps:	USGS Morena Reservoir; Thomas Brothers, San Diego County, page 408.

Corral Canyon

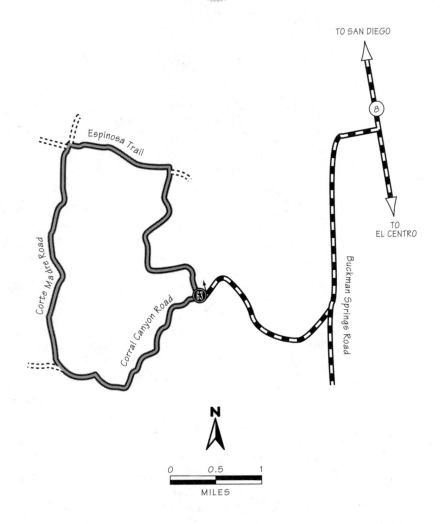

TO SAN DIEGO

8

TO
EL CENTRO

Espinosa Trail

Corte Madre Road

Corral Canyon Road

63

Buckman Springs Road

N

0   0.5   1

MILES

Access: From San Diego, where Interstates 805 and 8 meet at Qualcomm Stadium, go 60 miles east on I-8. Exit at Buckman Springs Road and head south. Approximately 2 miles past the freeway turn right at the sign for Corral Canyon O.R.V. Area. Drive another 5 miles until you get to the Four Corners parking lot.

Notes on the trail: From the Four Corners turn right and begin a steep climb north on Los Pinos Road. Continue straight on Los Pinos Road, pass the trail to the lookout tower at 2.2 miles and the Spur Meadow Trail at 3.1 miles. At 3.9 miles you get to a four-way junction. Turn left onto the Espinosa

The steep trail up Corral Canyon.

Trail and begin a rough, bumpy descent. Continue straight until you get to a four-way junction at Corte Madera Road, turn left and continue your descent. Continue straight through the gate at 7.3 miles and pass several trails that veer off the main road. At 10.6 miles turn left at the three-way junction and begin a short climb. At a three-way junction at 12.3 miles, turn left onto Corral Canyon Road. Continue straight past a few offshoot trails and the Corral Canyon Campground at 14.9 miles until you get back to Four Corners at 16.1 miles.

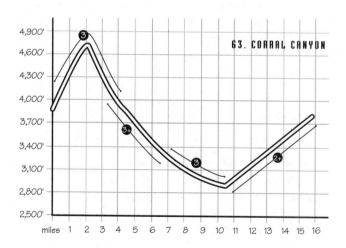

0.0 Head north, climb up Los Pinos Road.

2.2 Continue straight past trail to right that heads to lookout tower.

3.1 Continue straight past Spur Meadow Road on left.

3.9 Turn left at unmarked Espinosa Trail at four-way junction. Begin bumpy descent.

4.7 Continue straight past water tanks to left.

6.1 Continue straight past trail to left.

6.8 At four-way junction turn left onto Corte Madera Road.

7.3 Pass through gate.

9.0 Continue straight past trail to right.

10.2 Continue straight on main road past many trails that veer off to the left.

10.6 Turn left at three-way junction.

11.9 Continue straight past trail to right.

12.3 Turn left onto Corral Canyon Road.

13.3 Continue straight past trail to the right.

14.9 Pass Corral Canyon Campground.

16.1 The end.

Lake Morena

Location:	Approximately 60 miles east of San Diego.
Distance:	5.2-mile loop.
Time:	30 minutes.
Tread:	Mostly easy-rolling fireroad.
Aerobic level:	Easy.
Technical difficulty:	2.
Fees:	$5 day-use pass required.
Services:	A camp store and bathrooms are near the park entrance.
Water:	Water is available near the picnic area.
Highlights:	Easy family ride around the lake.
Hazards:	Rattlesnakes, severe heat.
Land status:	San Diego County Park.
Maps:	USGS Morena Reservoir; Thomas Brothers, San Diego County, page 408.

Lake Morena

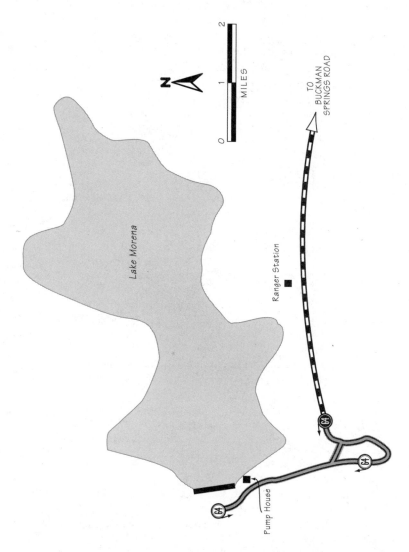

Access: From San Diego, where Interstates 805 and 8 meet at Qualcomm Stadium, go 60 miles east on I-8. Exit at Buckman Springs Road, and head south. Drive 4.5 miles to Oak Drive where you see a sign which reads, "Lake Morena." Turn right. Another 1.5 miles down the road, Oak Drive turns into Lake Morena Drive. Turn right at the sign for Lake Morena County Park. Go straight past the kiosk to the ranger's office to pay. From the ranger's office continue on the same road another one-half mile. The trailhead is off to the left just before the road deadends at the lake.

Notes on the trail: Ride back approximately 100 feet to the gated dirt road on the right. Ride along this road and at the 1-mile mark you come to a trail to the right which shortly deadends. Veer left past this trail. Within another tenth of a mile you see the old house off to the left and a trail that veers off to the left. Veer right and then veer left at another junction. At 1.7 miles you reach a big bend with a picnic table. Continue around the bend and the road gently drops until you reach the pumphouse at 2.7 miles. Continue past the pumphouse, pass through the gate, and begin a gentle climb until you get to the top of the dam at 2.9 miles. From here you turn around and head back. Just after the pumphouse at approximately 3.3 miles, you can turn left and head back to the car. This eliminates the loop out to the old picnic area.

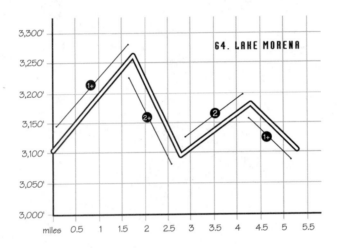

THE RIDE

- **0.0** Pass through the gate.
- **1.0** Veer left past dead-end trail to the right.
- **1.1** See old house off to the left. Veer right past the house and immediately veer left at another junction.
- **1.7** Reach old picnic area at big bend and begin gradual decent. Pass singletrack which heads off to the left.
- **2.7** Reach pumphouse and pass through gate.
- **2.9** Reach top of the dam and turn around.
- **3.3** Turn left at junction, head back to car.
- **5.2** The end.

Sierra Nevada/ Kern County

Mount Pinos Loop

Location:	In Frazier Park within the Los Padres National Forest.
Distance:	10.5 miles, one way, with a short out-and-back spur to the Mount Pinos Summit and a shuttle from the bottom of the McGill Trail to the Chula Vista parking lot.
Time:	1 hour.
Tread:	Combination singletrack, fireroad and paved road.
Aerobic level:	Easy since the majority of the ride is downhill with a shuttle. The spur to the Mount Pinos Summit is moderate.
Technical difficulty:	2+ overall with some Level 3 singletrack.
Fees:	Forest Adventure Pass required.
Services:	Pit toilets in the Chula Vista parking lot and McGill Campground. Full services back near the freeway.
Water:	No water available at the trailhead.
Highlights:	Fun, non-technical singletrack descent. Excellent for new riders to develop singletrack skills. Beautiful view overlooking Frazier Park and Mount Pinos Summit.
Hazards:	Watch for cars on Cuddy Valley Road between the bottom of Chula Vista Trail and McGill Trail.
Land status:	Los Padres National Forest.
Maps:	USGS Cuddy Valley.

Access: From Interstate 5, approximately 90 miles north of Los Angeles and 3 miles north of Gorman, exit at Frasier Park and go west. Frasier Mountain Park Road then turns into Cuddy Valley Road and approximately 13 miles from the freeway is the lower trailhead for the McGill Trail. Drop off your first car here. Continue up Cuddy Valley Road another 8 miles until you reach the Chula Vista parking lot. As you reach the parking lot, you see the trailhead for the Mount Pinos Summit straight ahead.

Mount Pinos Loop

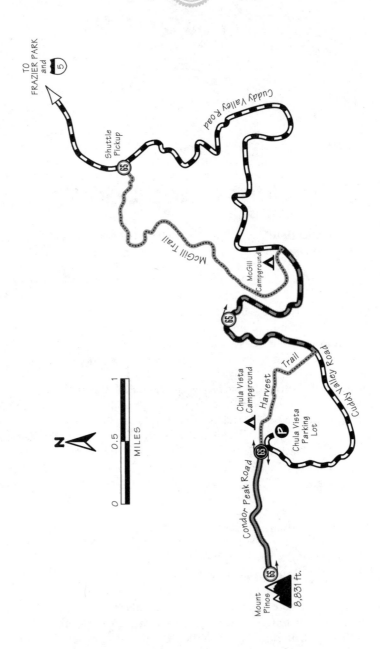

N

MILES
0   0.5   1

TO
FRAZIER PARK
and ⑤

Shuttle
Pickup

Cuddy Valley Road

McGill Trail

McGill
Campground

Chula Vista
Campground

Harvest
Trail

Cuddy Valley Road

Chula Vista
Parking
Lot

P

Condor Peak Road

Mount
Pinos

8,831 ft.

Enjoying the Mt. Pinos Loop.

Notes on the trail: From the Chula Vista parking lot begin your climb on the fireroad to the Mount Pinos Summit. The moderate climb appears a little tougher than it actually is because of the 8,450-foot elevation starting point. The fireroad climbs to the summit with an occasional gravelly section and a few ruts. At 0.3 mile you want to veer left past a little trail to the right. At 0.9 mile veer left at the junction and continue straight at 1.2 miles as you see a footpath to the left. At 1.7 miles the road splits. To the right are radio towers and to the left is the summit toward which you want to continue. At 1.9 miles you reach the summit. From the summit, bomb down toward the Chula Vista parking lot and, once back at the parking lot, ride toward the far left where you see a small singletrack that marks the beginning of the Chula Vista Trail. As you descend on the Chula Vista Trail you come to several trails that veer left toward picnic areas. Continue straight past them and veer right as you see a sign marking the Chula Vista Campground. At 4.2 miles veer right past the trail coming in from the left. At 4.8 miles you reach the Cuddy Valley Road. Turn left and ride down the paved road until you see the McGill Campground on the left at 6.5 miles. Turn into the McGill Campground and, when you reach the top of the short hill across from the forest information signs, you see the McGill Trailhead to the left. Begin a gradual climb until you descend at 7 miles. Pass a trail from the left. Here marks the final descent through fast, windy singletrack with a series of switchbacks. At 10.5 miles you come out to Cuddy Valley Road where you parked the first car.

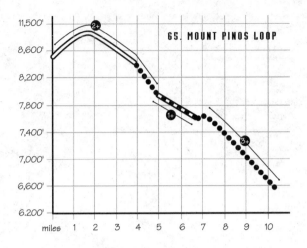

THE RIDE

0.0 From the Chula Vista parking lot begin climbing to the Mount Pinos Summit.

0.3 Veer left past the trail to right.

0.9 Veer left at the junction.

1.2 Continue straight past the singletrack to the right.

1.7 Veer left at the junction and ride toward the summit.

1.9 Top of Mount Pinos Summit. Head back down to Chula Vista parking lot.

3.8 At the Chula Vista parking lot, ride to the far left. The Chula Vista Trailhead is across from the building. Continue straight past a series of trails leading right toward picnic areas and veer right at the sign that reads, "Chula Vista Campground."

4.2 Veer left past the trail to the right.

4.8 Reach Cuddy Valley Road and turn left.

6.5 Turn left into McGill Campground.

6.7 At the top of the short hill turn left onto the McGill Trail directly across from the forest information signs.

7.0 Continue straight past a trail from the left and begin the final descent.

10.5 Reach the Cuddy Valley Road back at your first car.

Cannell Trail

Location:	The Cannell Trail starts high above the town of Kernville, which is approximately 50 miles northeast of Bakersfield.
Distance:	24 miles one way, but 7 miles can be shaved by starting at the Big Meadow Campground.
Time:	4.5 hours.
Tread:	Mostly singletrack with a few sections of fireroad.
Aerobic level:	The majority of this trail is downhill. While the overall climb of this ride is moderate, the lack of oxygen due to the elevation often makes it strenuous.
Technical difficulty:	3+ with some Level 4+ sections.
Fees:	Forest Adventure Pass required.
Services:	The town of Kernville has everything you need. After your ride you may even want to spend a day whitewater rafting with one of the many local rafting companies in town. *Mountain and River Adventures* offers guided overnight trips on the Cannell Trail. Not only do they guide you through some of the best singletrack in Southern California, they haul your gear and cook you gourmet mountain meals. *Mountain and River Adventures* also offers combined bike/raft trips. You can reach them at 800-861-6553. There are no services at the trailhead but 7 miles down the trail is Big Meadows Campground which has restrooms and fire pits.
Water:	There is no water along the trail. Bring plenty of your own water and food.
Highlights:	The entire trail is awesome singletrack which tests the ability of even the best riders. You see Giant Sequoias, brown bears, deer, and creeks chock-full of trout. An overnight stay can be had at either the Big Meadow Campground or Cannell Meadows Ranger Station, at the 12.6-mile mark. The Cannell Meadows Ranger Station was the first ranger station built in the Sequoia National Forest.
Hazards:	One of the co-authors came face-to-face with a baby brown bear while exploring the Cannell Trail. Narrow singletrack overlooking steep cliffs.
Land status:	Sequoia National Forest.
Maps:	USGS Sirretta Peak, Cannell Peak, Kernville; Thomas Brothers, Central Valley Cities, page 19.

Cannell Trail

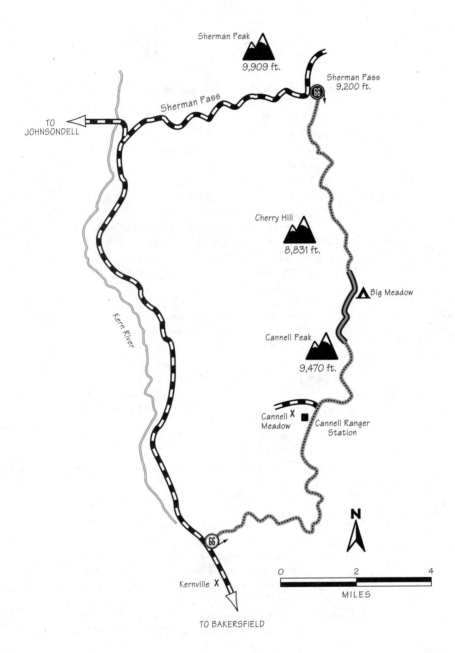

Sherman Peak
9,909 ft.

Sherman Pass
9,200 ft.

Sherman Pass

TO
JOHNSONDELL

Cherry Hill
8,831 ft.

Big Meadow

Kern River

Cannell Peak
9,470 ft.

Cannell
Meadow

Cannell Ranger
Station

66

Kernville

TO BAKERSFIELD

N

0   2   4
MILES

Access: This trail should be done as a car shuttle. One car can be left in the town of Kernville and the other at the trailhead. From Bakersfield take California Highway 178 east to Kernville as it begins to wind along the Lower Kern River. From Kernville go across the bridge at River Park and turn left on Sierra Way. After approximately 20 miles go right on Sherman Pass Road. Follow this road approximately 18 miles until you get to a small forest sign that says, "Sherman Pass Vista 9,200 feet." There is a cattle crossing there, followed by a small loop that overlooks the valley below. You can park your second car here overnight.

For a shorter ride you can start at the Big Meadow Campground. To get to Big Meadow Campground follow the directions above but after driving up Sherman Pass Road about 8 miles, turn right at Cherry Hill Road. Drive along this road over 10 miles until you get to the Big Meadows Campground.

Notes on the trail: From the overlook, go back to the cattle crossing and on the left side of the road is the trailhead marked as the Cannell Trail (33E32).

Begin down the sandy singletrack through the Giant Sequoias and after about 0.8 mile and a short climb you come to a paved road. Cross the road as the trail continues on the other side. The trail begins to drop a little faster and the sand becomes quite heavy in some sections as you drop down some narrow chutes. At approximately 1.3 miles, 1.5 miles, and 2.2 miles you come to dirt roads which you continue straight across. After you ride about 3 miles and drop 400 feet in elevation, you get to an opening in the trail. To the right you see Mosquito Meadows. After another quarter mile the trail merges with a paved road and you continue as the trail veers to the right of the road. After about 3.2 miles you cross a small stream and begin your ascent up Burning Desire. Here you climb from 8,920 feet to 9,360 feet within less than three-quarters of a mile. After this brutal climb you begin a windy descent which turns into Kidney Punch around 5.4 miles. Kidney Punch is a half-mile boulder field which requires technical maneuvering over large boulders and tree roots that run across the trail. Kidney Punch eases up after a while but the trail remains extremely narrow and technical. It turns into doubletrack and makes several stream crossings. After 7 miles you cross a dirt road and enter Big Meadows Campground. Big Meadows Campground is a great place to have lunch or camp for the night. Continue out of Big Meadows Campground on the dirt road for about 2 miles until you see a sign that marks Cherry Hill Road to the left and Cannell Meadow to the right. As you head right the dirt road begins to climb about 400 feet in a little over 1 mile. Although this would ordinarily be a mellow climb for most conditioned riders, the elevation adds to the aerobic factor. After reaching the peak at 10.2 miles, head down the other side. Within one-half mile you see a little singletrack to the right that takes you to Cannell Meadows. You begin a short technical climb up little rock steps as you climb a narrow singletrack along a 50-foot cliff. After reaching the top at 11.3 miles, begin your descent and see a trail off to the right at 11.5 miles. Continue straight for another mile down narrow, windy singletrack, which quickly becomes

HB Extreme Team at the Cannell Meadows ranger station.

more technical as it descends over rocks and tree roots. At 12.6 miles you come to a dirt road. You can either continue on the trail straight across the road or, if you turn right for a few hundred feet, you see a road to the left which takes you to the old Cannell Meadows Ranger Station. This was the first ranger station built in the Sequoia National Forest and is a great place to camp for the night. Although you must camp outside of the wood fence surrounding the ranger station, there is a fire pit inside the wood fence to the right of the ranger station. There is always plenty of wood there and you are welcome to enjoy a fire. Make sure you put it out before going to sleep. As you continue your ride at the 12.6-mile mark you immediately see two doubletrack trails crossing the Cannell Trail; continue on the singletrack past these two trails. At 13.2 and 13.4 miles you come to large meadow areas where you see a barely visible trail running through the grass. Go straight through the meadows and try to stay on the trail. At 13.5 miles you pass a dirt road and continue on the singletrack past the road. At 14.2 miles you cross one last meadow which takes you through wet grasslands for another quarter of a mile. At the end of this meadow you are adjacent to the road. Through the trees to the right, you can see the trail continue. After 14.6 miles you come to the road once again. Look through the trees to the right to find the trail as it continues toward a rocky technical section. This section travels for almost 1 mile as you rock-hop across streams. At 16.1 miles the trail merges with a dirt road where you veer to the right. Within the next one-half mile you come to two more roads where you stay to the right. At 16.7 miles you come to a gate which you have to open and pass through. You then travel for a little less than one-quarter mile on a narrow singletrack along the side of a cliff. At 17 miles, as you ride along the side of the mountain, you come to "The Gates" where you are able to look over the entire Kern River Valley and Lake Isabella. From here continue along the singletrack which becomes sandy and requires a great deal of technical ability. At 18.5 miles you enter White Knuckler 1, which is chock-full of rocks. At 18.9 miles you come to a short climb which quickly becomes a hike-a-bike for a few hundred feet. After reaching the top, you enter White Knuckler 2, which starts off very rocky and then leads into a series of switchbacks. At 19.8 miles you see a trail going off to the left which heads up the mountain. Continue toward the right, down the hill. At 20.2 miles you begin a series of some of the most technical switchbacks to be found as you drop through chutes while making switched turns. At 21.9 miles you pass through a gate and at 22.4 miles you come to a fork in the road with a forest sign. Turn left and climb until you reach the top at 22.6 miles where you then take the windy singletrack which veers to the right. At 22.9 miles you come to a series of dirt roads that head left. Continue straight but veer to the right. At 23.8 miles you reach the end of the Cannell Trail at Sierra Way. Turn left and head back to the town of Kernville.

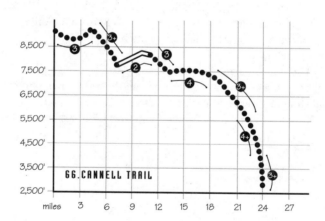

66. CANNELL TRAIL

THE RIDE

0.0 From the trailhead, ride down the sandy singletrack.

0.8 As you cross a paved road you see the trail continue onto the other side.

1.3 Cross the two dirt roads within a few hundred feet of each other and continue on the singletrack.

2.2 Cross the dirt road and continue on the singletrack.

3.0 Approach Mosquito Meadows.

3.1 Approach paved road and veer to singletrack on the right.

3.2	Cross stream and begin 440-vertical-foot climb up Burning Desire.
7.0	Reach Big Meadows Campground. Stay on Cherry Hill dirt road that veers right.
8.0	Pass road on the right which heads back to Sherman Pass Road.
9.0	Reach sign at Cherry Hill Road and turn right toward Cannell Meadows.
10.2	At top of fireroad. Head down fireroad.
10.7	Turn right onto singletrack.
11.5	Continue straight past trail to the right.
12.6	Reach dirt road. Continue straight on singletrack and straight past two immediate doubletracks or turn right at first dirt road and at 12.75 miles turn left to Cannell Ranger Station to rest or camp.
13.2	Cross through a meadow and ride through grass to trail at other end.
13.4	Cross through meadow and ride through grass to trail at other end.
13.5	Cross the dirt road and continue on the singletrack.
14.2	Cross through meadow and ride through grass to trail at other end.
14.4	Approach road and veer to the right through trees to locate singletrack. After another quarter mile you reach the road once again and have to look right through the trees to locate the trail.
16.1	Merge with dirt road and veer right.
16.4	You approach two roads coming in from the left. Continue on the road that veers right.
16.7	Open the gate and continue riding.
17.0	Ride along steep cliffs that travel down into Kern River Valley.
19.8	Continue right, past trail heading up the hill to the left.
21.9	Pass through gate.
22.4	At fork and forest sign, go left.
22.6	Pass through gate and take singletrack on the right down windy trail.
22.9	Head straight, veer right past three dirt roads heading left.
23.8	End of trail at Sierra Way. Turn left and ride 1.5 miles back to Kernville.

Minaret Summit/Mountain View

Location: Mammoth Mountain.

Distance: 14.5-mile loop.

Time: 2 hours (solid).

Tread: The first half of the climb is on pavement. The second half is on doubletrack and the ground is a soft pumice stone from Minaret Vista to Deadman Pass (but there is no traction problem). From Minaret Vista down to the Earthquake Fault is singletrack, sometimes on really soft pumice stone (which is why we do not recommend climbing this section).

Aerobic level: Strenuous.

Technical difficulty: 3.

Fees: None.

Services: Bathrooms at Earthquake Fault and at the main lodge and at Minaret Vista. There is an emergency repair bike shop at the main lodge.

Water: Available at the main lodge.

Highlights: Incredible views from a 10,000-foot elevation. An unbelievable downhill.

Hazards: There are two potential hazards—the altitude and the cold. We did the ride in mid July, and we still needed a jacket at the top.

Land status: Inyo National Forest.

Maps: USGS Mammoth Mountain, Old Mammoth; U.S. Department of Agriculture Map, Inyo National Forest.

Access: From Los Angeles take California Highway 14 east to U.S. Highway 395 north. After approximately 130 miles, exit to California Highway 203 and turn left toward Mammoth.

This could be a good shuttle ride, but we assume you have one car. Travel on Old Mammoth Road and turn north (toward the Main Lodge) on CA 203. Turn right, after approximately 2.5 miles, at the Earthquake Fault and park. This is where the ride ends.

Notes on the trail: Begin riding up California Highway 203 from the Earthquake Fault past the bike park and Main Lodge to Minaret Vista at 3.8 miles. This is where you change to dirt and begin a steep ascent to Deadman Pass. You reach Deadman Pass at 6.2 miles and, after a well deserved rest,

Minaret Summit/Mountain View

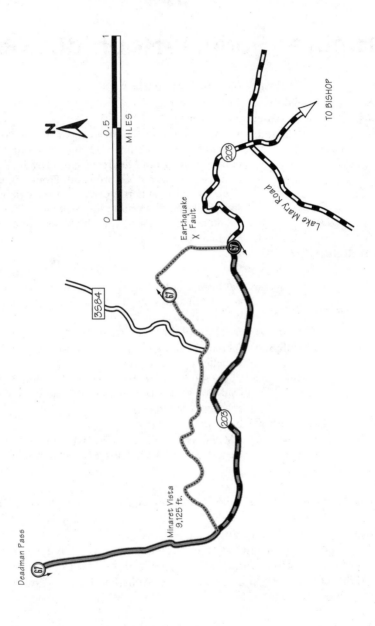

MILES

0   0.5   1

N

Deadman Pass

Minaret Vista
9,125 ft.

Earthquake
X Fault

3S84

203

Lake Mary Road

TO BISHOP

Mammoth police patrolling Mountain View Trail.

fly back down to Minaret Vista where you pick up the Mountain View Trail. This trail is an adventurous singletrack all the way back to the Earthquake Fault. Follow the signs for Mountain View Trail and at 11.5 miles turn right on 3S89. Then 100 yards up turn left when you see the Mountain View Trail marker. At 12 miles turn right on the fireroad and then make a sharp left at 12.5 miles as you see another Mountain View Trail marker. Continue on the trail until you reach the Earthquake Fault at 14.5 miles.

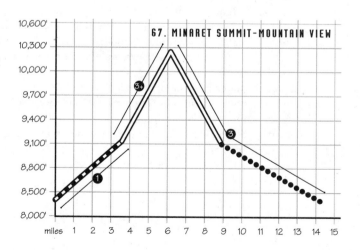

0.0 From the Earthquake Fault, ride paved California Highway 203 toward the Main Lodge.

2.5 Reach Main Lodge and continue past ranger stand.

3.8 Reach Minaret Vista Ranger Station. Make right onto dirt road, continue up.

6.2 After challenging ascent you reach Deadman Pass. Turn around and head down.

8.7 Back at Minaret Vista. Notice a car roadblock on the left and a sign that says, "No Motorcycles or Cars Beyond This Point." Take this trail.

11.5 Turn right at fireroad marked 3S89. Continue for approximately 100 yards and make a sharp left where the trail is marked for Mountain View.

12.0 Turn right onto fireroad.

12.5 Pick up Mountain View Trail by making sharp left at the Mountain View sign.

14.5 Back at Earthquake Fault.

Mammoth Mountain Bike Park

Location:	In the town of Mammoth Lakes in the Inyo National Forest.
Distance:	Network of over 70 miles of trails.
Time:	As much as you can handle.
Tread:	Nearly all singletrack.
Aerobic level:	Easy to strenuous.
Technical difficulty:	2–4. All trails are marked with level of difficulty.
Fees:	Adults $23, children $20.
Services:	A full bicycle repair and rental shop is available as well as a restaurant, patio barbecue, and bar. Hotels and restaurants are available a few miles back in the town of Mammoth.
Water:	Water is available at the bottom of the hill.
Highlights:	Over 70 miles of singletrack. Gondola or ski lift to the top. No climbing!
Hazards:	Steep cliffs. Loose gravel descents. Windy at the top.
Land status:	Inyo National Forest.
Maps:	USGS Mammoth Mountain.

Access: From Los Angeles take California Highway 14 east to U.S. Highway 395 north. After approximately 130 miles, exit California Highway 203 and turn left toward Mammoth.

Notes on the trail: The legendary ski resort of Mammoth Mountain opens to mountain bikes during the summer. The bike park boasts over 70 miles of singletrack in addition to the infamous Kamikaze Run. There are varying degrees of trails for all levels of riders. This is a great place to get started and also provides a challenge for the most advanced riders. Be sure to pick up a trail map at the main lodge to get a preview of the amazing network of trails. While many people climb some of the lower trails such as Paper Route and Up Town (which leads from town to the bike park), the bike park is designed around the gondola and a few of the many chairlifts. From the very top of Mammoth Mountain you have many options to get back to the bottom. These include the lightning fast Kamikaze Run used in pro-NORBA races, the 14-mile-long Off the Top, and the more technical Skid Mark. For those who like to take the easy way down, there are a myriad of trails including Paper Route and Beach Cruiser on the lower parts of the mountain.

Doc at Mammoth Bike Park overlooking Lake Mary.

Lower Rock Creek Trail

Location:	Off U.S. Highway 395 between Bishop and Mammoth Lakes in the Inyo National Forest.
Distance:	7.8 miles, one way with a car shuttle.
Time:	50 minutes.
Tread:	100 percent singletrack.
Aerobic level:	Moderate. Although it is all downhill with a car shuttle, the technical difficulty increases the heart rate.
Technical difficulty:	3–4 with a couple portages around rockslides.
Fees:	None.
Services:	The Paradise Restaurant is located at the bottom of the trail. Full services are available in the town of Bishop, approximately 9 miles below the lower trailhead, or in the town of Mammoth Lakes, 16 miles above the upper trailhead.
Water:	None available on the trail.
Highlights:	Bitchin' singletrack meandering along Rock Creek.
Hazards:	Rocky, technical sections. Extreme cold in early spring and late fall. Trail becomes covered with snow in the winter.
Land status:	Inyo National Forest.
Maps:	USGS Hammil Valley, Tom's Place.

Access: From the town of Mammoth Lakes at California Highway 203 and U.S. Highway 395, drive 26 miles to Paradise Road and turn right. Just past the turnoff, turn right on Lower Rock Creek Road and drive 3 miles to the Paradise Restaurant. Just to the right is the lower trailhead. Park your car off to the side of the road near the restaurant. Drive the second car approximately 7.5 miles up Lower Rock Creek Road. Just before reaching US 395 you see a Forest Service sign to the left and the trailhead just to the right of the road.

From the town of Bishop, drive approximately 9 miles north on US 395 and turn left on Paradise Road. Just past the turnoff, turn right on Lower Rock Creek Road and drive 3 miles to the Paradise Restaurant. Just to the right is the lower trailhead. Park your car off to the side of the road near the restaurant. Drive the second car approximately 7.5 miles up Lower Rock Creek Road. Just before reaching US 395, you see a Forest Service sign to the left and the trailhead just to the right of the road.

Notes on the trail: Ride past the trail markers at the trailhead and wind

Lower Rock Creek Trail

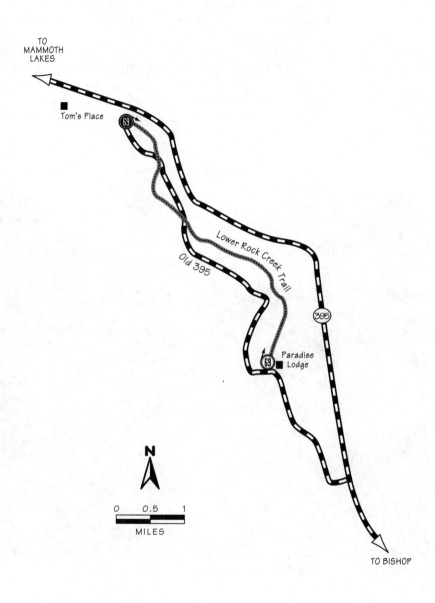

TO
MAMMOTH
LAKES

Tom's Place

69

Lower Rock Creek Trail

Old 395

395

69 Paradise
Lodge

N

0   0.5   1
MILES

TO BISHOP

down the singletrack as it meanders along Rock Creek over small rocks and bridges. At 2.2 miles you cross the road and see the trail continue on the other side off to the right. The trail becomes slightly steeper with tighter turns and sandy terrain. At 3.2 miles you cross the road again and continue on the trail straight across the road to the right. The trail quickly becomes more technical as it leads you over large rocks and hillsides. At 3.7 miles continue straight past a trail to the right. Keep riding as the trail continues to get more technical and bets get placed as to who can clean the most sections. At 7.5 miles the trail turns to a wider dirt road and you veer right. At 7.6 miles you cross the last bridge and come out at a dirt road. To the right is a small singletrack. You can either take the singletrack or the dirt road, both of which lead to the end of the trail at 7.8 miles.

Mountain Bike Doc rippin' Lower Rock Creek Trail.

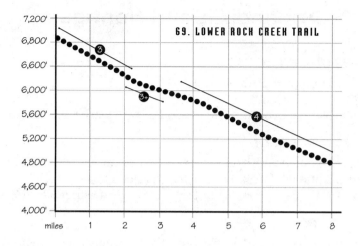

69. LOWER ROCK CREEK TRAIL

THE RIDE

0.0 Ride past the trail marker at the trailhead.

2.2 Cross the road and see the trail continue on the other side off to the right.

3.2 Cross the road again and continue on the trail on the other side of the road to the right.

3.7 Continue straight past the trail to the right.

7.5 Veer right as the trail becomes doubletrack.

7.6 Trail turns to dirt road straight ahead and singletrack to the right of the dirt road. Take either track.

7.8 The end.

Appendix: Land Managers

SAN LUIS OBISPO COUNTY

Montana de Oro State Park 805-528-0513
Morro Bay State Park 805-772-2560
Los Padres National Forest, Santa Lucia Ranger District 805-925-9538

SANTA BARBARA COUNTY

Los Padres National Forest, Supervisor's Headquarters 805-683-6711
Los Padres National Forest, Los Prietos District 805-967-3481
Los Padres National Forest, Santa Barbara Ranger District 805-967-3481

VENTURA COUNTY

Department of Parks and Recreation, Santa Monica Mountains District 805-987-3303
Point Mugu State Park 310-457-8143
Santa Monica Mountains National Recreation Area 805-370-2301

LOS ANGELES COUNTY

Angeles National Forest, Arroyo Seco Ranger District 818-790-1151
Department of Parks and Recreation, Santa Monica Mountains District 818-499-2112
Topanga State Park 818-880-0360, 310-454-8212
Malibu Creek State Park 818-880-0367
Will Rogers State Historical Park 310-454-8212

ORANGE COUNTY

Aliso/Wood Canyons Regional Park 714-831-2174
Cleveland National Forest, Trabuco District 714-736-1811
Crystal Cove State Park, Moro Canyon 714-494-3539
O'Neill Regional Park 949-858-9365
Peter's Canyon Regional Park 714-538-4400
Whiting Ranch Wilderness Park 714-589-4729

RIVERSIDE COUNTY

Bureau of Land Management 760-251-0812
Cleveland National Forest, Trabuco District 714-736-1811
Riverside County Parks 909-955-4310
Riverside City Parks and Recreation 909-715-3440
San Bernardino National Forest, San Jacinto Ranger District 760-659-2117

SAN BERNARDINO COUNTY

San Bernardino National Forest, Supervisor's Office 909-383-5588
San Bernardino National Forest, Big Bear Ranger District 909-866-3437
Chino Hills State Park 909-591-9834

SAN DIEGO COUNTY

Cuyamuca Rancho State Park 619-765-0755
Los Penasquitos Canyon Preserve 619-533-4067
Marian R. Bear Natural Park 619-525-8281
Mission Trails Regional Park 619-668-3275, 619-533-4051
San Diego County Parks Department 619-565-3600, 619-694-3049
San Diego Convention and Visitor's Bureau 619-236-1212
Cleveland National Forest, Headquarters 619-673-6180, 619-674-2901
Cleveland National Forest, Descanso District 619-445-6235

SIERRA NEVADA/KERN COUNTY

Inyo National Forest, Mammoth Ranger District 760-934-2505
Los Padres National Forest, Mount Pinos Ranger District 805-245-3731
Mammoth Mountain Bike Park 888-4-MAMMOTH
Sequoia National Forest, Cannell Meadows Ranger District 760-376-3781
Inyo National Forest, White Mountain Ranger District 760-873-2500

Authors' Picks

EPIC SINGLETRACK

Backbone Trail
Cannell Plunge
Holy Jim Trail
Islay Creek Trail
Mount Wilson Trail
Mount Lowe Railway
Noble Canyon Trail
Lower Rock Creek Trail
Santa Ana River Trail
San Juan Trail
Thomas Mountain/Ramona Trail

BEST FAMILY RIDES

Bluff Trail
Lake Hodges

Peter's Canyon
San Clemente Canyon
Big Sycamore Canyon (Ventura County)
Rocky Oaks Park
Palos Verdes

MOST PHYSICALLY STRENUOUS

Arroyo Burro Loop
Bulldog Loop
Harding Trucktrail
Minaret Summit/Mountain View
Mount Lowe Motorway
Mount Wilson Toll Road
Mount Wilson Trail

Glossary

ATB: All-terrain bicycle; a.k.a. mountain bike, sprocket rocket, fat-tire flyer.

ATV: All-terrain vehicle; in this book ATV refers to motorbikes and three- and four-wheelers designed for off-road use.

Bail: Getting off the bike, usually in a hurry, whether or not you mean to. Often a last resort.

Bunny hop: Leaping up while riding and lifting both wheels off the ground to jump over an obstacle (or for sheer joy).

Clamper cramps: That burning, cramping sensation in the hands during extended braking.

Clean: To ride without touching a foot (or other body part) to the ground; to ride a tough section successfully.

Clipless: A type of pedal with a binding that accepts a special cleat on the soles of bike shoes. The cleat clicks in, for more control and efficient pedaling, and out for safe landings (in theory).

Contour: A line on a topographic map showing a continuous elevation level over uneven ground. Also used as a verb to indicate a fairly easy or moderate grade: "The trail contours around the canyon rim before the final grunt to the top."

Dab: To put a foot or hand down (or hold onto or lean on a tree or other support) while riding. If you have to dab, then you haven't ridden that piece of trail **clean.**

Downfall: Trees that have fallen across the trail.

Doubletrack: A trail, jeep road, ATV route, or other track with two distinct ribbons of **tread**, typically with grass growing in between. No matter which side you choose, the other rut always looks smoother.

Endo: Lifting the rear wheel off the ground and riding (or abruptly not riding) on the front wheel only. Also known, at various degrees of control and finality, as a nose wheelie, "going over the handlebars," and a face plant.

Fall line: The angle and direction of a slope; the line you follow when gravity is in control and you aren't.

Graded: When a gravel road is scraped level to smooth out the washboards and potholes it has been graded. In this book, a road is listed as graded only if it is regularly maintained. Such roads are not necessarily graded every year.

Granny gear: The lowest (easiest) gear, a combination of the smallest of the three chainrings on the bottom bracket spindle (where the pedals and crank arms attach to the bike's frame) and the largest cog on the rear cluster. Shift down to your granny gear for serious climbing.

Hammer: To ride hard; derived from how it feels afterward: "I'm hammered."

Hammerhead: Someone who actually enjoys feeling **hammered.** A Type-A rider who goes hard and fast all the time.

Kelly hump: An abrupt mound of dirt across the road or trail. These are common on old logging roads and skidder tracks, placed there to block vehicle access. At high speeds, they become launching pads for bikes and inadvertent astronauts.

Line: The route (or trajectory) between or over obstacles or through turns. **Tread** or trail refers to the ground you're riding on; the line is the path you choose within the tread (and exists mostly in the eye of the beholder).

Off-the-seat: Moving your butt behind the bike seat and over the rear tire; used for control on extremely steep descents. This position increases braking power, helps prevent **endos,** and reduces skidding.

Portage: To carry the bike, usually up a steep hill, across unridable obstacles, or through a stream.

Quads: Thigh muscles (short for quadriceps) or maps in the USGS topographic series (short for quadrangles). Nice quads of either kind can help get you out of trouble in the backcountry.

Ratcheting: Also known as backpedaling; pedaling backward to avoid hitting rocks or other obstacles with the pedals.

Sidehill: Where the trail crosses a slope. If the **tread** is narrow, keep your inside (uphill) pedal up to avoid hitting the ground. If the tread tilts downhill, you may have to use some body language to keep the bike plumb or vertical to avoid slipping out.

Singletrack: A trail, game run, or other track with only one ribbon of **tread.** But this is like defining an orgasm as a muscle cramp. Good singletrack is pure fun.

Spur: A side road or trail that splits off from the main route.

Surf: Riding through loose gravel or sand, when the wheels sway from side to side. *Also* **heavy surf:** frequent and difficult obstacles.

Suspension: A bike with front suspension has a shock-absorbing fork or stem. Rear suspension absorbs shock between the rear wheel and frame. A bike with both is said to be fully suspended.

Switchbacks: When a trail goes up a steep slope, it zigzags or **switchbacks** across the **fall line** to ease the gradient of the climb. Well-designed switchbacks make a turn with at least an 8-foot radius and remain fairly level within the turn itself. These are rare, however, and cyclists often struggle to ride through sharply angled, sloping switchbacks.

Track stand: Balancing on a bike in one place, without rolling forward appreciably. Cock the front wheel to one side and bring that pedal up to the one or two o'clock position. Now control your side-to-side balance by applying pressure on the pedals and brakes and changing the angle of the front wheel, as needed. It takes practice but really comes in handy at stoplights, on **switchbacks,** and when trying to free a foot before falling.

Tread: The riding surface, particularly regarding **singletrack.**

Water bar: A log, rock, or other barrier placed in the **tread** to divert water off the trail and prevent erosion. Peeled logs can be slippery and cause bad falls, especially when they angle sharply across the trail.

Whoop-dee-doo: A series of kelly humps used to keep vehicles off trails. Watch your speed or do the dreaded top tube tango.

Index

About the Authors

Mark Ross and Brad Fine have known each other since diaperhood. Growing up together in the Los Angeles area, these two ventured into various extreme and endurance sports like surfing, skiing, running, and of course, mountain biking. They have mountain biked and surfed most of the California coastal area as well as sections of Baja and mainland Mexico. They have participated in mountain bike races, triathlons, 10K's, marathons, and adventure races. Their competitive goal is to complete the Eco Challenge and Raid Guiloise. While not hammering up trails or racing, Brad

Mark (left) and Brad in a pre-race photo at Lake Castaic.

works as a stockbroker and lives in the Southbay area with his wife Jessica. Mark works as an attorney and lives in Orange County with his wife Roseann.

FALCON GUIDES® Leading the Way™

FALCON GUIDES® are available for where-to-go hiking, mountain biking, rock climbing, walking, scenic driving, fishing, rockhounding, paddling, birding, wildlife viewing, and camping. We also have FalconGuides on essential outdoor skills and subjects and field identification. The following titles are currently available, but this list grows every year. For a free catalog with a complete list of titles, call FALCON toll-free at 1-800-582-2665.

MOUNTAIN BIKING GUIDES

Mountain Biking Arizona
Mountain Biking Colorado
Mountain Biking Georgia
Mountain Biking New Mexico
Mountain Biking New York
Mountain Biking Northern New England
Mountain Biking Oregon
Mountain Biking South Carolina
Mountain Biking Southern California
Mountain Biking Southern New England
Mountain Biking Utah
Mountain Biking Wisconsin
Mountain Biking Wyoming

LOCAL CYCLING SERIES

Fat Trax Bozeman
Mountain Biking Bend
Mountain Biking Boise
Mountain Biking Chequamegon
Mountain Biking Chico
Mountain Biking Colorado Springs
Mountain Biking Denver/Boulder
Mountain Biking Durango
Mountain Biking Flagstaff and Sedona
Mountain Biking Helena
Mountain Biking Moab
Mountain Biking Utah's St. George/Cedar City Area
Mountain Biking the White Mountains (West)

■ *To order any of these books, check with your local bookseller or call FALCON® at* **1-800-582-2665**.
Visit us on the world wide web at:
www.FalconOutdoors.com

FALCON®

FALCONGUIDES ® Leading the Way™

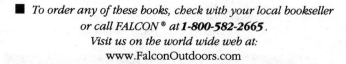

■ *To order any of these books, check with your local bookseller
or call FALCON ® at 1-800-582-2665.
Visit us on the world wide web at:
www.FalconOutdoors.com*

FALCON®

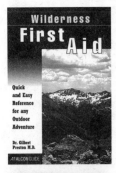

WILDERNESS FIRST AID

By Dr. Gilbert Preston M.D.
Enjoy the outdoors and face the inherent risks with confidence. By reading this easy-to-follow first-aid text, all outdoor enthusiasts can pack a little extra peace of mind on their next adventure. *Wilderness First Aid* offers expert medical advice for dealing with outdoor emergencies beyond the reach of 911. It easily fits in most backcountry first-aid kits.

LEAVE NO TRACE

By Will Harmon
The concept of "leave no trace" seems simple, but it actually gets fairly complicated. This handy quick-reference guidebook includes all the newest information on this growing and all-important subject. This book is written to help the outdoor enthusiast make the hundreds of decisions necessary to protect the natural landscape and still have an enjoyable wilderness experience. Part of the proceeds from the sale of this book go to continue leave-no-trace education efforts. The Official Manual of American Hiking Society.

BEAR AWARE

By Bill Schneider
Hiking in bear country can be very safe if hikers follow the guidelines summarized in this small, "packable" book. Extensively reviewed by bear experts, the book contains the latest information on the intriguing science of bear-human interactions. *Bear Aware* can not only make your hike safer, but it can help you avoid the fear of bears that can take the edge off your trip.

MOUNTAIN LION ALERT

By Steve Torres
Recent mountain lion attacks have received national attention. Although infrequent, lion attacks raise concern for public safety. *Mountain Lion Alert* contains helpful advice for mountain bikers, trail runners, horse riders, pet owners, and suburban landowners on how to reduce the chances of mountain lion-human conflicts.

Also Available

Wilderness Survival • Reading Weather • Backpacking Tips • Climbing Safely • Avalanche Aware • Desert Hiking Tips • Hiking with Dogs • Using GPS • Route Finding • Wild Country Companion

To order check with your local bookseller or
call FALCON® at **1-800-582-2665.**
www.FalconOutdoors.com